M000169000

THE Im PERFECT SPY

THE INSIDE STORY OF A CONVICTED SPY

THE
ImPERFECT
SPY

THE INSIDE STORY OF
A CONVICTED SPY

ANDY J. BYERS

VANDAMERE
PRESS

Published by
Vandamere Press
P.O. Box 149
St. Petersburg, FL 33731
USA

Copyright 2005
by
Andy J. Byers

ISBN 0-918339-66-9

Manufactured in the United States of America. All rights reserved, which includes the right to reproduce this book or any portion thereof in any form whatsoever, except as provided by U.S. Copyright Law. For information contact Vandamere Press.

Acknowledgments

Writing and researching George Trofimoff's story has been an exhaustive effort, and I am in debt to the many individuals who have aided me. This book would not have been possible without their help.

First, I want to express my gratitude to my wife, Doris, who has endured, with me, the agony of the loss of our good friend and great neighbor, George Trofimoff. She tolerated the many hours I devoted to research, correspondence, and writing with a calm and supportive attitude, and has helped by carefully proofreading my many rewrites. My highest appreciation goes to her.

Next, Trofimoff has been extremely helpful. I am continually amazed at his ability to remember and document names, dates, and places. He went to prison with no advance warning, and, with no notes, recorded and gave me these details completely from his memory. Using other sources, I have been able to independently verify much of what he told me. Regarding quotations, I have presented actual comments made by individuals I have interviewed or corresponded with, or those who have been quoted in the media or in court records; in the case of Trofimoff, many pages of his handwritten and typed notes provide the dialogue and quotations attributed to him in the text of the book. To my mind, his notes give credibility to the stories of his early life as he has documented with several hundred handwritten and typed pages. Therefore, I believe the descriptions he gave of his early life, up to the time of his transfer to Germany in the 1960s, are, in essence, true. Throughout this book, whenever he is quoted as "writing," or "saying," his words are taken from the notes he gave me, official court transcripts of telephone calls and videotapes, or exhibits entered during his trial.

Jutta, Trofimoff's wife, provided invaluable assistance, both serving as a messenger between her husband and me, and providing her own details to add to the story. She suffered terribly, emotionally as well as financially, during the years prior to and after the trial. I sincerely hope her life is more pleasant and fulfilled in the future.

Others providing invaluable assistance include Carol Jose, a wonderful published author, tutor, and dear friend. Without her great help and advice, I could never have written this book and managed to get it published. Maynard Allington, another fine novelist and friend, provided much assistance and advice, as well as authors Joseph H. Badal, William Coleman, Anna Flowers, John Nichols, Anthony

Sacco, and Alice Weiser. I also wish to acknowledge the following individuals: General (Ret.) William A. Knowlton; my West Point class-mates Peter A. (Pete) Abbruzzese, Jack V. Mackmull, Richard G. (Dick) Steuart, William F. (Bill) Ward, Jr., and Edward C. (Ed) West; Henry Evans, another West Point friend; my good friend and expert handwriting analyst Charles Richardson; Journalist Derald Everhart; Dr. James Papritan; political cartoonist Jeff Parker; the Butterworth sisters, Jean Robinson and Lucy Townsend; Attorney Robert J. Fiore; retired US Army Counter Intelligence Agent Rocco Rosano; retired CIA Agent Frederick Wettering; FBI Special Agents Anthony Wagner and Joe Navarro; KGB General (Ret.) Oleg D. Kalugin; Richard Russell of Brassey's; Trofimoff's ex-coworkers Walter Burgreeff, George Drozdza and his ex-wife, Irene, Nicholas Getmanoff, and Mike Moschetti. Victoria Strauss, Editor, *Writer Beware,* gave invalu-able assistance during my search for an agent, and Walter and Colleen Tomasulo (Technicorp) provided invaluable technical assistance in resolving the many difficult computer problems I experienced during the writing, rewriting, and editing of the book. Janice Walters' poem, "Bondage," provides an incredibly appropriate closing for the story. Last, but surely not least, is the great advice and assistance provided by my publisher, Art Brown. His suggestions have made the book a much more readable, entertaining and polished work. The detailed, expert, and professional editing of his editor, Patricia Berger, provid-ed the final touches to the manuscript, and Victor Weaver's great design work put the icing on the cake.

When I began listing those who provided assistance and input for the book, I became amazed at how many names arose, and still the list goes on and on. It is incredible that the contributions of so many indi-viduals were merged to produce the final work. While I have tried to name every individual, I'm sure some have been omitted. However, all of you know who you are. Please accept my sincere gratitude for all you have done to make this story as realistic, factual, and objective as possible.

Andy J. Byers
May 1, 2005

Foreword

General William A. Knowlton, US. Army (ret)

We have just passed the 60th Anniversary of VE Day—the end of combat in Europe for World War II. But for those of us remaining in the Occupation of Germany, VE Day marked the beginning of a growing realization that our Soviet allies and we might have different objectives in world power. The Cold War was becoming visible.

Those of us fortunate enough to be stationed in Berlin saw the change first-hand. Russian friends reported the change of tone of their command briefings. Then from a new post in counterintelligence in Frankfort, I had a chance to see the pool from which the Soviet penetration effort was manned. War had displaced millions of people and exposed them to a new way of life. Yet it is important that we not judge too hastily. From the children of this latter-day Diaspora came superb army officers to serve our nation. One became Chairman of the Joint Chiefs of Staff. But from this pool also came George Trofimoff, the highest ranking army officer to be found guilty of espionage against his adopted country.

This book is about Trofimoff. The author, himself a retired army officer, was a next door neighbor and friend of the Trofimoffs for five years. He and his wife were totally unsuspecting and devastated by the arrest and conviction of their neighbor. That led him to do this book on the amazing career of this KGB spy. He attended every session of the trial and also the sentencing hearing. Additionally, he did an immense amount of research, and was fortunate to have access to notes by Trofimoff on his early life.

The result presented here, is the exciting story of help repaid by treachery, of opportunity repaid by betrayal. While the "what" is always of singular importance in espionage cases, the "why" is often of more interest to the reader. Was the appeal of Mother Russia a key mover? But, he was born in Berlin. What role did the Russian church play in his recruitment? Was money, usually a significant player, important in this case? The answers to these questions and many others are well developed in Byers' book. Readers interested in intelligence and espionage, as well as those who just like a good read, will find this book a keeper.

Preface

Frederick L. Wettering
CIA Operations Officer (ret) and
Member of the Senior Intelligence Service

According to Soviet Intelligence (KGB) Major General Kalugin, agent "Markiz" was one of the KGB's most valuable sources of intelligence on the United States. "Markiz" supplied thousands of documents, inter alia, revealed American war plans in Europe, as well as the extent of American knowledge of Soviet military deployments and weaponry. This spy collected over $300,000 in payments from the KGB, which awarded him the coveted Order of the Red Banner for his service to the "Motherland." That spy was named by the FBI and General Kalugin as George Trofimoff, who is described as the most senior American army officer convicted of espionage. Trofimoff was also identified as a spy by KGB defector Vasili Mitrokhin and a British Secret Intelligence Service (MI-6) representative.

Andy Byers, a retired U.S. Army colonel who was a neighbor of Trofimoff in a Florida retirement community has written a detailed, very readable biography of Trofimoff. Colonel Byers makes several original research contributions. He describes his own social contacts with Trofimoff, which are followed by an extensive correspondence while in custody. Trofimoff also gave Byers a lengthy autobiography which Byers has woven into his book. The author also interviewed Trofimoff's wife, the arresting FBI Agent-in-Charge, and several other acquaintances of Trofimoff. He attended the trial and obtained both the trial transcript and FBI indictment which are also effectively woven into the narrative.

As a former CIA operations officer who worked in counterintelligence, I found this book to be a valuable addition to the literature. It reflects the validity of studies like the Defense Department's PERSER-AC report on why spies spy. These studies have provided indicators absolutely vital for counterintelligence officers in terms of identifying characteristics of potential and real spies. These studies note that spies are often narcissistic and egotistical to a fault, and Byers develops these aspects of Trofimoff's character. The need for money, the flagrant spending on self (such as Trofimoff's love of fast cars and attractive young women), the inability to sustain long-term relationships with a spouse (Trofimoff was married five times and admittedly spent little time with wives or three children) are all red flag indicators which should have been spotted. The KGB since its inception in 1917 (as the Cheka), has sought informants abroad among émigré Russians (which Trofimoff was). And every spy service looks for a person with evident weaknesses who has access to secret information. All these add up to an indictment of Army Counterintelligence, which ironically is the organization for which Trofimoff worked during his productive spying years (1962-1987) in Nuremberg, Germany.

Trofimoff, as the author relates, maintained what I call the "Alger Hiss Defense," denying everything. This often is a sound defense against an espionage charge, which requires strict proof standards for conviction, but does not work when the accused admits his wrongdoing, as Trofimoff did, to an FBI agent using the false-flag technique, wherein the agent posed as a KGB officer.

The book demonstrates how the FBI has pursued and convicted former spies using this false-flag technique. This method was effective in developing sufficient court-presentable evidence to try George Trofimoff, as well as others identified as formerly spying for the Soviet Union such as Robert Lipka, Earl Pitts, David Boone, and the "red diaper" spies—Theresa Squillacote and Kurt Stand. All these Americans were spies, but the American intelligence community only became aware of their espionage after they stopped. Conviction in court in such cases is unlikely unless they admit to their former espionage activities. This false-flag technique has proven an effective means of getting them to do so, as the author relates in useful detail. The author also introduces the reader to the seemingly mystic, but in fact very real and very useful science of graphological analysis, used by counterintelligence agencies around the world.

In sum, Colonel Byers has produced an informative new book which is a very layman-friendly read and still has enough detail to satisfy most intelligence buffs.

Prologue

George and Jutta Trofimoff were next-door neighbors of my wife, Doris, and me, from early 1996 until June 2000. During those years, Trofimoff was, to us, anything but "The Perfect Spy" as the media later dubbed him. He was nothing like James Bond or other spies of literary or movie fame. On the contrary, he was, to us, simply another retired military officer—an ordinary resident of our close-knit neighborhood, the Indian River Colony Club (IRCC), an upper middle class community in Melbourne, FL.

We first met the Trofimoffs in mid-1995 when we visited the lot we had selected for our retirement home. As we walked over the lot, a tall man with close-cut, receding grayish hair emerged from the house next door and approached us. His shorts accentuated the contrasts among his long, thin legs, his expanded paunch, and his wide, expansive chest. At his side was a young, pretty lady. He introduced himself as George Trofimoff, welcoming us with a friendly smile and outstretched hand. He introduced us to his wife, saying that they were married a few years ago while he was working in Germany. "We'll be your neighbors when you move in," he said.

After I introduced Doris and myself, Jutta greeted us with a friendly smile. She had a strong German accent and her English was halting at first. As time passed and with constant tutoring by Trofimoff, we could see steady improvement. Trofimoff explained that Jutta worked in Germany with a travel agency at the Nuremberg airport and learned her English serving customers. With her shoulder-length blonde hair and brown eyes, she was a vivacious, beautiful lady. Trofimoff showed obvious pride in his young wife.

"We've been looking forward to meeting you," he said. "Your name has been on the sign posted on this lot for a long time now, and we've wondered when you would show up. Where are you moving from? When do you expect to move in?"

I explained that we lived in New Jersey. We had been told that our house should be ready in a few months, and we hoped to move in early the next year.

"Just remember, when you're ready to move in and need a place to stay before or while your furniture arrives, you have a bedroom reserved next door." The couple insisted that we walk through their home, which was tastefully decorated with comfortable and handsome furniture. Trofimoff pointed to one of two guest bedrooms, saying that it would be ours when we arrived.

As we drove away, the Trofimoffs waved good-bye. Both Doris and I agreed that it appeared that we would have great neighbors. It was a wonderful surprise and a great pleasure to be greeted so warmly by our soon-to-be neighbors.

Our initial impression proved to be correct. I will always remember the day we moved into our new home. As soon as we arrived, Trofimoff appeared.

"Don't worry about dinner tonight," he said. "You're eating with us."

What a reception they had for us! Several neighbors attended, and Trofimoff toasted our arrival with champagne, followed by a delicious steak dinner. In my entire military career of more than 20 years, we had never been treated so royally upon our arrival at a new home.

As the days and weeks passed, our friendship with our new neighbors grew and prospered. Both Trofimoff and I enjoyed cooking. Almost every week one couple would entertain the other with dinner, with each of us men trying to outdo the other with gourmet meals (he usually won). They did not play bridge, but we introduced them to the game SKIP-BO. Playing a few rounds of that game became a ritual to be followed after every dinner. Trofimoff and I were always partners against the two ladies, and much friendly banter accompanied each session.

We exchanged house keys with them, and whenever either couple was to be absent for a few days, it became routine for the other to watch their neighbor's house, pick up the mail, etc. Upon our return from our first absence of a few days, we were pleasantly surprised to find fresh milk, juice, fruit, and a loaf of bread in our refrigerator.

The Trofimoffs had a large cat they brought with them from Germany, and we took care of the cat whenever they were away. Trofimoff loved to hold and caress the cat, and it was clear that the affection was mutual. The real proof of the cat's love for Trofimoff would become apparent later.

On one of our first visits, Doris observed that the pink tile on their kitchen counters was very pretty, and asked Jutta if she had selected the color. Jutta replied that pink was her favorite color, and that Trofimoff, knowing her preferences, made the decisions for the house on a visit he made to Florida to finalize details. Everything in the house was first rate—furniture, kitchen appliances, cookware, draperies, etc. An open fireplace stood between the living and dining areas, and Trofimoff engaged a stonemason to finish off both sides with beautiful flagstone facing. In addition to lightning arrestors and a security alarm system, he landscaped the lot beautifully with large graceful palms and other plants. A bubbling fountain cascaded into the swimming pool in the enclosed "bird cage" at the rear of their house. The pool was surrounded with lush tropical plants and several colorful ceramic leopards. I told Trofimoff that in my opinion the house was exquisite, and there was nothing more he could do for his home.

"Well," he replied, "I want Jutta's home to be perfect. It wasn't easy for her to leave her family in Germany, and I want her to be happy here." Clearly, he spared no expense and did everything possible to make a good life for her in their new home.

When it came to food and drink, Trofimoff served nothing but the best. He stocked the finest liquors and wine and always had a collection of premium nuts and snacks, which he ordered from specialty mail order houses. He kept a supply of premium steaks in his freezer and often visited nearby Orlando to purchase wild game for his gourmet meals. He truly enjoyed the good life, and he was a wonderful host who enjoyed sharing with his friends.

During our first Christmas at the Indian River Colony Club (IRCC), Jutta's mother visited for the holidays. It soon became clear that she adored Trofimoff. (With his engaging personality, everyone who knew him for any length of time thought highly of him.) Jutta's mother was a small, sprightly, friendly lady in her eighties who loved life. Trofimoff tried to convince her to move to the United States permanently and live with him and Jutta. Fortunately (as later events would disclose), that eventuality never materialized. In her broken English, she voiced her love for her son-in-law, saying that she would visit often but could not leave her German home for good.

That first Christmas, Trofimoff asked us to join them for dinner. When I asked if I could help him, he vehemently stated that he did not need or want any help, and that his meal would be a real German feast. And feast it was! He prepared a large goose, a long-standing German tradition, with kraut, spatzle, and other old-world delicacies. Complemented with excellent German Rheinpfaltz wine, the meal was followed by a superb dessert prepared by Jutta, and topped off with espresso and fiery schnapps. "Good for your stomach after a rich meal," Trofimoff said.

For News Year's Eve that year, we all dressed splendidly to attend the ball at our club's entertainment center, Colony Hall. Trofimoff, the epitome of pomp and dignity, gloried in the opportunity to dress formally and display his miniature military ribbons on his wide chest. Later, we all returned to the Trofimoff home to enjoy another of his specialties, oxtail soup, which had been simmering on his stove for days. From that time on, Doris and I always looked forward to his oxtail soup, regularly served each New Year's Eve.

Trofimoff and I became very close. Weekly, we visited a nearby fitness center where we exercised and enjoyed the relaxation of a sauna afterward. We soon discovered that we both enjoyed a friendly game of poker in an ongoing game with other retired officers in the Melbourne area. Trofimoff suggested that the two of us have our own game, so together we organized a low-stakes weekly session with other members of our community.

We had our differences, but each respected and enjoyed the companionship of the other. I became fascinated with the tales of his early life in Berlin during World War II and the difficulties he overcame in evading members of the German and Russian military forces, eventually making his way to Paris, France and, later, immigrating to the United States. Even then, I had thoughts of writing the fascinating story of his life, but I procrastinated and never got started until several years later.

Trofimoff was very proud of his Russian heritage and spoke often of his father, who, he said, won an assignment to the court of Tsar Nicholas II as a personal page. He also spoke frequently and proudly of his foster brother, Igor Susemihl, whom he grew up with in Berlin during the war years. Igor, several years older than Trofimoff, was his "big brother" tutor and protector as they grew up, and they came to love each other as blood brothers, a relationship that would last throughout their lives. Igor became a priest in the Russian Orthodox Church and was eventually promoted to Metropolitan, which, according to Trofimoff, corresponds to a cardinal in the Catholic Church.

"My brother tells me he will leave money for me when he dies," Trofimoff told us more than once. "He says it will be difficult to send it, and it will have to come through church channels."

As time passed, Doris and I continued to enjoy the close friendship of the Trofimoffs, who had become "perfect neighbors." It soon became apparent that Trofimoff had overextended himself financially.

During our evenings together, he often spoke of his money problems. In his desire to live the good life and obtain the best of everything for himself and Jutta, he assumed a second mortgage on his home and accumulated a large credit card debt.

"The interest on the credit cards is killing me," he confided to us many times. "I have to find a job to pay off my debts."

Finding steady employment in a retirement area such as Florida is never easy, and when one reaches the age of 70 years (Trofimoff was born in 1927), it is practically impossible. He tried for some time and went through a few unsuccessful interviews until he realized he had set an impossible goal for himself. Not only did Trofimoff need the extra income, but also he was fast becoming bored with his daily routine. Both he and Jutta were excellent tennis players, but he developed serious knee problems and was forced to stop playing. Jutta, however, continued to play almost daily with the community tennis group, leaving Trofimoff alone in the house with nothing to do. In desperation, he decided to take a job with a local super market, bagging groceries.

He confided to Doris and me that the pay was terrible, but he had to get out of the house and do something. "At least in this job I will be out with other people, and even though it will take a long time, I can eventually get my credit card debt under control. I have no other choice."

He was proud, with an enormous ego. He begged us not to tell his friends that he bagged groceries for the added income. "Just tell them that since I can't play tennis anymore, I get bored spending every day alone in the house, and I need to get out and mix with other people."

Doris and I continued to enjoy the good life in IRCC, and our two wonderful neighbors made our life even better. We knew Trofimoff had financial problems, but we were satisfied that he would work himself out of his difficulties. We thought, that, if his brother leaves him an inheritance, his problems might be solved. We had no idea of how deep in debt he had fallen, nor did we have any inkling of the violent storm, which even then was rumbling just under the surface of our relationship, a storm to soon erupt with disastrous consequences and drive our quiet community into chaos.

Contents

THE MITROKHIN ARCHIVE

Trust not him with your secrets, who, when left alone in
your room, turns over your papers.
—Johann Kaspar Laveter,
Aphorisms on Man, circa 1788, No. 302

Vasili Mitrokhin, an employee of the KGB, was head archivist of
the KGB's First Chief Directorate from 1972 until he retired in 1985.
Prior to retiring, he regularly removed key files from storage, copied
their contents on pieces of paper, and smuggled them past the security guards in his shoes or trousers. At home, he transcribed the notes
into notebooks or typed and filed them in envelopes organized by
regions of the world. Over the years, as the records accumulated, he
buried them in metal trunks under his house.[1,2]

Disillusioned with his government, he traveled to Latvia in 1992,
taking samples of his documents with him. He walked into the
American embassy in Riga and asked if he could defect.

Incredibly, the Central Intelligence Agency (CIA) officers at the
embassy who handled defectors, overwhelmed at that time by hundreds of Russians trying to get to the West, said they were not interested. Regarding Mitrokhin, their attitude was that, after all, he was
not a spy, but essentially a librarian, and they had no interest in talking with him. To them, the documents carried by Mitrokhin were
clearly not originals and could easily have been fakes.[3]

Paul Redmond, then head of CIA counter-intelligence, pleaded,
with no success, for the U. S. authorities to bring in Mitrokhin. When

the full extent of the material Mitrokhin delivered became known, Redmond was quoted as saying of the CIA's rejection of Mitrokhin, "It was . . . in my view a breathtakingly stupid thing."[4]

Rebuffed by the Americans, Mitrokhin did not give up. Undeterred, on March 24, 1992, he went to the British Embassy in Latvia.[5] The British reaction to Mitrokhin's request for asylum differed from his experience with the Americans. A young female diplomat who interviewed him described him as "young, attractive, and sympathetic, as well fluent in Russian." He identified himself with his passport, his Communist Party card, and his KGB pension certificate, and told her he had with him important material from KGB files. While he went through his bag to dig his notes out from under his food and clothes he told the diplomat he had worked for the KGB's First Chief Directorate from 1948-87. He handed over ten envelopes crammed with 2,000 closely-typed pages from KGB files. His hostess ordered tea, and while Mitrokhin sipped his first cup of English tea, she read some of his notes, asking questions about them. He told her that the notes were only a part of his vast archive, which included material on KGB operations in Britain.[6]

At the British embassy, a British Secret Intelligence Service (BSIS) (which corresponds to the U. S. CIA) agent spotted his potential, and after a series of in-depth interviews and consultations with headquarters, Mitrokhin was formally accepted as a BSIS agent.[7] Impressed with Mitrokhin's material, British officials agreed to help him defect and provide safe passage to England for him and his family. He agreed to return later to meet representatives of the BSIS, and to discuss plans for a visit to Britain. On June 11, he returned to the embassy bringing a rucksack with more archival material. Most of this visit concerned plans for a visit to England, and on September 7, BSIS agents escorted him to England. During this visit he made final arrangements for moving his family and his archives. The BSIS returned him to Russia on October 13 so he could finalize plans for his move. On November 7, he and his family arrived at the embassy. A few days later their new life began, 18 years after he started accumulating the notes for his archives.[8]

The KGB keeps several different sets of files on its own employees and officers as well as on all agents working for them. From 1972 to 1985, Mitrokhin was in charge of, and had full access to, all top-secret KGB files, files that were meticulously maintained. After retiring in 1985, Mitrokhin continued to work, organizing his purloined records until 1992, when he decided to make his move after years of careful planning. After his defection, the British helped him smuggle out of Russia six trunks full of notes and copied archive material exposing the KGB's espionage activities against the West during the Cold War.

When Mitrokhin and his files were safe in England, the BSIS assumed responsibility for evaluating the information. The BSIS, also known as Military Intelligence Department 6, or, more familiarly, as MI6, the agency made famous by the master fictional spy, James Bond, assigned a 30-year veteran to work full-time with the defector. The BSIS agent, fluent in spoken and written Russian and an expert in Russian constitution, government, and history, worked with Mitrokhin for six years translating and organizing the defector's notes.[10]

The Mitrokhin files covered the gamut of KGB clandestine operations all over the world. David Major, a former FBI counterintelligence agent, said, "This is probably one of the most, if not the most, important defector that I've seen in the 20th century."[11]

Revelations from the Mitrokhin papers included the KGB's attempts to recruit Cyrus Vance (later U. S. Secretary of State); a campaign to discredit Ronald Reagan, which began some five years before he became president; attempts to discredit U. S. civil rights leaders, such as Martin Luther King Jr.; and a bizarre, vengeful scheme to break both legs of ballet dancer Rudolf Nureyev, who had defected from Russia in 1961. Mitrokhin's material also revealed how the KGB stashed weapons, radios, and money in secret hiding places in the United States. While it is not known whether any of those caches in the United States were ever located, Mitrokhin did lead police to similar locations in Switzerland, which were booby-trapped with explosives.[12]

The papers revealed details on what the Soviets did, tried to do, and thought about doing. They listened to telephone calls of U. S. officials like Henry Kissinger, placed spies in companies like General Electric and IBM, and tapped the telephones and fax machines of major defense contractors. The KGB developed plans for sabotaging major dams in the western United States and also targeted the Port of New York, amassing details of work schedules and identifying weak points in port security .[13]

Former Department of Justice prosecutor John Martin stated "[Mitrokhin] is really making a massive contribution to our understanding of Soviet activities going back a very long time . . . It was great. This very simple Russian, this bureaucrat, was disgusted with the evil and immoral regime under which he operated. He was not recruited by Western intelligence, he was not paid. For over a decade he diligently and studiously copied KGB files. What a swell kick in the ass."[14]

Mitrokhin's detailed information covered Soviet activities from the Bolshevik Revolution to the 1980s. When his defection became known, U. S. government sources were reported as saying that the revelations had energized at least a dozen espionage cases, some of which had been languishing for many years. One example was the case of Robert Lipka, who spied for the Soviets in the late 1960s when he was a clerk at the U. S. National Security Agency. The FBI's investigation of the case could not proceed until Mitrokhin's information became available. Lipka was convicted and given an 18-year sentence.

At the time, officials said that other cases could soon reach the courts. "There were hundreds of cases or leads opened," said Robert "Bear" Bryant, deputy director of the FBI at that time. Other U. S. officials warned at the time that anyone who had spied for the Soviets and thought he was safe should guess again.[15]

Another FBI announcement described Mitrokhin's material as "the most detailed and extensive pool of CI (Counter Intelligence) ever received by the FBI." The CIA described Mitrokhin's material as "the biggest CI bonanza of the postwar period."[16]

Among the documents in the Mitrokhin Archive were extracts of many that had been delivered to the Soviets by an agent using the various code names of "Markiz," "Konsul," and "Antey." Some of the papers described how a KGB agent, a clergyman with the code name of "Ikar", had recruited that agent.[17] American counterintelligence may have been slow to get started, but like a dog with a bone, they now had hold of something and wouldn't stop until the full story was completely unearthed.

Chapter

2

THE TROFIMOFF FAMILY HISTORY AND EARLY YEARS IN BERLIN

The imagination of a boy is healthy, and the mature
imagination of a man is healthy; but there is a space of life
between, in which the soul is in a ferment, the character
undecided, the way of life uncertain, the ambition thick-sided.
—John Keats,
Preface to *Endymion* (1918)

George Trofimoff was born in Berlin, Germany, in 1927. After immigrating to America in 1947, he enlisted in the U. S. Army in 1948, became a U. S. citizen in 1951, and received a commission in the U. S. Army reserve in 1953. His father, Wladimir Wladimirovich Trofimoff, was born in St. Petersburg in January 1896. Wladimir Ivanovich Trofimoff, George's grandfather, was a descendant of high Russian nobility dating back to the days of Ivan the Terrible, Peter the Great, and the Romanov succession down to Nicholas II. Wladimir earned a commission in the Imperial Tsarist Army and retired as a Colonel of Artillery. He returned to active duty during World War I to serve against the Austro-German invaders, attaining the rank of Brigadier General of the General Staff of the Imperial Russian Army.[1]

Wladimir Ivanovich and his wife, like most members of the Russian nobility, were wealthy owners of large estates and lands in the provincial regions of Russia and owned a family mansion in St. Petersburg.[2] The Trofimoff family, as many other wealthy members of

5

George Trofimoff's grandfather, Wladimir Ivanovich Trofimoff, date unknown. (Author's collection)

the Russian nobility, lost everything during the revolution. Trofimoff writes that the Bolsheviks shot and killed his grandfather in St. Petersburg. His widow, suffering from the Bolshevik rule of "No work—no eat," starved to death there in 1932-33.[3]

In accordance with family tradition, Wladimir, their only son (Trofimoff's father), entered the exclusive Pagen Corps Academy in St. Petersburg. Graduating with top honors in 1913, he spent the following year with the family of Tsar Nicholas II as a personal page (Leib Page), a singular honor reserved for graduates of the academy.[4,5] Later, as a Cornet (Second Lieutenant) of Cavalry, he joined the Imperial Guards of His Majesty's Grodno Hussar Regiment in St. Petersburg. That unit served in the front against the Austro-German forces. George Trofimoff, in his notes, states that during that conflict

George Trofimoff's father, Wladimir Trofimoff, as a cadet at the exclusive Pagen Corps Academy in St. Petersburg, Russia (circa 1913) and mother, Ekaterina Kartali (date unknown) a popular pianist. (Author's collection)

his father received numerous citations and medals.[6]

After the events of October 1917, war broke out between the White Forces and the Bolshevik Red Armies. George Trofimoff's father, along with other remnants of his regiment, served with the White Forces. In 1919, the White Forces attacked the Bolshevik Red Armies from all directions, but despite assistance from the United States, France, and Great Britain, they were unsuccessful. The conflict lasted until November 1920 when the White Forces were defeated.

With the collapse of the White Forces, George Torfimoff's father, then a Major of Cavalry, fled Russia through Finland. Eventually, he found his way to Berlin, Germany, where he had to find a means of support. An excellent amateur guitarist, he soon started performing in several Berlin music halls.[7]

In 1926 Wladimir married Ekaterina Kartali, a popular pianist. Ekaterina gave birth to their only son, George, on March 9, 1927, and in June 1928, she died of blood poisoning resulting from throat surgery. Wladimir, struggling to exist, did not have adequate means to support his son and was desperate to find a solution to the problem.[8]

After the death of his wife, Wladimir Trofimoff approached Baron von Ruckteschell, a classmate of his at the Pagen Corps Academy, and asked if he and his wife would take his son for a short while until he could make other arrangements. As with most Russian refugees in Berlin at that time, the couple lost their parents and all their possessions during the revolution and were in dire financial straits. Even so, they agreed to take care of the baby Trofimoff for a few months. The Baroness, a graduate of the Smolny Institute, a finishing school for aristocratic girls of the high nobility in St. Petersburg, agreed to become his godmother. Later, the institute would become the Bolshevik headquarters.[9]

Another Russian refugee, Wladimir Scharawoff, resided in Berlin at this time with his family. Scharawoff, a former Lieutenant of the Russian Imperial Army, had, like Trofimoff's father, fought with the White Forces against the Bolsheviks. After the collapse of the White Armies, he fled to Berlin where he met and married the widow Antonina Susemihl, who had escaped from the Ukraine after losing her husband, all her property, and the remainder of her family. Her son Igor (born in July 1918) and two sisters-in-law, Elisabeth and Lydia, came with her to Berlin. At the time of Antonina's marriage to Scharawoff, Elisabeth worked in a nursing home for old people in a suburb of Berlin, and Lydia remained with the Scharawoffs, keeping house and helping with a day care center for young Russian refugee children established by the family.[10]

Baron and Baroness von Ruckteschell were able to keep the young Trofimoff for only a short while, and, with no other options, his father became desperate and went to the Scharawoffs, stressing that he could not take care of his son and that the Scharawoffs were his only hope. Lydia, attracted to the baby boy, offered to assume responsibility for his care and assured the Scharawoffs that, if they agreed to accept the baby, she would serve as his nanny for as long as he needed her. She added that Antonina's young son Igor needed a companion and had offered to help her in caring for the Trofimoff baby.

After much consideration and with Lydia's urging and Igor's professed willingness to help, the Scharawoffs relented, and in late 1928, at the age of one and one-half years, the young Trofimoff was admitted to the day care center with Lydia as his nanny and Igor as his foster brother.[11]

Young George Trofimoff with his father, circa 1934. (Author's collection)

The Scharawoffs closed the day care operation a few years later, and the family accepted Trofimoff as a foster child. Later Trofimoff wrote, "This is how I became a foster member of the family and Igor my foster brother. Until the age of ten or eleven, I did not know I was not their natural son. I often wondered why I had two fathers, because my real father visited me at least once a week; my father was 'Papa' and my foster father was 'Papa Volodya.' My foster mother was just 'Mama.' I thought that I was really something special . . . The family was poor but we were all very happy."[12]

The elder Scharawoff obtained a job as a mail clerk for the German Ministry of Commerce and studied business administration in the evenings. Antonina taught Russian language, literature, and history at a Russian school. At first, the entire curriculum of the school was taught in the Russian language by Russian émigrés who had fled Russia during and after the revolution, but in 1935 the school became a fully accredited German institution. From that time on, all instruction was given in German. However, Russian language, history, and literature continued to be mandatory subjects.[13]

Both Trofimoff and Igor attended this school. Igor began in 1924 at the age of six and attended until he graduated twelve years later, and Trofimoff started in 1932, attending until 1943 when the school was closed and evacuated because of Allied bombings. Trofimoff, then sixteen years old, transferred to a private school until the continuous Allied bombings forced its relocation to Poland.[14]

Life was hard for poor Russian émigrés in wartime Berlin. The Scharawoffs lived in decrepit, converted wooden barracks in Spandau, a suburb of Berlin. The converted apartment consisted of just two rooms, a small kitchen, and a tiny room no larger than a walk-in closet, which served as a bedroom for the two foster brothers. Igor's bed was a folding cot and Trofimoff's was a converted crib. In the darkness, before going to sleep, they often discussed and fantasized on what they wanted to be as adults. Trofimoff remembers that at times he wanted to become a fireman or a train engineer; at other times, he thought he would like to be a streetcar conductor. Igor, on the other hand, had consistent dreams of becoming a surgeon.[15]

The two boys took a 45-minute streetcar ride to school each day. During those school years, they developed lifetime bonds. "Igor was always my 'big brother,' " Trofimoff recalls in his notes. "We played together at home; he took me riding on his bike; and in school he was always my 'protector.' I was a sickly child plagued by constant ear infections and other diseases, missing school on many occasions for a week or two at a time. Igor always helped me with homework to catch up with the rest of the class."[16]

Their relationship was not always rosy. Igor, as with many older brothers, sometimes became tyrannical with his younger brother. Trofimoff tells of one incident:

> At one time, for my birthday, I must have been four or five years old, I received a snow white teddy bear— almost as large as I was at the time. Without losing any time, Igor explained that the teddy had a bad stomachache and needed 'surgery' to feel better. He proceeded to cut the belly of my teddy with and pulled out the kapok from the inside.
>
> I watched all this with great interest, but when Igor refused to put the stuffing back, I burst out in tears. Igor grabbed the bear and hit me with it.

Trofimoff recalls that the noise of his wailing brought Lydia, who ordered Igor to repair the bear's stomach. "Needless to say," he writes, "Igor never touched this bear again."[17]

Trofimoff's nanny, Lydia, was a persuasive influence on the young boy during his formative years. "Lydia Susemihl was not only my nanny when I was a baby, but she was my tutor and mentor, always pushing me to improve my scholastic efforts, which were never very efficient. Without my nanny, I would have been most certainly stuck in 9th or 10th grade for a second year."[18]

All members of the Scharawoff family were devout members of the Russian Orthodox Church. Trofimoff and Igor became altar boys in a church located a few blocks from their school and were kept busy with church activities.[19]

Trofimoff remembers that church as a real "jewel." Interior walls of an apartment were removed to create one large room where some 200 to 300 persons could stand (Russian Orthodox Church members stand during services as there are no pews). Hand-painted religious scenes covered the walls, and many valuable icons, gold-plated and studded with gems, donated by members of the Russian nobility living in Berlin, were on pedestals throughout the church. Many candles and oil lamps in colored glass containers added to the beauty and solemnity of the church.[20]

The basement of the church housed a library with an extensive collection of Russian literary classics. While Trofimoff was too young at that time to appreciate the heavier classics, he remembers reading extensively: Pushkin's *Fairy Tales*, translations of Grimm and Hans Christian Anderson stories, and the novels of James Fennimore Cooper, Jack London, and other adventure classics.

Trofimoff and Igor received Russian Orthodox lessons in school during the week and attended children's bible classes in church after Sunday services. The entire family attended church on Saturday evenings, Sunday mornings, and before and during all Russian Orthodox holidays.

"During the fasting period before Easter," Trofimoff writes, "especially during the Passion week, we were in church almost six hours each day, to include the Midnight Mass which lasted until three o'clock in the morning. This last week we ate only salt herring, boiled potatoes with sunflower seed oil and dry bread."[21]

After the fasting period, the Scharawoff family enjoyed the Russian Easter feast, a celebration they had saved and sacrificed for throughout the year. ". . . what a feast," Trofimoff writes. "We saved and saved for many months to be able to have a true Russian feast at Easter, and we always had it!"[22]

The traditional Russian Christmas holiday was a somber, solemn affair, a great contrast to the feasting and celebrations Russian families enjoyed after their Easter fast. However, an entirely different Christmas celebration, organized by Lydia, a dedicated Lutheran, took place each year in the Scharawoff home. Lydia attended services in her own Lutheran church and did not participate in the continuous Russian Orthodox worshipping practiced by the Scharawoffs during Easter.

Trofimoff recalls many fond memories of his nanny, who had a profound influence on his development. "She always insisted that Igor and I accompany her to a Lutheran Christmas Mass . . . Lydia's sister Elisabeth used to come and spend a week or two before and during Christmas at our home to prepare all the German 'goodies' so mandatory in a German family . . . Those were the two happiest holidays in our lives: Russian Easter and German Christmas."[23]

The Scharawoffs moved frequently, whenever better housing became available. In the mid-1930s, they relocated to the Bavarian quarter of Berlin, very close to their church and Trofimoff and Igor's school. Trofimoff remembers that the new home was a vast improvement over the old, tiny barracks in Spandau. "It was a three-bedroom apartment on the 6th floor of an apartment building with a view of the Berlin rooftops, with a small bath and small kitchen with a natural gas cooking stove. We did have running hot and cold water but the rooms had to be heated with coal stoves. Nevertheless, it was an improvement, especially since we were able to walk to school and to church."[24]

It was during this period that Trofimoff and his foster brother became separated. Igor graduated from high school in 1936 and enrolled in a German university and medical school in Berlin. In 1937 he became an apprentice deacon of the Russian Orthodox Church, and in early 1942, he married a Russian émigré from Austria. Drafted into the German Army and commissioned a Lieutenant, he was sent to the Eastern front and was severely wounded. Returning to Berlin and discharged from the army, he became a Russian Orthodox priest. Trofimoff recalls seeing Igor in Berlin in late 1944, shortly after Igor's wife gave birth to a baby son, Nicholas. "This was the last time I saw Igor and his family until 1962," he writes.[25]

After that brief encounter, the two foster brothers lost contact for many years. Susemihl and his family, along with his parents Wladimir and Antonina Scharawoff, emigrated to Australia at the end of the war. Later, Igor divorced his wife, became a monk, and advanced rapidly through the Russian Orthodox Church to become a bishop, archbishop, Metropolitan, and finally Patriarch of Vienna and Austria.

In 1938 the Scharawoffs made another improvement in their living conditions by moving again. Trofimoff writes: "What a blessing! On the fourth floor and no more carrying buckets of coal up six floors! It is in this area that we first experienced the true nature of the Nazis. This whole area was inhabited by many Jewish people, especially refugees from . . . Russia and Poland . . . It was the infamous *Kristallnacht* . . . We were really scared. After all, we were also refugees from Russia. How did the Nazis know we were not Jewish?" The riots occurring on *Kristallnacht*[26] were particularly frightening.[27]

When Trofimoff posed this question to his foster father, the answer reinforced his pride in his family heritage and his sense of invincibility, which would be a hallmark of his later years. He writes: "Well, my two 'fathers' later explained to me that several years before the *Kristallnacht* occurred, all Russian refugees in Berlin had to prove ancestry being 'Arien' [sic]. Fortunately, the Trofimoffs and the Scharawoffs and most of the Russian émigrés in Berlin were descendants of the old hereditary Russian nobility and were registered in various ancestral records in European libraries, easily proving their 'Arien' [sic] ancestry."[28]

Even so, many Jewish Russian émigrés did not escape the Nazi atrocities. "Several of my classmates, male and female," writes Trofimoff, "disappeared from our school during the period 1939 to

1941. After the war a few of them surfaced in England and the United States. Most of them were never heard from again."[29]

Soon after *Kristallnacht*, Trofimoff became very sick and was hospitalized with double pneumonia. He writes that he hovered close to death for several days; when he recovered, doctors announced that he was weak and susceptible to tuberculosis. The good fortune that was to follow Trofimoff for much of his life, which began when he was accepted to the Scharawoff family, continued when in February 1939, German Health Authorities arranged for him to be sent to a convalescent center in Davos, Switzerland.[30]

Trofimoff writes of his six months in Switzerland, "For me it was a marvelous time. The food was excellent, the medical facilities the best in Europe. The 80 or so children . . . were well taken care of . . . about 60 of us were pronounced completely cured and no longer apt to get TB, and were returned to Berlin on August 31, 1939.

"I will never forget this date because when we woke up the next morning, 1 September 1939, the Germans had invaded Poland. Two days later England and France declared war on Germany."[31]

World War II was underway, bringing more problems to the already perilous existence of the Scharawoff family. While they were not directly or personally affected by the conflict, many changes came about which made their life in Berlin more miserable and difficult than before. Trofimoff writes:

> The day the Germans invaded Poland, all food disappeared from the shelves of grocery stores and even small shops. During that same week, ration cards for meat, dairy products, bread and all food staples were issued. The allotted quantities were small but not extreme. As time went by, the amounts were diminished.[32]
>
> After the first bombing raid in Berlin in March of 1943, life became very difficult: a struggle to stay alive, being hungry most of the time and being miserable all of the time.[33]

Earlier, Trofimoff joined a Russian Boy and Girl Scout organization, supervised by the parent organization in England, but in 1940 it was outlawed in Germany because of the English influence. "This was pretty rough on us kids," he writes, "because it was a wonderful organization where Russian tradition was maintained."[34]

In mid-1941 the Germans allowed the formation of a new organi-

zation, called the National Organization of Russian Youth (NORM),
and Trofimoff enrolled. "Every year, during summer, we had a big
camp . . . These camps were wonderful for our Russian émigré
morale," he writes. "We had large bonfires under the old Russian
'White, Blue and Red' flag and we sang the old Russian National
Anthem and old nostalgic Russian songs . . . our lectures about the
Revolution and the Bolsheviks, Soviets, and Communists in general
became more detailed and profound. Combined with information
that most of us had received from our parents, we developed a deep,
solid hatred for anything connected with Communism." (Trofimoff's
notes state that due to increased levels of Allied bombings and lack of
participation, NORM was disbanded in late 1943.)[35]

Trofimoff recalls that the Allied bombing of Berlin got off to a slow
start in late 1941, and raids were sporadic during 1942. "At first, only
two or three bombs were dropped at any one time, and then only in
widely dispersed areas. The raids were so infrequent that they became
a curiosity. We actually went by streetcar to view such singular bomb
results. Nevertheless, the air raids were a constant irritant."[36]

The frequency and duration of Allied bombings of Berlin increased
steadily until the winter of 1943 when the raids, a nuisance at the
beginning, became very dangerous. Trofimoff describes these times:
"The bombing appeared to be systematic with disastrous results.
Whole sections of Berlin disappeared overnight."[37]

In 1943 Trofimoff's father married a former singer of Russian
Gypsy songs who had performed in German movies depicting life in
Russia during the reign of the tsars. Shortly after his marriage,
Wladimir asked his son to live with them in their new Berlin home
and Trofimoff bade farewell to his foster family. He recalls that his
father, after attending night school, became an electronics engineer,
working for an electronics firm. "He had a comfortable income but
worked very hard . . . He invented many parts for electronics technology and obtained 30 to 40 patents."[38]

Trofimoff describes how his entire family almost lost their lives
during one of the nightly air raids in 1944. Their apartment building
suffered a direct hit and was completely destroyed, along with the
apartment buildings on both sides. They were buried by debris; the
entrances to the passages to adjacent buildings were blocked by rub-
ble. They attempted to signal their plight by banging on water and
gas pipes, but as the entire block was destroyed, no one heard their
signals and they remained imprisoned for more than 72 hours before

being rescued. During that time they subsisted on a few emergency rations they had stockpiled in the basement, some coffee and tea in thermos bottles, and a trickle of water they obtained from the underground pipes. When rescuers reached them, they were amazed to see that the raid had leveled the entire block.[39]

After this raid the electronics company which employed the elder Trofimoff moved its operation, and Wladimir and his wife left Berlin with the firm. Trofimoff lost contact with his parents until 1947 when he was in Paris, but he did not see them until Christmas 1949, when, as a member of the U. S. Army, he was assigned to Germany.[40]

Trofimoff's school closed because of the bombings and he eventually transferred to a private school, which also closed. He evacuated to Poland and in October/November 1944 received a draft notice from the German Army with directions to report to the local German Military Headquarters for processing and a physical examination. He writes, "I was classified 1A, given a military passbook and told to go to my godmother's in Berlin, to wait for final reporting orders."[41]

Trofimoff decided to evade the draft notice. He stayed with his godmother until she obtained travel ration coupons, extra clothing, and money to pay for his travel by express train to Dresden. His military passbook allowed him to travel freely at half-price.[42]

While staying with his godmother, Trofimoff visited the church he had previously attended and encountered his foster brother, Igor, who by then had become a priest in the church. Igor told Trofimoff of an early 1944 air raid that had destroyed the entire area where the Scharawoffs lived, including their home. Igor also told George that his nanny, Lydia, died of cancer in late 1943. The two foster brothers would not meet again until late in 1962 when Susemihl passed through Frankfurt/Main, Germany, on his return from Australia.[43]

In late November Trofimoff left his godmother's home and took an express train to Dresden. He stayed with his aunt, Countess von Adlerberg and her son, Alexander, for four days before taking another train to Prague, where he hoped to find friends of his godmother. He did not know it at the time, but this was the last time he would see his aunt and her son, as they both perished in the firestorm resulting from a massive air raid on 22-23 February 1945.[44]

Unable to locate his godmother's friends in Prague, Trofimoff boarded a local train to Pilsen in early December where he continued his journey to the west on foot. His long, solo journey across Europe, and eventually to America, was just beginning.

Chapter

3

FROM PILSEN TO PARIS

Dame Fortune is a fickle gypsy,
And always blind, and often tipsy;
Sometimes for years and years together,
She'll bless you with the sunniest weather,
Bestowing honour, pudding, pence,
You can't imagine why or whence; —
Then in a moment—Presto, pass! —
Your joys are withered like the grass.
—Winthrop Mackworth Praed (1802-1939),
The Haunted Tree

At Pilsen, the end of the line, Trofimoff stepped off the small, still hissing train, surveying the countryside. Almost deserted, it was bleak and unfriendly, and he was not quite sure which direction to take. Not knowing what the future would bring, he slung his knapsack over his back, selected a likely looking road, and started walking.

"Conditions in this part of Czechoslovakia were disorganized and hectic," he writes. "My situation was desperate and very dangerous. Most Czechs hated the Germans and their occupation forces, but there were some who collaborated with them and informed on any strangers in their areas, and even on their neighbors."[1] Trofimoff had to be very careful. He knew to be wary of native Czechs; at the same time, as a German deserter, he had to avoid German soldiers who were everywhere. "The only thing that helped me was the fact that it had become quite obvious at that time that the Germans were losing the war and that's why most people in rural areas were sympathetic to people like myself."[2]

Most of the population spoke some German and Trofimoff communicated reasonably well. Most of the farms were cared for only by old men and women, and, to his favor, they were happy to have a young and willing hand like George helping with the fieldwork.

Trofimoff spent several months moving through the countryside, looking for work and refuge in rural farms, staying away from villages. Recognizing his danger, he says he kept moving, "never remaining in one place for more than two or three days until early April, 1945, when I found a farm with two old women who hid me from retreating German troops, fed me, and generally took care of me asking nothing in return except a little work in the barn and in the house itself."[3]

Trofimoff recalls that this area was overrun with fleeing German soldiers as well as remnants of the Russian Liberation Army (ROA). "The villages in the area were full of rumors and news on the radio were [sic] incomplete and misleading."[4] He remembers one rumor reporting that units of the ROA surrendered to advancing Soviet forces. "Additional rumors, which were later confirmed by fleeing members of the ROA, stated that all officers and senior NCOs were separated from the rest of the troops and machine-gunned by Soviet tanks. The lower rank soldiers were loaded into boxcars, sealed therein and transported directly to Siberia. I personally observed Soviet troops shooting at fleeing unarmed German soldiers."[5]

Trofimoff says that the local population was terrified by the many rumors of Soviet atrocities. He was particularly concerned, "especially as I was the son of a Russian émigré."[6]

Trofimoff heard that U. S. troops had arrived in the vicinity of Passau, further to the west, and because of his precarious situation, he decided to leave his "haven" with the two old ladies and seek safety with U. S. forces. He had reports of a line of demarcation, established somewhere between his current location and the Czechoslovakian-German border. This line was reportedly guarded by Soviet troops who would permit no one to pass to the west.

His two benefactors were disappointed to lose his help. Trofimoff writes that they gave him some bread and a few boiled eggs for his backpack, wishing him good luck on his journey. He started walking through the countryside, avoiding larger roads, but was soon confronted by two drunken Russian soldiers, one astride an old nag of a horse. "They started cursing me in Russian, saying that I was a German soldier . . . I denied it vehemently, but to no avail. They put a rope around my neck and started dragging me . . ."[7]

They came to a large meadow enclosed by a barbed wire fence, and the two soldiers pushed Trofimoff toward the enclosure to join a group of 200-300 German Army prisoners of war. Another large group of German prisoners soon arrived. At the same time, a group of old people, mostly women and several small children, were milling around outside the gate.

"As the German soldiers were entering the compound, I slowly pushed myself through this group and mingled with the group of women and children, trying to be as inconspicuous as possible."[8] The women noticed his predicament and shielded him from the Soviet guards as the group moved away from the enclosure to a nearby village. With luck, ingenuity, and the aid of the women, Trofimoff was free after only an hour of captivity.

Trofimoff left again as soon as darkness fell. After several hours, "I heard loud talking, laughing and even singing by soldiers who were supposed to be guarding the demarcation line. The sentries were easily seen because they smoked and had some petroleum lanterns."[9]

Trofimoff dropped to the ground and crawled on his belly through the line of sentries. Just as he thought he had broken through safely, he heard a barrage of machine gun fire from his rear. "I became panicky, jumped up and started running, bumping into trees, going through bushes and brambles . . . I was really lucky to get away with just some scratches and bruises."[10]

The next morning he resumed his walk to Passau. As he stopped and rested at farmhouses, he heard that the Germans had unconditionally surrendered to the Allies, and he realized that at last the war was over. "What a joy and relief. For me this was the end of privation, hunger, and the danger of being shot for desertion."[11]

Trofimoff tells how, enroute to Passau, he hitched rides on farm carts, and at other times joined bands of other refugees. Reaching Passau after some ten days, he stopped at a bridge crossing the Danube River. Since leaving Pilsen, he had traveled more than 100 miles, mostly on foot.

The crossing was guarded by U. S. Army soldiers, who checked the papers of anyone attempting to cross. "I stood there undecided at what to do. The only papers I had was [sic] my old German-Issue 'Nansen' passport, which identified me as a Russian émigré born in Berlin of 'stateless' citizenship. The other document was a 'Wherpass,' a soldier's book of the German Army.

"While I was standing there . . . a U. S. Army jeep stopped next to me asking for directions to the *Rathaus* (City Hall). I happened to see a street sign pointing to its location. So, in my broken school English, I explained to the American soldier (later I knew that he was a lieutenant) how to get to the City Hall. He was surprised at my English and asked me if I would help him to interpret while he had some business with the local police. I was only too happy to oblige and that is how I landed as a kitchen police (KP)/interpreter with the 660th Medical Clearing Company."[12,13]

Good fortune continued to follow Trofimoff as he became a temporary addition to the U. S. Army unit, where he provided interpreter service and worked as a helper in the unit's kitchen.

"It was a wonderful time for me. My English improved within a few days and, additionally, I began to look like a human being again . . . It is difficult to describe how happy I actually became. The soldiers were very nice to me; they gave me all necessary items of clothing, U. S. Army uniforms without insignia . . . even a helmet liner, and all of this in brand new condition. They were sharing all of their rations, cigarettes, tobacco, cigars, chocolate, candy, toilet articles—everything! On payday, they passed a helmet liner, and everyone contributed whatever he wanted in U. S. script money and even some German money. The total usually exceeded the pay of a private in the army."[14]

Shortly after joining the unit, Trofimoff was taken to an intelligence officer for a security check. He recalls that "The interviewing Major was polite but very negative in his attitude until I produced my 'stateless' passport and my Military Book (Wehrpass)."[15] The German Army document proved that, although Trofimoff had been drafted, he was never inducted into the German Army, and the passport established his "stateless" identity. The Major became more friendly and receptive to Trofimoff's story but retained his papers, saying they would be checked out. About two weeks later the Major summoned him back to his office. " . . . the Major handed me my passport wishing me 'Good Luck' for the future, saying that . . . my passport was a perfectly valid identification document."[16]

Trofimoff tells how he spent about three "happy" months with the clearing company, working in the kitchen and frequently interpreting for the lieutenant. During periods of free time, he played softball and pitched horseshoes (a game he had never heard of before) with the soldiers. "It was a wonderful time for a young man who had just spent years of hunger and other privations for five years of his youth."[17]

The good times for Trofimoff came to an end when the company received orders to move to Le Havre, France, for transfer to the Pacific Theater of Operations. The company commander called Trofimoff to his office to break the news. He said that the unit had orders to relocate to the Far East, and would leave shortly for Le Havre. He told Trofimoff that he could not take him with the unit to the Far East, but that he could drop him off at any place on the way to Le Havre.

Trofimoff was aware that his godfather, who served with his father as a member of the White Forces, had moved to Paris sometime in 1933-34 and was living there along with a large contingent of other Russian émigrés. He asked to be taken there. The unit left in early July 1945, stopping in tent camps along the way. Trofimoff spent three more nights with his American friends, and on the next evening he was dropped off in Paris.

After enduring years of poverty and hardship growing up in wartime Berlin, a perilous journey on foot from Pilsen to Passau, and three months with the U. S. Army unit, a young eighteen-year-old George Trofimoff found himself alone on a street corner in Montmartre, Paris, at ten o'clock in the evening in July, 1945. His worldly possessions, consisting of clothing and provisions donated by the American soldiers, were contained in two U. S. Army duffel bags.

For many months he had survived under the harshest of conditions, using his personality and wits, while he learned how to avail himself of any and all opportunities, taking full advantage of the help (and, where necessary, the weakness) of others. Now, with his meager possessions and a mere $65 in U. S. script and some 200 worthless Reich marks in his pocket, he was convinced that the good fortune that had followed him during the first years of his life would continue. Confident that success would be his in the future, he was ready to meet the challenges of his adult life.

"And so here I was in Paris! What a shock! After almost six years of deprivation, hunger, cold and general misery," Trofimoff writes, "I find myself in the city of light, overwhelmed by noise, movement of vehicles and people with a general sense of well-being and contentment."[18]

Standing alone under a street lantern, wearing a U. S. Army uniform with no insignia, with only a limited knowledge of the French language, Trofimoff did not know what to do or where to turn. He had no way of locating his godfather or other Russian émigrés, and he had no identification other than his Nazi-issued passport and a letter saying that he had worked for a short time for the U. S. Army in Germany, certifying only that he was honest and diligent in his work. He knew that without a French visa or other legal identification papers, these documents were not sufficient to justify his presence in Paris and would probably lead to trouble if he tried to use them.

Suddenly, the good fortune that had followed him since his Berlin days returned when he heard footsteps behind him. Turning around, he saw a young French lady wearing the uniform of the French Auxiliary Forces. Trofimoff writes that the young lady, in halting English, asked how she could help him.

He was delighted to hear words spoken in English, but he didn't know how to explain his circumstances. His notes reveal his desperation, relating that he lied and blurted out that he had missed his convoy for Le Havre. He told the young lady that he was lost in Paris with no place to stay and didn't know what to do.

The young lady introduced herself, he writes, telling him that her brother was in the French Army, serving in Germany. She told him that her brother's room was empty and that she was sure her parents would he happy to have an American soldier as a guest. Trofimoff's notes tell how she offered to take him to her parents' home.[19]

Trofimoff was not a U. S. Army soldier, and he was embarrassed because of his lie. He recalls that he realized that beggars can't be choosers, and he accepted the offer of assistance.

His new friend hailed a taxi and soon they were at her home. Trofimoff writes that while his new hosts were surprised at receiving such a late houseguest, they welcomed him enthusiastically, offering bread, cheese, sausage and a carafe of red wine. They then led him to their son's room where he slept soundly until mid-morning. He recalls awaking to the delectable aroma of hot coffee.

After a breakfast of café au lait and brioches, Trofimoff realized he could not continue to lie to this family and, at the same time, take advantage of their hospitality. He related his true story with his hosts' daughter translating. He was pleasantly surprised to find generous compassion as they demonstrated a sincere desire to help him get settled in Paris.

Trofimoff writes that his hosts emphasized that the first and most important thing was for him to get a job—any job.[20] With no legal papers, he had to take whatever job was available. His benefactors suggested that he try to find work at the *Gare du Nord* where, they told him, manual labor was always needed. He applied for work, but as a foreigner with no papers, he was hired at half-pay to shovel coal.

Trofimoff recalls that the work was backbreaking and the pay minimal. After three weeks he realized he had to make a change. "I decided that I could not continue living like this, always afraid of being arrested for lack of documentation. I told my hosts that I decided to try to get legalized."[21]

He went to the Parisian police headquarters to apply for identification papers and a permit allowing him to work and reside in France. As he sat, uneasy and worried about his interview, he heard two elderly ladies speaking Russian. Astounded by his good luck, he wasted no time in interrupting their conversation, telling them how happy he was to hear the Russian language. "As soon as they heard the details of my being in Paris, they immediately stood up, grabbed me by the arm, and left the waiting room."[22]

The ladies never spoke again until they had him outside the building where they explained that his chances of getting the documents he needed were zero, as he had entered France illegally from Germany, a country the French despised. They assured him that they wanted to help him find his way through the French bureaucracy, but they insisted first that they wanted to help him find a place to live with some of the many Russian émigrés in Paris.[23] What great luck, Trofimoff thought, as the ladies led him to a small Citroen automobile and drove him to the home of his French friends to retrieve his few belongings. His hosts and their daughter regretted his departure but wished him good luck, inviting him to visit them at any time.

Trofimoff's new Russian friends introduced him to many émigré families, and with their help, he soon obtained temporary residence papers. He writes that for some three months he lived with several different families, all poor. He kept moving from one family to another until late 1945 when good fortune struck again.

"A Russian lady, the widow of a deceased former Czarist general, took pity on me and treated me like the son she never had."[24] She offered him a tiny room in her four-room apartment and purchased a complete wardrobe for him. "It was the first real suit of my life." [25]Trofimoff writes that he stayed with this lady for almost a full year.

Once in the Russian community, Trofimoff began attending the Russian Orthodox Church. His notes describe the importance of the church to all Russian émigrés: "It was not just a place to worship but also a meeting place for people who were lost and people who tried to find friends and relatives who had been dispersed all over Europe during the war."[26]

Trofimoff wanted information on the whereabouts of his godfather, a Grand Romanov Duke. One Sunday, after services, he approached several individuals standing outside the church to ask for any information they might have. He writes that most everyone knew the grand duke, but that he spent most of his time in the Riviera and probably would not return to Paris until the fall.

Trofimoff writes that from his discussions at the church he learned that a group of young Russian émigrés was enrolled in a school located on the outskirts of Paris, similar to the cadet schools in Russia prior to the revolution. "The young people also told me that there were two or three men among that group who had lived in Germany during the war . . . One was actually in my class and his name was Shurik Mitkaleff . . . And what a happy reunion it was next Sunday. Shurik was there and we recognized each other and became the best, almost inseparable, friends during the next three years."[27]

Trofimoff writes that Shurik's parents were very poor. His father was an invalid as a result of wounds suffered during World War I and with the White Armies during the Revolution. His mother eked out a meager living as a private seamstress. "Shurik had just started working as an apprentice for hand-painting on silks and other fabrics in a studio which had been opened by a Russian émigré family, and he introduced me to the owners of the studio who hired me immediately."[28]

Trofimoff's lucky star was still shining brightly! The friends completed their apprenticeship and began working full time. "The studio had very large orders from the U. S. A. and we were working 10–12 hours a day making very good money," Trofimoff writes. [29]

As time passed, Trofimoff's circle of friends grew rapidly. "Shurik had meanwhile introduced me to many of his friends in the Russian émigré youth group."[30] Trofimoff's new circle of friends were Russian youths, children of the older émigrés who were members of the "upper crust" of Russian society, "privileged Russia." Trofimoff and his friends enjoyed an extensive social life, with " . . . private parties at home with Russian 'Zakuski' (appetizers), lots of vodka, and some champagne and wine. Additionally, some of the older Russian émigré groups organized larger parties in a private club or in a Russian restaurant. We, of course, attended all of them and had a wonderful time."[31]

Trofimoff writes about the "Union of Soviet Patriots," an organization very active in Paris at that time. Supported by the Soviet Embassy, the group held large balls and parties frequently. "These parties were attended mostly by older people of lower social positions like former laborers and farmers in the old Czarist Russia, who had not been able to achieve a better life abroad and decided to return to the USSR . . . A few of these people with their children had already left their homes in France for the USSR and were writing to their friends in France, giving glowing accounts of their new jobs and the 'wonderful new life.' They were also suggesting to their friends to follow suite [sic] and join them in their 'homeland.' "[32]

Trofimoff's friends, sons and daughters of former Czarist officers and members of the old nobility, still harbored feelings of superiority over the lower classes. They deeply resented the activities and political leanings of the "Union of Soviet Patriots" and decided to make a political statement of their own. He writes of the ensuing events:

"About twenty of us, boys and girls of about 18 to 20 years of age, attended one of these parties and started to provoke the elderly participants and their offsprings by engaging them in arguments about the pros and cons of the Revolution. We reminded them of what the Bolsheviks did to the officers in the Armed Forces and to members of the noble families . . . We reminded them of the atrocities perpetrated by Stalin, Beria, and cohorts in the Ukraine in the years of 1931–1933, when over three million peasants were systematically starved to death.[33]

"Soon, some of these arguments became very heated and loud, and fisticuffs started flying, quickly developing into a near-riot. We had a couple of very 'tough' guys in our group, and we proceeded to demolish the premises. First we broke the telephones, then we tore down the portraits of Stalin, Lenin, and Marx, and then we continued by breaking the mirrors behind the bar and upending the tables with all of the delicacies, the vodka, the cognac, the Krim champagne and wines. Needless to say, we did not have much of a chance once the 'goons,' probably members of the Soviet Embassy, arrived on the scene and joined the fracas. We departed from the premises in a hurry, just before the French police arrived, and vanished through the nearby metro subway."[34]

While Trofimoff and his friends tried for a repeat of this fracas, which apparently resembled saloon free-for-alls depicted in old John

Wayne movies, they were unsuccessful, for they were never admitted to future affairs. "Looking back today, the incident was probably foolish, but we had to show the Russian émigré community in Paris that the old Czarist Russian spirit was still alive among the Russian youths, descendants of the old monarchist nobility, who fought the Communist Bolsheviks during the revolution as members of the 'White Armies.' "[35]

Trofimoff's participation in these insurrections against the lower-class "dark people" emphasized the depth of his love for "Mother Russia" and the nobility from which he was descended. The passion and pride in his aristocratic background were to consume him and guide his actions throughout his life.

With all the socializing among the young Russians, the inevitable happened: Trofimoff had his first love affair. He writes, "I fell in love, for the first time in my adolescent life, with a Russian émigré girl. Irina Grineva was the great-great-granddaughter of a heroine who had played the major role in an old Russian literature classic, the novel, *The Captain's Daughter,* by Alexander Pushkin . . . Irina's father was a former Captain of these Imperial Cossacks, and also fought against the Bolsheviks during the period of the revolution 1917–1919."[36]

Trofimoff and his friend Shurik spent many hours in Irina's home, fascinated by her father's stories about life in the Caucasus and his battles against the Red Armies of the Bolsheviks. "We learned much about pre-World War I Russian history and about life in general in places other than St. Petersburg and Moscow."[37] Trofimoff's Russian history education had come to an abrupt halt with the Allied bombings of Berlin during the war, and the stories of Irina's father helped to bridge the gap in his knowledge of his homeland's history. Much as he enjoyed his sessions with Irina's father, he reports that his love affair was short-lived and soon faded. "I wanted to make my life in the United States and Irina did not want to leave Paris under any circumstances."[38]

Trofimoff and Shurik's employment as silk painters was on the wane, as the once-large volume of orders from the United States for hand-painted ties and scarves began to decline rapidly. Soon they had work for only one or two days each week, and the two decided to go into the business on their own.

"Shurik was a very gifted designer and artist and I had by then become an excellent painter."[39] Pooling their resources to buy equipment and silk material, they created a collection of original-design silk scarves with various motifs and different color combinations. Their plan was not to sell individual scarves, but to obtain orders by displaying the samples to exclusive Parisian shops. Unable to gain access to any of these shops and frustrated by their failures, they were dejected until Trofimoff's lucky Parisian star sparkled once more. In a small perfume shop, they encountered a gracious lady manager.

"She suggested that we visit her sister, who worked at the Pate film studios as a makeup specialist . . . she immediately called her sister on the phone and arranged a meeting at the studios the next morning."[40]

During their visit to the film studio, they obtained several orders for scarves. "We had met many people at the Pate studios and our reputation grew for a while, resulting in a number of additional orders for our scarves, giving us sufficient work for the next five to six months."[41]

Business success was only a part of the luck falling on Trofimoff as a result of their introduction to the Pate studios. "For me, this episode changed the course of my life in Paris. I met Mr. Sergei Karpov who was the chief makeup artist at the Pate studios and was also a Russian émigré, former officer of the Czarist Imperial Guards . . . He invited us to the studio's restaurant for an apperitif [sic] and wanted to know more about our backgrounds . . . I explained that I came from Berlin and that I was the son of a graduate of the Pagan Cadett [sic] Corps Academy in St. Petersburg. Mr. Karpov became all excited and decided to call his sister immediately to tell her all about me. He explained that he had married a member of the French embassy in St. Petersburg before and during World War I, and that she would probably swoon when she heard that the son of Wladimir Wladimirovich Trofimoff was in Paris."[42]

Trofimoff's good fortune continued as he and Shurik were invited for dinner at the home of Mr. and Mrs. Maurice Thiebault, Karpov's sister. Trofimoff writes that the Thiebaults insisted that he move to their apartment as soon as possible, " . . . and stay with them as long as I was in Paris or as long as I wanted to. Mrs. Thiebault was a member of an old nobility Russian family, which was well acquainted with my father's family in St. Petersburg. She and my father were friends as children and were corresponding after the escape from Russia during the revolution. Her husband, Maurice Thiebault, was the son of a French banker who was a financial advisor (attaché) at the French embassy at St. Petersburg before and during World War I."[43]

Trofimoff's good luck appeared to be running out when he and Shurik experienced difficulties selling their scarves at the Pate studios. The two young men were not old enough to have a commercial license, and Trofimoff, with only temporary residence papers, did not have a worker's permit.

Trofimoff had heard of The Society of Friends (Quakers) and decided to ask for their assistance in obtaining a worker's permit. "I was interviewed by a very cordial middle-aged gentleman, a Mr. Thomas R. Bodine, who explained to me that the Society could not help me with any identification documents in France, but could and would help me emigrate to the United States."[44]

Trofimoff told Mr. Bodine it was his dream to immigrate to the United States, but with no relatives or friends there to sponsor him for immigration, he had never expected to have that opportunity. "Mr. Bodine asked me to write a short biography, and promised to forward it with his own letter to his 'Friends' in the United States."[45]

Bodine was also helpful in finding some work for Trofimoff while he waited to hear from the United States. The yard in back of the society's building needed to be cleaned out, and there were logs to be cut and split. Trofimoff asked if Shurik could help, as he also needed work, and the two of them completed the task in a short time. Bodine paid them generously and promised to advise Trofimoff when he heard from his "Friends" in the United States.

"I was really surprised when, two weeks later, I received a personal letter from a Mr. Paul Butterworth in which he informed me that the Society of Friends had decided to help me emigrate to the United States and that two Affidavits of Support had already been mailed to the American Embassy in Paris."[46] His lucky star was now shining across the Atlantic!

At the US Embassy, Trofimoff submitted his application for a visa and was told that since Affidavits of Support were already on file, no difficulties were anticipated. The American emigration quota for individuals born in Germany was high, and he was told to expect a short waiting period.

Trofimoff relates how, during his entire stay in Paris, he searched for his parents in every possible way, including queries to the police and the International Red Cross, with no results. He had not contacted his parents since he was separated from them in late 1944. "The good thing was," he writes, "that my parents had not been reported as casualties after the air raids, and I still hoped to find them."[47] Now, as his dream of emigrating to the United States was soon to be realized, he was concerned that he might never see or contact his parents again.

Waiting for approval of his emigration visa to the United States, Trofimoff became acquainted with a group of graduates of the Pagen Academy. This group, consisting of former officers of the various Imperial Guards Regiments in Czarist Russia, held traditional annual dinner reunions. As Trofimoff was the son of a graduate of the Academy and a godson of one member of the group, he was invited to attend one of the dinners in 1947. He writes, "This was an all-men affair with much traditional toasting to the late Czar and his butchered family, interspersed with reminiscing discussions about the glorious past of the various Imperial Guards Regiments and nostalgic memories of events at the Pagen Academy.

"During a lull in the conversation, one of the older gentlemen asked for general attention, and then proceeded to ask if anyone present knew or heard of one 'Goga' (my nickname since childhood), the son of Wladimar Wladimirovich Trofimoff, one of their former classmates. This, of course, produced a babble of excited voices and gestures all pointing in my direction. I got up and approached the old gentleman, identifying myself as this 'Goga.'

"He looked at me very closely and then jumped up and hugged me and kissed me on both cheeks, explaining that he was General Lampe, lately from Berlin, Germany, a good friend of my late grandfather in St. Petersburg and a friend of my father in Berlin, and that he knew me as a little boy in Berlin. He went on to tell me that my father was alive, and that he lived with his wife, my stepmother . . . in a small town not far from Cologne, and that he was looking for me all over Europe."[48]

Trofimoff writes that the next morning he sent a telegram to his father saying that he was alive and well. "Two days later, I received a return telegram from my father, and now all was in order with the Trofimoff family."[49]

Trofimoff reports that the Thiebault family immediately initiated procedures for obtaining a visa for his father's visit to Paris, but as the French did not want any visitors from Germany, approval of the visa was delayed. Trofimoff received his visa to the United States on November 1. Since U. S. Immigration regulations required that approved visas were to be used within 60 days of issue, Mr. Bodine obtained first-class booking for Trofimoff on a French luxury liner, to depart Le Havre on December 8. His father received his visa to visit Paris on December 4, but it would be three weeks after Trofimoff's arrival in the United States that he would receive a letter from the Thiebaults with that news. The combination of good fortune, which brought Trofimoff to the United States, countered by bad luck in the delayed approval of his father's visa by the French, eliminated all chances of a reunion of Trofimoff and his father at that time.

Trofimoff left Paris on December 7, arriving at Le Havre on December 8 to board the French liner *de Grasse*. "I had a total of $50 in my pocket and was very uncomfortable traveling first class. However, I should not have worried about it, as we were greeted aboard ship with the notification that the *de Grasse* would probably not sail because of a strike . . . That evening, all passengers had to disembark and we were sent to Paris by train, where we were offered transportation to New York by plane. Those of us who accepted went by train to Amsterdam, where we boarded a KLM Royal Dutch airliner to New York. Before I left Amsterdam, I cabled Mr. Paul Butterworth informing him of my arrival in New York, La Guardia Field, at '4.25 Dec.' (without specifying the date). [50]

"It is difficult for me to describe all of my feelings during this three-day period. I traveled on two trains, spent one day in first class on a luxury liner, and then some 20 hours on the most modern plane of that period, namely a Super Constellation, also in 1st Class. The experience, to say the least, was overwhelming."[51]

At the age of twenty, Trofimoff's new life in America was beginning.

Chapter

4

EMIGRATION TO THE UNITED STATES

So at last I was going to America! Really, really going, at last!
The boundaries burst. The arch of heaven soared. A million
suns shone out from every star. The winds rushed in from outer
space, roaring in my ears, America! America!

—Mary Antin,
The Promised Land (1912)

Overwhelmed by his good fortune and eagerly anticipating his new life in the United States, Trofimoff's first experiences upon his arrival in New York proved to be anticlimatic, as his feelings of euphoria soon vanished with his first encounter with a New York cabbie.

"I was expecting to be met by someone from the 'Friends' in Hartford, but no one was there. After checking with information and having Mr. Butterworth paged without results, I decided to continue my travel on my own."[1] It was late in the day, he was near exhaustion, and he didn't want to be lost in a strange, unfamiliar place like New York City after dark.

An attendant in the information booth at the airport suggested that he travel by bus to Pennsylvania Station. "I bought a ticket for the surprising low price of $1.20, and 45 minutes later, I disembarked at the RR station . . . I was informed that the train for Hartford, Connecticut, had already left a few minutes ago, but that I could catch another train from Grand Central Station in about 30 minutes."[2]

He decided to take a taxi to Grand Central, and after a ride up and down several New York City streets, he arrived there, only to discover that he was just a few blocks from where he hailed the cab. "He (the driver) charged me $4.80 plus an extra dollar for my large but almost empty bag, and I thought, welcome to the United States! The taxi driver saw me coming! Anyway, I bought a ticket for $4.60 (a pleasant surprise, compared to the taxi fare) and boarded the train, arriving in Hartford at 9 PM. It was dark outside and the station was almost empty with most windows shuttered and dark, but a few taxis were parked at the curb outside.

"I did not really know where to go, but I had two addresses in my wallet: one was for Mr. Butterworth at Sunset Farms, West Hartford; the other was for Miss Elizabeth T. Williams at 15 Woodland Street in Hartford."[3]

Dismounting from the train, he met a more understanding cabbie. "This taxi driver was honest and suggested that I go to the Woodland Street address as it was only about fifteen blocks away, and that the fare would be less than $5.00, which put my mind at ease about money."[4] By now, his cash was disappearing rapidly and he was all too happy to take the cabbie's advice.

After a short drive, the taxi arrived at a home which stunned Trofimoff. His notes describe it as large two-story building, whose full details could not be clearly seen in the evening's darkness. With everything covered with snow, it was, to him, a fairy tale castle he had never expected to see. Walking up the sidewalk in the new-fallen snow, he left deep tracks and his dress shoes filled with the white crystals. By then, it was after 10 PM and his breath created swirls of vapor in the frigid, crisp air. He was reluctant to ring the doorbell at so late an hour, but he realized he had no other choice.

A lady with silver gray hair opened the door. She had a questioning expression on her face and obviously had no idea who the late visitor was. When she asked how she could be of help, George became flustered, stuttering as he introduced himself.

"I'm G-G-George T-T-Trofimoff." The cold and his embarrassment combined to make him stutter. With no sign of recognition on the lady's face, he went on. "You know George, George from Paris, France."[5]

Trofimoff writes in his notes that when she realized who he was, her face lit up. "She became all excited and practically pulled me into the house, demanding to know how I got to Hartford so 'early' as she had not expected my arrival until the 25th of December.[6] She invited me into the living room and introduced me to her mother, with whom she was having a late snack.

"I was invited to partake of the snack, while Miss Williams, who told me to call her 'Bumble' like all of her friends did, started to call some of her friends to inform them of my arrival."[7]

Trofimoff's notes go on to relate that the Butterworths (Paul and Libby) soon arrived and greeted him warmly. It was decided that he would remain with Bumble for a few days before moving in with the Butterworths, who told Trofimoff to address them as "Uncle Paul" and "Aunt Libby." He had suddenly become a new and honored member of the Butterworth family.

"Two days later," Trofimoff writes, "Uncle Paul picked me up at Bumble's home and took me out to Sunset Farms in West Hartford, a large park-like estate with several homes located far away from each other among ancient oaks and huge fir trees with a pond, a tennis court, and just the most beautiful place on earth I had ever seen.[8] I was introduced to Uncle Paul's two beautiful daughters, Jeanie and Lucy,[9] who were spending the holidays at home on vacation from college. The whole Butterworth family made me feel at home as a member of their family."[10] Trofimoff's emigration to the United States began with the same good fortune he had enjoyed throughout his young life.

Uncle Paul's first order of business with Trofimoff was to get new clothes for him. Early the next day, they went to a men's store in West Hartford on a buying spree like the young Trofimoff had never seen. Uncle Paul saw that he was provided with a dark blue business suit, white shirts, ties, socks and a pair of black dress shoes. He added a sports jacket, two pairs of slacks, sport shirts, brown loafers, and, clearly implying that the young man was expected to do more than take life easy, work clothes: corduroy slacks, heavy work boots, and a thick, warm pullover sweater. Underwear, handkerchiefs, and a trench coat with a removable lining completed the new wardrobe.

They next visited a drugstore where Uncle Paul helped Trofimoff select an assortment of toilet articles.

"I kept protesting all the time," he writes, "because I did not want Uncle Paul to spend so much money, but to avail; he responded that all of this was necessary for a new start in life for a young man who had just arrived in the United States."[11]

Back at the Butterworth's home, the two sat down to discuss Trofimoff's future. His first wish, Trofimoff told Uncle Paul, was get a job and attend night school to improve his English.

"Second, I thanked him for his hospitality but also told him that I did not want to impose on him and his family, and that I wanted to live on my own, somewhere near my future place of work and the school I was going to attend."[12]

Trofimoff writes that Uncle Paul agreed with his ideas, but suggested that he proceed slowly and wait until after the holidays, when he would help Trofimoff make necessary arrangements. He first wanted him to meet the people who supported his coming to the United States, the members of the Society of Friends, "Quakers," who had contributed to his travel and other expenses.

The entire family, Paul, Libby and daughters Lucy and Jeanie took Trofimoff to the next Sunday Hartford Friends meeting for worship. The informal service, quite a contrast to the formal services he had experienced in the Russian Orthodox Church, was something new for him. "The service was informal but very impressive because of its simplicity expressed in silent prayers and subsequent sharing of thoughts and feelings of all attendees. I was introduced to the group and asked to give a speech. It was difficult for me with my limited English, but I managed to at least thank everyone present for all they had done for me."[13]

"Uncle Paul" and "Aunt Libby," members of the Society of Friends, sponsored a stateless George Trofimoff 's emigration to the United States in 1947. (Author's collection)

As his English improved, Trofimoff spoke at the Quaker Meeting House frequently, describing his early years and recounting the experiences and hardships he endured during his life in Berlin and his travels through Europe to Paris. "During these presentations, I never failed to tell the group how most Europeans, including myself, hated the Communists in general and the Soviets in particular."[14] In his talks he emphasized how his experiences and the hardships endured by his grandparents and his father worked together to develop his deep dislike for the Bolsheviks and Soviets. He told of atrocities committed by Soviet troops and Communists he had observed firsthand, describing in vivid terms how the Soviet Army treated their own comrades who had been captured by German forces.

"Many East European people had observed and experienced how Soviet troops and their NKVD Commissars committed atrocities . . . They saw with their own eyes, as I did, how the Soviet Army treated their own 'liberated' former soldiers who became German prisoners of war (POWs) . . . and then transported them not to their homes, but directly to the labor camps in Siberia."[15]

At Uncle Paul's request, Trofimoff agreed to give his talks to students at Hartford colleges. "I agreed, because I wanted the young people to know how terrible Communism was and how dangerous it was to even think that it could somehow benefit the people in the United States."[16] As in Paris, his words and actions clearly demonstrated that his deep, continuing love for "Mother Russia" and his revulsion at the Bolshevik overthrow of the Romanov aristocracy fueled his hatred for the Communists and Soviets.

Trofimoff felt that his words did not have his desired effect on the students. "Unfortunately, although there was interest shown during my presentations, there was considerable skepticism expressed. Too much 'propaganda,' glorifying the Soviets as Allies during World War II, had been imposed on their young minds, and it would probably take years . . . before they would start to believe what I told them in early 1948."[17]

Trofimoff insisted that he wanted work in order to make some money to help with the expenses of his stay at the Butterworth home. Uncle Paul suggested he could make some pocket change by helping clear the woods around the house, as many trees needed old and dead limbs removed. The opportunity to be outside and get some exercise while enjoying the beautiful New England winter pleased the young man.

Christmas in America was another new experience for Trofimoff. "What surprised me was that Christmas Eve was not being celebrated like it was in Germany and France."[18] He vividly remembers the Christmas Day dinner, with carol singing and gift-giving. As he started to open a package somewhat larger than a shoebox, he tried to guess its contents. He wondered: another pair of shoes? Opening the package, his eyes widened and he could not contain himself. "I received a pair of brand-new Canadian ice hockey skates . . . a great present because when I was a kid in Berlin, I always dreamed of such a pair."[19]

The happy times of the Christmas holidays would not last forever. Soon after Christmas, Trofimoff decided to seek his American citizenship. At the first opportunity Uncle Paul drove him to the Hartford Post Office, ". . . where I signed the 'The Declaration of Intention to Become an American Citizen.' "[20] They next went to the YMCA near the State Capital where Uncle Paul made arrangements for a rental room. Next, they went to the Hartford Hospital where Uncle Paul used his influence as a member of the Board of Directors to obtain a job for Trofimoff as a medical orderly.

Trofimoff was overwhelmed by his good fortune, which continued as he enrolled in Business Administration and English classes at Hillyer College. Uncle Paul paid his tuition of $150. When he protested this new expense, Uncle Paul told him that The Society of Friends wanted him to have a solid start in America and that, when Trofimoff "had his feet on the ground," he could consider repaying what was being invested in his future.

After moving to his YMCA room and starting classes, Trofimoff's day followed a standard routine. "I worked from 7 AM to 4 PM Monday through Friday at the hospital and went to night school at Hillyer College four nights a week from 6 PM to 10 PM."[21] He did well with English, but reports that bookkeeping and accounting were difficult for him. Trofimoff writes:

> From childhood, I always had trouble with math, and now it was even worse, as I had to learn everything all over again, and to make it worse, with different methods and terminology. Not having the necessary command of the English language did not make it any easier, and I began to wonder whether business administration was the proper choice for my college education . . . I was ready to give up and the new draft law

helped me make up my mind.

I decided to inquire about enlistment opportunities at the Army Recruiting Office in the Hartford Post Office instead of waiting for the draft to call me. When the recruiting sergeant heard of my qualifications as a Russian, German, and French linguist, he got all excited and told me that the army was the place for me. He proceeded to describe possible immediate assignments for me, starting with basic training at Fort Ord, California, and subsequent assignment to the Army Language School in Monterey, California, first as a student and later probably as an instructor, being a 'native' linguist. We also discussed the possibility and requirements of becoming a commissioned officer. All of this information sounded marvelous to me, especially since the service would start in California. I went to see Uncle Paul and asked for his advice. He was not enthusiastic about it, being a Quaker, but admitted that it would probably be the best for me, especially since I did not seem to care too much for the business courses. And so, with Uncle Paul's permission and good luck wishes, I enlisted in the U. S. Army on July 19, 1948.[22,23]

After only a few short months in America, Trofimoff's life had suddenly reached another significant turning point. A new phase of his life, which would lead him all over the world and into international intelligence activities, had begun.

Chapter

5

THE ARMY
YEARS

Man is a military animal,
Glories in gunpowder, and loves parade.
—Philip James Bailey,
Festus, A Metropolis (1839)

After enlisting in the army on July 19, 1948, Trofimoff received orders to report to Fort Ord, California, for basic training. He received a Pullman sleeper ticket to San Francisco, a bus ticket to Fort Ord, and meal tickets for seven days. He had only a few days to wind up his affairs in Hartford before leaving for his new life.[1]

The Butterworths were surprised that he would leave so soon. Uncle Paul told him that, even though he had stated his intent to enlist, the family had barely come to know him in the short time he had been with them; they had never expected him to leave so soon. The next few days were hectic while Trofimoff prepared to leave. He visited "Bumble" Williams and her mother to say good-bye and thank them for their hospitality. After sad farewells from Uncle Paul, Aunt Libby, Jeanie, and Lucy, he took a local train to New York's Grand Central Station where he boarded a New York Central train for Chicago.

Trofimoff was on his own for the travel to California, and his notes express his astonishment with the fact that he, as a mere recruit, was allowed to travel by himself across the United States. After spending his first night in a Pullman berth, he arrived in Chicago with a few spare hours to see that city while changing trains.

During the next leg of his journey George drank in the beauty of the western American landscape and arrived in San Francisco for a two-day visit before boarding a bus to Monterey, California, where he took a military bus to Fort Ord for a 13-week basic training course. During the first week Trofimoff became an acting squad leader, keeping that position throughout the duration of the course. Before basic training was completed, he traveled by jeep to the U. S. Army Language School in Monterey for an interview and a test of his Russian language ability. He recalls that as a "native" in Russian and German languages, he was assigned to a Russian language class, which was to graduate in November, but he first returned to Fort Ord to complete basic training. Upon returning to the language school, he became an assistant instructor and was immediately promoted to Private First Class and, the next day, to Corporal.

The cold war was growing in importance. With the Soviets flexing their muscles in Europe, more trouble was expected. "The U. S. Army decided to organize a new type of military intelligence unit," Trofimoff writes. "One of the first such units was the 525th Headquarters Intelligence Detachment (HID), organized at Fort Bragg, NC . . . It was filled up with linguists from such countries as the USSR, Poland, Czechoslovakia, Hungary, Greece, Japan, Korea, and China."[2]

Trofimoff's assignment as an instructor at the language school was cut short, and in early 1949, he was sent to Fort Bragg to become one of the first soldiers assigned to the new unit.

"The 525th HID was engaged in field and basic intelligence training, primarily for the interrogation of prisoners of war and other basic intelligence specialties."[3] In July 1949, with other linguists (three Russian, two Polish, and two Czech), Trofimoff was sent to Fort Riley, Kansas, for advanced training in aerial photography interpretation, order of battle, and prisoner of war interrogation. The training lasted until October when they were sent back to Fort Bragg to rejoin their unit, which by then had been designated the 525th Military Intelligence Platoon. Later, the unit was enlarged to become the 525th Military Intelligence Company with three subordinate platoons, each with some forty to forty-five linguists assigned by geographic area. Trofimoff became a member of the 526th Platoon, whose members consisted mainly of specialists in all Slavic languages.[4] He, then, was "in on the ground floor," at the beginning of a new thrust in U. S. Army intelligence activities, an assignment that would develop into a lifetime career in intelligence.

In late 1949 a team consisting of a major, a sergeant, and two corporals (Trofimoff was one of the two) was sent to Frankfurt, Germany, on a temporary assignment. His notes reveal that he was engaged for six months interrogating military deserters from Soviet Army units stationed in East Germany. The deserters were of low to medium rank, mostly privates, some sergeants, and an occasional lieutenant. He also assisted the CIA in the interrogation of a Soviet Army Artillery captain, who provided considerable up-to-date information on Soviet artillery tactics as well as detailed technical information on some of the latest Soviet artillery equipment.

Trofimoff was happy to be in Germany at this time. His father and stepmother resided in Dieringhausen, a small village some 90 kilometers from Cologne. He was allowed to take a 15-day vacation and he sent them a telegram, announcing that he was in Germany and would visit them during the Christmas holidays. Telegraph services were still unreliable, and he had no way of knowing if his message was received.

Food was strictly rationed, and fresh produce was limited, available only on a barter basis. In the post exchange (PX), Trofimoff bought as many rationed goods as he could carry: cigarettes, tobacco, cigars, coffee, tea, and alcoholic beverages, as well as many non-rationed items (clothing, canned food, etc.), which he packed into one large duffel bag along with the rationed items. He knew that these items would be useful to his parents in trading for fresh produce from local farmers. Clothing items were practically unavailable, and since they could be used for barter, they were more desirable than money. He bought the largest canned ham available in the PX, and, from a local farmer, his finest and biggest goose. With a duffel bag filled to overflowing and the slaughtered goose tightly wrapped in paper, he was ready for the trip to his parents' home and a grand Christmas reunion.[5]

In those days, there were practically no direct trains. Trofimoff remembers that several transfers were required to get to Cologne. He left early in the morning on Christmas Eve, and with the duffel bag in one hand and the bulky goose in the other, he was a spectacle and the center of attraction for all passengers as he struggled from one train to another. He finally reached Cologne late in the afternoon and boarded a local to Dieringhausen. The last leg of his journey was only 90 kilometers, but the trip took more than three hours and it was after

Sergeant First Class George Trofimoff, Headquarters Intelligence Detachment, Ft. Bragg, North Carolina, 1951 (Author's collection)

dark when he staggered off the train with his duffel bag and goose.

Trofimoff writes that Christmas Eve is one of the most important holidays in Germany, when all families gather first in church and then return to their homes. Stores and restaurants are closed, and the village Trofimoff's parents lived in had no streetlights and no local transportation. He asked for directions at the train station and was told that he was on Koellner Strasse, his parents' street, but that their home was some three kilometers away.[6]

The night was pitch black and the cold penetrating, but Trofimoff was serene. Everything was covered with a fresh snowfall, which crunched under his boots. He recalls that Koellner Strasse was devoid of people, but he passed several churches conducting Christmas services with people singing Christmas carols. As he neared another church, services had just ended and people were streaming into the street. He asked one person if he knew where Herr Trofimoff's radio shop was located and was told the shop was just a few doors down the street, across from the church. He had arrived![7]

Trofimoff's father's shop, on the first floor of a three-story building, was dark. The entire building was dark, except for one dim light in a third floor window. There were three buttons near the entrance without names, and he pushed one at random several times. Chimes rang from somewhere in the building and the topmost window opened. His notes describe this reunion in vivid detail.

Trofimoff recognized the voice of his stepmother, obviously annoyed, asking "Who is there?"

He replied, "This is Goga—you know, Goga, your son!"[8]

A long silence followed. The next thing Trofimoff heard was the sound of two people storming down the stairs. Finally the door burst open, and they fell into each other's arms. The joy for all was great, and the tears flowed like rivers.[9]

The two weeks Trofimoff spent with his family were like a dream for all three. The goose was cooked, and with the other items he brought, the reunited family enjoyed a wonderful Christmas feast. His parents unpacked the many scarce items in his duffel bag. As they admired and counted each item, they were overwhelmed, telling him that they would be able to barter for many items they could not obtain otherwise. They expected to live and eat comfortably for at least a year.[10]

After the visit with his parents, Trofimoff returned to Oberursel. His interrogator responsibilities kept him busy for the next five months when he received orders to return to Fort Bragg. Before leaving, he obtained a five-day pass to visit his parents again.

In late May, the team returned to Fort Bragg, and Trofimoff resumed his duties as an instructor in Russian, German, and POW interrogation techniques. It was an exciting time for him; new organizational and operational concepts for intelligence activities were being developed, and he was again in the forefront of this rapidly changing field. His dedication to his duties paid off with rapid advancement; his roommate and close friend at Fort Bragg during 1950–1951 writes:

> . . . Right at the very beginning I was introduced to George who immediately underscored to me that he was an RA (Regular Army) All the Way,[11] and obviously very proud of it . . .
>
> Subsequently, having generally similar ethnic backgrounds—both sons of former 'white officers,' both absorbed in fierce fury and hate of ANYTHING Soviet . . . both grateful to the United States for giving us HOME and immensely proud of being in the service—we had become close friends. I guess our dedication, the kind that only youth can possess, reflected in our bearing, our performance of duties and even our appearance. We ALWAYS looked 'sharp' (as much as anybody can look sharp in fatigues). I guess our efforts were positively noticed somewhere above, and we both soon progressed ahead of our contemporaries to become 'NON-COMS.'[12] I believe sometime in the latter part of 1951, the group received a whole bunch of draftees. George and I were summoned to the Chief of Staff of the Group and told that we were selected to form a training company and take it through the full infantry basic training.[13]

In September 1951, Trofimoff reported to the U. S. District Court in Raleigh, NC, to appear for citizenship processing. He writes that he reported to the court in his Sergeant's uniform, with two Master Sergeants as witnesses, and was sworn in. It was, to Trofimoff, a great, important day in his life. Upon return to his unit, a celebration was held with many of his peers, who, like Trofimoff, were émigrés from Europe who had joined the U. S. Army to fight, they all proclaimed, worldwide Communism.[14]

Trofimoff's duties with the training company ended with the transfer of the 526th MI Platoon to Germany. In October he left with the platoon for New York to board a troop transport, sailing to Bremerhaven, Germany. From there, the platoon traveled by train to Frankfurt, Germany. In Frankfurt, Trofimoff and two other Russian linguists interrogated Soviet defectors and deserters. Trofimoff says that the CIA "borrowed" his services, and for three months he interrogated special Soviet deserters.[15]

Trofimoff's notes describe the greatest surprise of his life, when, on March 9, 1953, he was notified that the President of the United States had commissioned him as a Second Lieutenant, Military Intelligence, in the United States Army Reserve (USAR). He had applied for the commission soon after becoming a US citizen, and had almost given up hope that the application would be approved. The fact that the commission was awarded on his birthday added to his elation, and a big celebration followed. A few days later, he visited his parents to share his good fortune with them.[16] (When Trofimoff received his commission, he remained in the U. S. Army Inactive Reserve and continued to serve on active duty as a noncommissioned officer.)

The number of Soviet deserters slowed to a trickle, and by mid-1953 it stopped completely. Trofimoff became the senior member of a border interrogation team, and while the working hours were sometimes demanding, he recalls that the assignment was a great one. In those days there was no wall between the two Germanys, and crossing the border was an easy task. There were many defectors from East Germany and they usually crossed at night.[17]

Trofimoff's European assignment ended in October 1954, and he embarked on a U. S. Navy transport headed for New York. He requested a ten-day delay enroute and stopped to visit the Butterworth family. Trofimoff recalls that it was a wonderful time. Uncle Paul and Aunt Libby greeted him like a long-lost son and took him to his old room, which still contained his prized ice skates. Later, Uncle Paul took him to a car dealer and helped him buy a used, like-new Pontiac Chieftain, which he drove to Fort Bragg.[18]

After the excitement of his interrogation assignments in Germany, Trofimoff's duties at Fort Bragg were a letdown. He became an instructor again and participated in some projects translating from Russian to English. He writes that he was frustrated by this assignment, stating that anyone could do the training and translation projects, but very few were qualified to interrogate actual deserters and defectors from Communist countries. He felt that his abilities were being squandered, and he longed for the excitement and self-satisfaction of his previous duties.[19]

Trofimoff had a new girl friend, Frances, whom he met while she visited friends in Fayetteville, N. C. After meeting him, she remained in the area. The two became serious and were married in June, leaving for a honeymoon in Daytona Beach, Florida.

Upon return to Fort Bragg, Trofimoff's frustrations with his boring duties continued, and he began a search for a new and more challenging assignment. His quest for new responsibilities would send him to new, unexpected and exciting adventures on the far side of the world.

In his quest for more challenging responsibilities, Trofimoff noticed an announcement describing two openings for intelligence-qualified noncommissioned officers (NCOs) in Military Advisory positions overseas and he wasted no time in applying. He writes that he told Frances he might not be accepted, as he was only partially qualified, but that it was an opportunity too good to be missed.[20] In mid-September he received instructions to report to Washington, D. C., for interviews by several officials who delved into his background and explored his fluency in French. After hours of probing interviews he was told that he was accepted, and that he should return to Fort Bragg to wait for further developments.[21]

He soon received orders to attend a special training course in Washington.[22] Frances was not allowed to be with him during the training, and he was told that with no family quarters in the as-yet-unidentified country she would not be allowed to join him there. During his training Trofimoff learned that he would be a member of a two-man team attached to a group of military advisers in Laos. The team's duties, as "end-use-observers" would be to assess the quality and utilization of U. S. assistance provided to the Laotians. He was told further that he could expect to spend a lot of time traveling throughout the outer provinces of Laos evaluating Laotian and Montagnard units.

Trofimoff, never having been in that part of the world, was eager to get started. His partner, "Bob," an ex-captain, was familiar with the area but did not speak French, and Trofimoff became the team's interpreter.

After a final visit with Frances, Trofimoff returned to Washington, and he and his partner left in March 1956 for Laos. They arrived in

Vientiane, the Laotian capital, at the height of the summer dry season. Trofimoff's notes reveal that the 104-degree heat was stifling, and even with little rain, the heavy humidity blanketed everything. "The 'airport,' if one could call it that," he writes, "consisted of just a small concrete air-traffic control tower, and a large shed built of bamboo with a sheet metal roof used as an arrival/departure passenger terminal."[23]

After briefings on local conditions at the American Embassy, the team went to the American compound, a collection of tents and wooden buildings on stilts. They were again welcomed by a group of former U. S. Army officers. The group, called the Programs Evaluation Office (PEO), led by a retired Brigadier General, was responsible for overseeing the use of equipment and financial aid provided by the American Government. Trofimoff's team was attached to the PEO.

As a commissioned officer in the U. S. Army reserve, Trofimoff could retain his reserve commission in an inactive status and simultaneously remain on active duty in an enlisted status. In Laos, he was given an honorable discharge from his enlisted position so that he could be given a civil service assignment, attached to the Laotian Embassy. However, he still retained his reserve commission.

The team's new home was a tent on a wooden platform. "It wasn't the Hilton," Trofimoff writes, "but it was snug and equipped with the ever-present mosquito net."[24] During the next few days, the team prepared for field trips, stocking up on medical needs such as antimalarial pills, diarrhea prevention medicine, heat-rash cream, etc.

Trofimoff's notes describe his first experience visiting Laotian units. "At the end of April, the team finally scheduled our first field trips . . . the initial trips were made by jeep with a Laotian captain as liaison officer and a Laotian soldier as driver. The team was greeted with enthusiasm at all units, and was shown all of the facilities with detailed briefings on weapons, equipment, and personnel."[25] At first, the team had difficulty with the native food, but soon realized that the meals were an important part of their visits, and they endured the strange food, their suffering disguised as far as possible.

Trofimoff's request to have Frances join him was approved, and she arrived in Bangkok. Trofimoff was given a week to help her become familiar with local conditions. He writes, "It was a new honeymoon, this time in exotic oriental surroundings, but too short." He returned to Laos and Frances stayed in her hotel while plans were made to build permanent housing for them in Vientiane."[26]

With Trofimoff's return to Vientiane, the team visited remote provinces until the monsoon season arrived and he was free to fly to Bangkok to visit Frances. He writes that she could not adjust to the loneliness, and the separation and life in a strange country were too much for her to handle. After his return to Laos, she was advised by U. S. Embassy personnel to return to the United States and seek a divorce on grounds of desertion. Trofimoff did not contest the divorce, and his first marriage, doomed from the beginning, was over. [27]

The team visited many remote villages and areas during the next three years, and at each location they received royal treatment from their hosts. A typical visit was to the Savannakhet Province and the famous Plaines des Jarres, a picturesque valley scattered with large "jarres" of unknown origin.

Upon arrival at the airfield, a member of the royal family, who introduced himself as the commander of the Savannakhet Military Region, welcomed the team. He took them with great fanfare to his headquarters where they received a thorough briefing on the military situation, followed by a sumptuous dinner in a local Chinese restaurant. This was the first magnificent meal the team had enjoyed since its arrival in Laos. It was a 12-course formal Chinese dinner with huge amounts of Siamese Scotch whiskey and some very succulent Chinese specialties, including the famous "100-years" eggs and three courses of Peking duck.[28]

Christmas and New Year holidays were spent with the American community in Vientiane, and soon the team was planning another round of field trips. Activities during 1956–1957 were largely a repeat of 1955 with visits to other local and remote units and villages. Feted almost constantly by the Laotians,[29] Trofimoff's love of the good life grew without bounds, and he began to believe that the "good life" of fine food and drink would be his forever.

Routine activities continued until late 1957 when the team left for the extreme northern part of Laos near the Chinese border. The team traveled first by air and then went as far into the mountains as possible by jeep. The journey continued to the north on horseback with Montagnard guides through a very picturesque area, which grew wilder and higher. As they approached the Chinese border, they proceeded on foot.

Trofimoff writes, "The group proceeded in file on the trail, with a Laotian soldier on point. He was about 10 meters in front of the next man, who was a Montagnard guide. As the soldier went around a bend in the trail. he suddenly cried out in pain. The Montagnard who followed him pulled his machete from his sash and hurried around the bend . . . the point soldier was bitten by a king cobra just below the knee and was in mortal danger. Two of the Montagnards grabbed the soldier, threw him on the ground, and chopped off his leg, just above the knee."[30]

A tourniquet was applied, a fire was started, and the wound was cauterized with a hot machete. Trofimoff provided dressings, tetanus and morphine and the soldier was removed on a litter pulled by one of the horses. What a way to lose a leg, Trofimoff thought.

Trofimoff writes that before leaving on their next visit, the team was notified that they were invited by a local village chief to participate in a tiger hunt. Neither had suitable rifles, so arrangements were made for the loan of two M-1 rifles from the Embassy Marine Guards.[31]

Bob and Trofimoff were assisted in mounting an elephant and instructed to do nothing but sit tight, hold onto their seats, and wait until told to shoot. The guides prodded the elephants forward to a valley covered with tall grasses, some bushes and a few trees. A large group of natives gathered on the opposite end, and they began to move forward toward the elephants, making loud noises to force any tigers lurking in the tall grass to flee toward the hunters.

The hunt was concluded when the beaters reached the elephants with no tigers appearing. The villagers were disappointed with the results, and both Trofimoff and Bob were pleased to have participated in the colorful and exciting event. However, they were just as happy that no tigers had been encountered, as they had no desire to kill such a magnificent animal.[32]

Several additional visits were made to local Montagnard villages. Upon returning to Vientiane both team members were advised that threats had been made against their lives, and their assignment in Laos was to be terminated. Trofimoff left the next day for Bangkok where he remained for a few days of shopping before going on to Hong Kong.[33]

In late 1958 Trofimoff was in Washington, his assignment in Laos completed. During three dangerous and exciting years, his ability to survive under difficult environments and situations became even stronger than before. The royal treatment, great food, copious Scotch and fine French brandy convinced him even more that good fortune and fine living would be his forever.

Trofimoff's first attempt at finding a job after his return to America took him to the Army's Civilian Personnel Office in the Pentagon. There he was told that all civil service positions in the area were restricted to registered civil service personnel. In desperation, he took a position selling encyclopedias, but he soon quit because he could not accept the sales system that pressured people into buying products which they really did not need.

Undaunted, Trofimoff returned to the Pentagon to be told that positions for intelligence specialists were available in Fort Shafter, Hawaii, and he decided to travel to Hawaii. He spent most of his meager savings on airfare and arrived in Hawaii in late December 1958.

Still a survivor, his luck stayed with him, and in January 1959 he obtained a position as an Intelligence Analyst in Headquarters, U. S. Army Pacific. He writes that he was welcomed with open arms, as he was the first American with current firsthand knowledge of Laos and its political, military, and economic situation. He prepared a strategic vulnerability study of the entire area and was soon known as an expert on all aspects of the region. "It was nice place to find one's self after the jungles of Laos," he notes.[34]

George developed a love of fine automobiles and bought a new Plymouth Fury convertible, writing that he traveled all over the island, seeing its wonderful mountains, waterfalls, and beaches, spending all his free time either on the beach . . . or the public tennis courts.[35]

Trofimoff 's notes tell of his meeting Edwina Lee and her family playing tennis. He soon became friends with the family and they invited him to their home. He fell in love with Edwina, and they were married a few months later in Honolulu's Mormon Temple. His notes describe the wedding reception: "It was a beautiful ceremony with the *Hawaiian Wedding Song* as background music . . . The reception took place in the Officers' Club in Fort Schafter . . . with all the trimmings of a Hawaiian luau."[36]

The young couple moved in with Edwina's parents and enjoyed a happy marriage for several months when, unexpectedly, George received notice that his position in Hawaii was to be eliminated. With his low seniority, his job would be lost, and to remain employed, he had to accept a transfer to Seoul, Korea. Unfortunately, dependents were not allowed in Korea at that time, and the couple would have to live separately for at least one year. George didn't want to go through another period of unemployment, and with Edwina's consent, he decided to go to Korea.[37]

Trofimoff's room in Korea was a far cry from the comfortable home he had shared with Edwina and her family. "It was really just the bare necessities and a considerable disappointment after the nice home in Hawaii." He remembers that his duties kept him busy, but that nearby tennis courts, available for weekend play, provided some diversion.[38]

In February 1961, Trofimoff planned to take a brief vacation in Hawaii when he received word that his father had died. It was very bad news because his father was only 66 years old and apparently in fairly good health. He obtained emergency leave, but when he arrived in Germany, he discovered that his father had already been buried. To be near and help his stepmother, he decided to look for a position in Germany. His luck held when he visited the Frankfurt Civilian Personnel Office. He was hired immediately, with a reduction from his current grade of GS-11 to GS-9. He told his future boss that he would need some time in Korea to complete his obligation there, and it was agreed that he would return to Seoul and report to Germany by the first of March.

Returning to Korea, Trofimoff stopped in Hawaii to visit Edwina. To his surprise, her father told him that she refused to meet with him and wanted a divorce. Trofimoff had half-expected this to happen since she had not been allowed to join him in Korea. He agreed to the divorce, signed the necessary papers, and returned to Korea.[39]

In each of Trofimoff's two marriages, he demonstrated that working and living where he wanted to be—self-satisfaction—was far more important than staying with his wife and preserving his marriage. With the failure of his second marriage, his ego, expressed by his love of self without full regard for others in his life, began to emerge as a predominant characteristic, a characteristic that would remain with him for many years.

Trofimoff arrived in Frankfurt, Germany, in March 1961. He joined a local sports club and while playing tennis, "I met Mrs. Liselotte Richter and her daughter, Alexa, with whom I fell in love and married on October 13, 1961. We moved into a rental apartment close to work."[40] With Alexa, Trofimoff fathered three children: Nicole, born on December 1, 1963; Natalie (Natasha), born on June 17, 1965; and Alexander, born on June 19, 1967.[41] At first, Trofimoff and Alexa owned a small Plymouth, but as the family grew in size, Trofimoff's love of cars was rekindled and he purchased a new Ambassador station wagon.

Trofimoff's next assignment was to a clandestine mail-screening group (Station "K") located at the Rhein Main U. S. Air Force Base near Frankfurt. As chief of the operation, he supervised some nine to twelve German employees who screened mail (to and from the USSR), which looked as if it might contain useful information. His notes describe the operation:

> The mail was steamed open, photographed, screened for intelligence type of information, particularly concerning life within the Soviet Union, and then closed again and forwarded as addressed. The difficult part of this exercise was the fact that mail could not be held for more than a 24-hour delay and had to be handled in such a manner as to not leave any traces. Even the glue used was untraceable.
>
> There were days when station 'K' had to work two 12-hour shifts to be able to cover the volume of mail. As many as a thousand or more letters were opened daily and photographed routinely with a very elaborate vertical photographic equipment setup.[42]

In 1962, Trofimoff's foster brother, Igor Susemihl, then a Metropolitan[43] in the Russian Orthodox Church, returned to Germany from Australia. Igor, passing through Frankfurt, called Trofimoff from the airport. "I rushed out to the Rhein Main airport to meet him," Trofimoff writes. "We had less than one hour to exchange family news as Igor continued on his trip, but from then on, we corresponded frequently."[44] This encounter at the Rhein Main airport, the first time the two foster brothers had seen each other since their brief meeting in Igor's church in Berlin in 1944, renewed their childhood relationship. Their close association would continue for many years thereafter.

Trofimoff writes, ". . . Igor became the bishop for Munich and moved permanently to that city. As long as I was still living in and near Frankfurt, I visited him once a year for a weekend, while passing through Munich . . . Later, when I moved to the Nuremberg JIC, I visited him more often, every two or three months."[45]

In 1963 the unit Trofimoff was assigned to at the Rhein Main U.S. Air Force Base was reduced in size. As Trofimoff was the last-hired employee, he was the first to go, but he was immediately assigned to another unit at Camp King located on the outskirts of Frankfurt that had a vacancy for a Russian/German linguist. "I became an interrogator of primarily Russian, but also East German, deserters and defectors, a job for which I was well-qualified." In his new position he was promoted to the grade of GS-10 and was also able to continue his career as an officer in the US Army Reserve.[46]

In August 1968 the Nuremberg Joint Interrogation Center (JIC) became very busy interrogating refugees, and, along with ten to twelve other interrogators, Trofimoff was assigned there temporarily to help with the unexpected workload. "We were extremely busy for the next three or four weeks, screening as many as 200 refugees per day."[47]

When he returned to Camp King, Trofimoff was offered a permanent transfer to the JIC as civilian chief of the U. S. Army element, with a promotion to GS-12. (Later, he would receive one more promotion, to GS-13, which was his grade when he retired from civil service in 1995.) "I accepted the permanent transfer to the JIC in November,1968, but without my family . . . I had to first find a place for us to live."[48]

Chapter
6

THE NUREMBERG JOINT INTERROGATION CENTER

A secret's safe
'Twixt you, me, and the gate post.
—Robert Browning,
The Inn Album, 1875

In the mid-1960s, the Cold War between the United States and the Soviet Union was at its height. This open rivalry between the two superpowers, beginning with Churchill's warning in 1946 that an "Iron Curtain" was descending across Europe, would dominate world politics for more than 40 years. The Cold War was waged on political, economic, and propaganda fronts with a constant threat of nuclear war.

The East German blockade of its borders with West Germany in 1948, the establishment of the North Atlantic Treaty Organization (NATO) in 1949, the signing of the Warsaw Pact by the Soviet Union and seven other eastern European nations in 1955, the erection of the Berlin wall in 1961 and the belligerent nature of the Soviets reflected in the invasion of Czechoslovakia by Soviet Bloc countries in 1989 all added to the tension between the United States, its NATO allies, and the Soviet Union.

With the buildup of Soviet Bloc forces, the need for intelligence within NATO increased daily. A primary source of this intelligence was the large flow to the West of refugees from Soviet Bloc countries. To tap into this reservoir of information, NATO forces established a series of Joint Interrogation Centers (JICs) located along the

Front entrance to the Nuremberg Joint Interrogation Center. (U.S. Justice Dept.)

border between West Germany and the Soviet Bloc and Warsaw Pact countries.[1,2]

JIC responsibilities were to screen all refugees crossing into West Germany to determine if they possessed any intelligence that might be helpful to NATO agencies, and then interrogate, or refer to higher echelons, those individuals suspected of having such information. The organization, mission, and operation of the JICs were defined by mutual agreements among the NATO forces.

Trofimoff arrived in Nuremberg for his assignment to the JIC without his family, but Alexa joined him with the children after he arrived and they rented a three-bedroom bungalow. The house was located on the route of the Army's school bus, and they experienced no trouble getting their oldest daughter to school, but Alexa had to drive their second daughter to kindergarten. They acquired a small second car and soon settled down to a routine family life.

The Nuremberg JIC, in a two-story building (with an attic and a basement), consisted of four elements, called partners:

- Partner I, the German element, the host, was the largest group in the JIC with a staff consisting of some 40 members of the German *Bunde Nachrichten Dienst* (BND). [3]
- Partner II, the U. S. Army Element, with a French Liaison Section attached, consisted of three Department of the Army civilians (DACs), two Warrant Officers, two NCOs, and several interrogators. Trofimoff, the senior DAC, was in charge of operations. All individuals spoke German and at least one East European language. Later the military personnel were replaced with DACs.
- Partner III, the U. S. Air Force Element, supervised by a Department of the Air Force civilian (DAFC), consisted of three DAFCs.
- Partner IV, the British element, consisted of one civilian Polish/Russian linguist.

The administrative offices of the German element were in the basement along with a heavy-duty shredder, a large vault, and controls for the security system. German personnel occupied the first floor; the second floor housed the other three partners; and the attic contained interrogation rooms used by all occupants when conducting interrogations.

Interrogations by the U. S. Army element followed guidelines contained in intelligence collection requirements published by U. S. intelligence organizations. Intelligence collection requirements were clas-

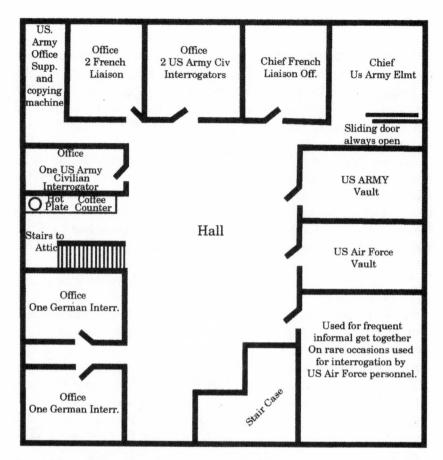

Second floor layout of working spaces at the Nuremberg Joint Interrogation Center. (U.S. Justice Dept.)

sified documents (usually SECRET). They listed intelligence requirements and often contained summaries of intelligence available to the agency publishing the document(s). Prior to interviewing a potential source, interrogators reviewed appropriate intelligence collection requirements to learn what information to look for during the interrogation as well as to evaluate the accuracy of any answers they obtained.

Interrogation results were drafted by interrogators, checked for accuracy, and turned over to Partner I who forwarded them to BND offices in Munich. They were then passed to the U. S. Army's 5th Military Intelligence (MI) Company where they were edited, typed, and distributed.

Partner I was responsible for security of the JIC. At the close of each day, desks of all personnel were checked for any paper, including personal mail. The fact that personnel other than German citizens worked at the JIC was classified, so any trace of non-German personnel was hidden from view. German security personnel controlled entry to the JIC; identification was verified for all those entering, and all those entering or leaving the premises were subject to search.

The U. S. Army and U. S. Air Force elements each had a security vault on the second floor; the Army's vault was adjacent to Trofimoff's office. Heavy steel doors with a triple combination mechanical lock, a triple combination electronic lock, and a safe key secured each vault. There was an outer grill door, locked with a key if no one was in the vault, and inside, a motion detector provided additional security. German personnel were responsible for energizing the alarm system at closing time and neutralizing it each morning. Two persons operated controls simultaneously, each with a key. With the system activated, any attempt to open the door to either vault would trigger an alarm at the local police station.

Members of the U. S. Army element were cleared for access to SECRET material, and controls existed to provide security for handling classified documents. In his notes, Trofimoff writes that no one, including the Officer in Charge, was permitted to remove SECRET material from the saferoom for any purpose.[4]

In the U. S. Army element, everyone trusted one another. The concept of mutual trust was a key element in the handling and safeguarding of classified documents. Several individuals, who were members of the JIC when Trofimoff was the chief of the U. S. Army element, confirmed the importance of mutual trust.

Michael Moschetti, a JIC interrogator, said, " . . . the whole atmosphere in our JIC was one of complete trust . . ."[5]

Eugene Drozdza, who worked at the JIC as an interrogator from 1970 to 1979, said, "I don't recall any log being present where we would be required to annotate our removal or returning the document . . . we would just go and just pull it out without anybody's permission . . . we didn't have to annotate anywhere that we were removing this document from the file cabinet . . . there was no log or other document to sign when I did so."[6]

Another interrogator, Arthur Farash, confirmed the mutual trust among the JIC staff: "Absolutely. As I say, we were soldiers, we had to trust each other."[7]

In addition to his responsibilities at the JIC, Trofimoff became heavily involved with his Army Reserve duties, and his relationship with Alexa began to deteriorate because of his heavy workload.[8] His notes reveal that he was teaching a class of the Branch Officer's Career Course, and simultaneously taking a resident/nonresident course with the Army's Command and General Staff College (C&GSC) on weekends and at night, all in addition to his job of supervising the activities of the JIC. He writes that the JIC was in a much-neglected state and needed considerable effort and extra work from all of the assigned personnel.[9]

George Trofimoff recognized the need to improve his relationship with his family, and he rented an apartment on the Italian shore. He writes that everyone was enthusiastic about the idea, but that he remained with his family for only a few days when he returned to Munich to teach more classes. This separation was the final blow to the relationship between Trofimoff and Alexa, and they decided to separate; Trofimoff rented a small bachelor apartment in downtown Nuremberg, and Alexa took the children with her to Frankfurt.[10]

Trofimoff's notes reveal that at this time his financial problems first surfaced, and that he received a lot of help from his foster brother, Igor, who then lived in Munich where he headed a Russian Orthodox Church.

Trofimoff writes that during the first months and later years of his separation form Alexa Igor provided considerable moral and financial help, and that soon after his separation from Alexa, Igor had a serious talk with him.

"He explained that he was making enough money for both of us," Trofimoff writes, "that he had a special aid fund to help Russian refugees, that he was the uncle of my children, and that he therefore had the right to help me financially or any other way he pleased."

Trofimoff was only too happy to accept, as the separation had placed a tremendous strain on him, emotionally and financially. In his notes he admits that without his brother's help, his family would have had considerable difficulties leading a normal life.[12]

Later, Igor had this to say about his financial support for Trofimoff: ". . . I lent [sic] him money twice, once DM 500.00 and once DM 600.00 . . . I do remember clearly that he was moving from Frankfurt to Nuremberg at that time and that his acute cash difficulty arose from purchasing furniture by his wife."[13]

Trofimoff's notes regarding the extensive assistance provided by

Igor Susemihl, date unknown. (U.S. Justice Dept.)

his foster brother certainly seem to belie Igor's assertion that he helped Trofimoff on only two occasions, and suggest that his foster brother had deep financial pockets well beyond the means of a priest. Apparently he did not question the logic of a priest saying he earned enough to support himself in addition to providing substantial support to Trofimoff's family.

Trofimoff's relationship with Igor continued after their 1962 meeting in Frankfurt. His notes describe how his entanglement with Igor and the KGB began. In the beginning, his discussions with Igor were very informal. "There were no photographs, there was just talking. He would ask me something and I would tell him something."[14]

As the frequency of their meetings increased, Igor began to pose very simple questions to George, asking for his opinion on various matters.[15]   During their discussions, George told his brother that he needed financial help for some furniture his wife had bought, and Igor loaned him some 5,000 marks. Later, when George needed more, Igor gave it to him, saying that it did not have to be repaid, and that if he needed more, he could get it for him.[16] In a short time, Igor, using traditional KGB recruiting tactics, had maneuvered Trofimoff into a vise that would grip him tightly for many years.

Trofimoff's notes reveal that after his separation from Alexa, his personal life continued routinely for the next few years. The workload at the JIC stabilized with the number of defectors significantly decreasing. He was promoted to Major in the U. S. Army Reserve (USAR) and taught all phases of the C&GSC courses to active-duty Army officers. Teaching took a considerable portion of his time with very little time remaining for his family. His long work hours, coupled with a time-consuming hobby of playing tennis, caused him to be so absorbed in his own personal life that he became more and more estranged from his children. He writes that he took his children to be with him in Nuremberg for a few weeks during one summer vacation, and on one occasion he took them on a four-week trip to Los Angeles and Honolulu. He visited them in Frankfurt whenever possible, but as his reserve duties and tennis interests took more and more of his time, his visits with the children became less frequent. He writes that as time passed, he missed important events like birthdays, football and soccer games, and high school graduation exercises.[17] Self-absorption in his work, his personal life, and tennis had become more important to Trofimoff than his own children, and he began to lead the life of a happy, free-spending bachelor.

In December 1970, some German friends from the tennis club invited Trofimoff to spend the Christmas holidays with them and a recently widowed lady in a hotel pension in Bad Ischl, Austria. Not wanting to spend the holidays in solitude, he gladly accepted. His notes relate that three married couples, the widow and he went in two luxurious cars, a Mercedes and a BMW, to Austria. They parked the cars and were picked up by a van, which took them up a mountain through deep snow to a hotel-pension. He writes that the setting was magnificent, high in the Austrian Alps."[18]

After that holiday, the same four couples repeated the trip in 1971-72. Trofimoff's relationship with the widow continued cordially for about two years, on and off, but never developed to the degree hoped for by the other couples.[19]

Trofimoff's carefree bachelor life continued, with the rest of the time between 1972 and 1977 devoted to work, tennis, and several girlfriends, some of whom he lived with for limited periods, and some who were just weekend dalliances. He writes that nothing serious developed. He had enough of a bachelor's life and wanted to have a steady home and family again.[20]

At that time, Trofimoff found his fourth wife, an eighteen-year old

George Trofimoff with a friend, somewhere in Europe, circa 1975. (Author's collection)

girl, Marion. He, a man of 52, married her in late 1978. He writes that his children never forgave him, even though they came to Nuremberg a few times and spent a few days. "Somehow, they never liked her much, although she tried her best to befriend them. But most of all, they held it against me that I married again, and not to their mother."[21]

Trofimoff's predilection for young women was a major factor in the failure of his relationship with his children, and the estrangement from them was never fully reconciled.[22]

Trofimoff's youngest daughter, Natasha, now lives in California and maintains some contact with him, while his other children remain estranged from him. His daughter, Nicole, lives in Germany, and Alexander, his only son and the youngest of the three, according to a report received by the author, is married, with children. Reportedly he lives in New Jersey and commutes to work in New York. While the author has had limited correspondence with Natasha, no contact has been possible with Nicole or Alexander.

During his assignment to the JIC, Trofimoff was highly respected by his coworkers and subordinates. Interrogator Arthur Farash gave his opinion of Trofimoff: "He was a very strict, upstanding person . . . in some way he might have been considered a little arrogant, probably to his credit, but in general he had a very good reputation."[23] Eugene Drozdza, another JIC interrogator, in a discussion with the author, emphasized that Trofimoff was a fine boss. "He often let us get away with big, long lunches. He frequently let us depart early. While he was generous and diplomatic most of the time, he was very temperamental and could blow up very easily, with little provocation."[24] When asked if he knew Trofimoff's wife, Alexa, he replied. "Yes, their relationship was loose—in my opinion, she was not the kind of person you could rely on. I don't think I would want her as a wife."[25]

Asked to comment on Marion, he said, "She was beautiful, and a nice person. George showered her with 'goodies,' buying gifts from mail order catalogs."[26]

Bernhard Frenkel served two different tours at the Nuremberg JIC as an interrogator under Trofimoff's supervision. Asked to describe his boss' reputation for honesty and trustworthiness, he said, "Excellent . . . One hundred percent trustworthy, of good character, and a good individual to work for."[27]

Regarding Trofimoff's financial situation, one interrogator who had worked for George at the JIC told the author confidentially that his observations of Trofimoff's spending habits raised questions in his mind. "George's standard of living was obviously higher than the rest of us. We were all receiving basically the same amount of pay, but George's spending was considerably higher than I could afford. He was spending a lot of money on clothes, apartments for his girl friends, and on cars. I couldn't help but wonder how his pay could support such a life style."[28]

Asked if he ever considered reporting his concerns to higher authorities, He replied, "After thinking about the situation, I realized that he spent a lot of time with his reserve activities and was getting paid for that. Besides, I knew how the Army's CI (Counter Intelligence) people tended to make mountains out of molehills. I had no desire to become mixed up in a security investigation, so I decided to say nothing."[29]

It is apparent that Trofimoff was admired and liked by the families of his co-workers. In an extended telephone conversation with the author, Mrs. Irene Drozdza, the ex-wife of Eugene Drozda, had this to say: "I first met George in 1970, shortly after the birth of my daughter. George was extremely charming and charismatic, and I grew to like him very much. My family, like his, were white Russians who were forced out of Russia during the revolution, so we had a lot in common. I really enjoyed the opportunity to speak Russian with someone and recall the old Russian traditions and songs. He was really Russian in his heart."[30]

She went on to say that she and her husband, Gene, were often invited to Trofimoff's house, and she emphasized how proud he was of his epicurean skills. "On one occasion, he cooked a wonderful meal for us," she recalled. "The first course was a delicious, clear broth. When I told him what a delicious soup he was serving, he exploded. 'Soup!' he said, 'I stand over a hot stove for four hours making this great bouillon, and you call it soup!' "[31]

Mrs. Drozdza remembers Trofimoff telling her that he and Alexa had three children and they were stopping with that number. "He was very generous and wanted me to take the clothing his children had outgrown as they would have no use for it. All of the clothing was beautiful and obviously very expensive, just like designer clothes.

"George loved fancy cars and night clubs and lived very high. It was clear to both me and Gene that he was much better off financially than any other American in the JIC. Even though his civil service rank was one grade higher than my husband's, the higher grade could not account for his plusher lifestyle."[32]

Asked how well she knew Trofimoff's two wives, Alexa and Marion, she replied, "I didn't know Marion very well, but Alexa was very nice. George was very sad after Alexa left him."[33]

The Drozdzas moved to Chicago in 1979, and in 1986 they separated. For some time Mrs. Drozdza had no contact with Trofimoff, but after her separation she and her daughter frequently visited her mother in Germany, and on each trip to Germany they visited Trofimoff. Asked if she ever had any suspicion that Trofimoff was involved in espionage or other illegal activities, she responded vehemently. "No indication at all! Never! Never! If he did what he is charged with, it would be horrible—contemptible—no excuses for his acts!" Nevertheless, she stated that she still felt sorry for him. "Tell him that I pray for him,"[34] she said.

Mrs. Drozdza said that her daughter, too, "liked him a lot." She said that her daughter remembers Trofimoff fondly, as he related very well with her, talking with her about her life in America, her schools, her life plans, etc. Her daughter also remembers Marion. "Marion was very nice to my daughter," Mrs. Drozda said. "She was tall and very pretty. The fact that each of them was very tall was a factor in their good relationship."[35]

Mrs. Drozdza's final comment was very telling: "Engaging and likable as George was, he was definitely a snob, who viewed the world as 'me' and 'them.' "[36]

Trofimoff writes that after his marriage to Marion, they lived in a rented apartment for a short time until they leased a new house on the outskirts of Nuremberg. He worked hard in landscaping their home, but their five-year lease was terminated prematurely. They were given an option to buy the house without a down payment, or else vacate it within 45 days. To them, the offer sounded like a wonderful idea, and so they bought it.[37]

They visited Igor frequently. In his notes Trofimoff describes one dinner they enjoyed with him in the small Austrian resort town of Zell am See. The dinner, consisting of succulent rack of venison, cranberries, mushrooms, and *spatzle*, followed by a flambé dessert, espresso, and an apricot cordial, was a true gourmet delight. He writes that it was another one of those memorable occasions, never to be forgotten.[38]

Tragedy struck shortly after they bought the house when the value of the U. S. dollar collapsed and Trofimoff was unable to meet his mortgage payments. Even though Igor helped again, Trofimoff could not stem the rising debts, and they had to sell the house.[39] With the sale of their home, they rented a house in Nuremberg. After three pleasant years in their new home, the shock of losing it and the subsequent move to a dismal rented house was, as Trofimoff's notes reveal, "the beginning of the end of our marriage . . . the 'happy' marriage was finished . . . I was 32 years older than she, and the generation gap could not be breached."[40]

Trofimoff tried to improve matters by developing Marion's interest in tennis and having her take driving lessons, but he was unsuccessful. Marion became involved with a younger man and not surprisingly, Trofimoff's fourth marriage, while it did not end formally in divorce for several years, was a failure.[41]

In addition to his duties as a civilian at the JIC, Trofimoff continued to keep busy on weekends with his U. S. Army Reserve career and was promoted to Colonel, U. S. Army Reserve, in 1980. His military career came to an end when he was retired and placed in the Retired Reserves in 1985.

During the next few years Trofimoff's health declined. He became a diabetic, his cholesterol level was high, and his blood pressure exceeded normal readings. In the fall of 1990, his doctor prescribed a 30-day convalescent medical leave in a spa (a five-star luxury hotel

Trofimoff's home in Nuremberg.

operated by the Austrian government). He was placed on a strict regime of exercises and a 1,000-calorie diet. He writes that he played at least three hours of tennis each day and spent some time swimming.[42]

In his first week at the spa, Trofimoff noticed an attractive lady sitting all by herself at a table in the dining room, but an opportunity to meet her did not arise for some time. One day he saw her playing on the tennis courts, and later in the evening, noticed her with her opponent having a drink at the bar. Trofimoff joined them and reports that, after her friend retired, they introduced themselves. "I did not want to miss my chance, and asked . . . for a tennis match the next morning. And this is how it started."[43]

Mutually attracted to each other, Trofimoff reports that they met frequently during the next two days, and when Jutta left he gave her a parting gift. "I surprised Jutta by making her a present of some locally crafted earrings, each with two black pearls, which she had admired . . . She burst out in 'happy' tears and told me a little more about herself."[44]

He writes that when she left, he stood in front of her door early in the morning to help her with her bags. "We embraced and kissed very warmly, and I promised to visit her soon. I was deeply in love for the first time in many years, and I wasn't going to give up on this chance." [45]

Jutta told the author about the time she first met Trofimoff:

> It was the last two days before I was to leave the spa and return home. I was sitting at the bar having a beer, when he approached and introduced himself. He was very nice and charming—he was, at the first, always 'Mr. Trofimoff' to me. He asked me to go with him to a nearby casino. After a few hours, we returned to the spa, and we each went to our own room. The next morning, when he found out I was leaving soon, he asked me to stay for a few days, but I told him I had plans to leave. It was my daughter's birthday, and I could not remain any longer. He continued to insist that I stay longer, so I agreed to stay one more night.[46]

The author asked Jutta if she was, at that time, actively looking for a husband. "Of course not," she replied. "I was married before, living in Spain. After two years there, I returned to Germany and was divorced, and after that my doctor arranged for me to go to the spa to recover from a liver operation. I never get [sic] married after 18 years!" [47]

Asked if she had expected to see Trofimoff again after she left the spa, Jutta replied, "We had exchanged addresses and he asked if he could visit me sometime, but he gave no date for a visit."[48]

Trofimoff writes that his time at the spa was scheduled to continue for ten more days, but he could not wait. To him, the spa was no longer the same without Jutta, so he canceled his remaining time.[49]

He drove back to Nuremberg and on to Jutta's home, "I made it in time . . . to obtain a large bouquet of roses . . . and then rang the bell at Jutta's apartment. The surprise was great, and we both cried from happiness . . . Jutta did not allow me to drive the 160 km back to Nuremberg, and I remained with her and her daughter Sandra over the weekend."[50]

Jutta recalls her surprise when she opened her door to Trofimoff's ring. "All I could see was my door filled with beautiful roses. George had brought me the largest, most beautiful bouquet of roses I had ever seen and only when I heard his voice did I realize who was behind them. The first words he spoke were, 'I love you, and I want to marry you.' We went out for dinner, and he stayed in the apartment with me and my daughter for the weekend."[51]

When asked how her family liked Trofimoff, Jutta replied, "He charmed everyone. His communication with my daughter and my mother was unbelievable . . . he loved my daughter like his own, and everyone loved him."[52]

"He visited me almost weekly for a year, and continued to ask me to marry him, but I always refused. Finally," she said, "George went to my mom and said, 'I'd like to marry Jutta.' My mom then said to him 'Why ask me? Ask her!' "[53]

Trofimoff writes that his courtship of Jutta continued over several months, despite the difficulties of having to drive over 300 km every weekend, summer or winter. He had meanwhile met Jutta's mother, sister, and the rest of the family and, after he obtained his divorce from Marion, he asked Jutta's mother for the hand of her daughter in marriage.[54]

After Jutta finally said "yes," the couple decided to get married. The required "red tape" with the German authorities was so lengthy and expensive that they decided to get married in Los Angeles. Trofimoff asked his daughter Natasha to make arrangements for the marriage in a local chapel.[55]

Jutta, however, offers a slightly different version. "We flew to the United States," she told the author. "George asked me on the airplane if I would marry him on my birthday, and I said 'yes.' "[56]

"And you didn't know he had it planned with Natasha?"

"I never knew," she answered.[57]

They were married in Los Angeles on October 23, 1991, with Trofimoff's good friend and former coworker Walter (Vova) Bugreef as best man. As a wedding present, Vova gave them the keys to his beach house near San Diego, where they spent one full week on their honeymoon.[58] They had a brief visit with Natasha before returning to Nuremberg where they moved into Trofimoff's rented house.

In Nuremberg, Jutta became the manager of a large travel center and agency in the local airport. Trofimoff's notes point out that one big advantage (of Jutta' s job) was frequent travel to exclusive hotels in resorts throughout Europe. They were able to take advantage of free, all expense paid, trips on three or four occasions, each time for a full week, all meals included, in five-star hotels.[59] Trofimoff was still enjoying his passion for the good life!

The newly-weds enjoyed their life together, and in the summer of 1992, they decided to visit the United States to explore locations for their retirement. In Melbourne, Florida, they were introduced to The Indian River Colony Club (IRCC), a new community with membership limited to active, retired, or honorably discharged military officers or their widows. "Jutta and I just looked at each other and did not even have to consult."[60] After selecting a lot and a model home, they returned to Germany and began to prepare for retirement and move to the United States.

Trofimoff recalls that after their visit to Florida, his foster brother, Igor, and his housekeeper-friend came to visit in Nuremberg and meet Jutta. He writes that they had Igor's favorite food, but they didn't stay overnight. While Igor and his housekeeper agreed to come again later, somehow the return visit never materialized.[61]

In September 1993, Trofimoff's doctor decided that because of their poor health they both needed another convalescent rest, and arrangements were made for another visit to the same spa where they met in 1990. They spent four wonderful weeks together, thinking of nothing except their anticipated retirement and move to the Florida home. The hotel manager and the bartender both remembered them well, and the manager arranged a special candlelight dinner. Trofimoff writes, "The manager, chef, maitre d' hotel, bartender, and all of the waiters and waitresses all sang an Austrian song for us, and the local press made photographs."[62] It was another one of those pleasant events never to be forgotten.

Trofimoff returned to Florida in mid-1994 to finalize plans for their new home. His notes reveal that they needed approximately $10,000 for an initial payment, which they did not have at that moment. A good friend agreed to lend the money.[63] (This contradicts Jutta's version, who told the author that they planned to use a retirement bonus Trofimoff had been promised for the down payment, but, when it was canceled, she obtained the money from her mother).[64]

In August 1994, Trofimoff applied for an advertised "early retirement" program with a bonus payment of $25,000 for 31 December 1994. They made arrangements to have their household goods packed and shipped, and gave notice to the owners of the rented house. A farewell Christmas party was scheduled for December 17 with all of Trofimoff's American employees from the JIC and all of Jutta's employees from her travel office invited.[65]

Relocation plans completed, the Trofimoffs began cleaning out their home. They had no warning of events which would erupt on December 14, events that would alter their lives forever.

Chapter
7

ARRESTS AND HEARINGS IN GERMANY

He who is bent on doing evil can never want occasion.
—Pubilius Syrus,
Maxim 459, circa 42 B.C.

On December 14, 1994, at about 6:00 a. m., Trofimoff, partially dressed, answered the doorbell of his Nuremberg home. At the door stood Norbeth Buchbender and other agents of the German Federal Office of Criminal Investigation (known as the BKA),[1] with U. S. Army Counter Intelligence (CI) agents. Jutta, following her usual routine, had left earlier for her job at the travel agency in the Nuremberg airport.

"When I opened the door, (they) informed me that they had a search warrant for the house and that I was under the suspicion of having committed espionage against NATO[2] and the Federal Republic of Germany, and that they wanted to question me about it."[3]

Trofimoff agreed to the search and called an attorney, who suggested that he comply with Buchbender's request to accompany him to the Nuremberg police station.

In the meantime, Jutta says she was in her office at about 6:30 a. m. when she received a call from an individual identifying himself as an FBI agent. "He asked me to return home at once, but would not tell me what the emergency was, other than that my house was being inspected and my presence was needed."[4]

Later, when she arrived at her home, she remembers that several agents of the German government and the FBI met her. "They told me

George had been arrested on charges of espionage and was being held in jail in Nuremberg."[5]

The agents questioned Jutta at length and asked her to accompany them to their offices. She told the author, "I said to them, 'I am not leaving this house.' After they called their office, they told me I did not have to go with them, but they wanted to question me about George's activities."[6]

Jutta remembers how the agents went through everything (all boxes, packed in anticipation of their move to America, were opened) and several pictures, address books, and other items were taken. The interrogation continued until approximately 5:00 p. m. When the agents left, they told her they would return the next morning with more questions.

"When the agents returned the next morning," she said, "they returned all the items taken the previous day. They continued to ask me more questions until midafternoon."[7]

Jutta recalls that at about 11 p. m. on December 15, she received a call from an attorney in Karlsruhe telling her he was George's attorney. "He told me that German law required a speedy hearing, and that George and Igor Susemihl were scheduled to appear before the Supreme Court Judge before midnight. When he told me that he would call me the next morning, I answered, 'You will not call me tomorrow! Call me immediately when you have news.' "[8] At about midnight she received a call stating that Trofimoff was released and on his way home.

Trofimoff's describes the events of that day: "About eight or more men and women entered the house and proceeded with the search, while I was allowed to finish my shaving, get dressed, and accompany a four-man team to their office in town. For the next eight to ten hours, I was thoroughly interrogated by the BKA agents."[9]

Trofimoff's uncanny ability to accurately recall details of his past is demonstrated in his description of an event described for him by the BKA agents. His handwritten notes were transcribed from memory in his Florida jail, some eight years after his interrogation:

> During the interrogation I was told by the German agents that a Soviet defector, who went over to the British SIS[10] in 1992, claimed to have seen 50 to 80 volumes with 'thousands' of pages of classified documents (photographs) in the KGB archives in Moscow, where he had worked until 1984, documents which

had allegedly been furnished by an American officer with three cover names, through a priest of the Russian Orthodox Church, to the Soviet KGB. Although my name was not mentioned anywhere by this defector, the suspicion fell on my brother and me. I was also told that Igor was being interrogated in Munich at the same time as I was.[11]

Trofimoff was interrogated by Buchbender from 8:30 a. m. to 5:05 p. m. and held overnight in the Nuremberg Police Headquarters.[12] He was first given an opportunity to make a statement in which he gave details of his life story, beginning with his birth in Berlin, his life with his foster parents and his foster brother, Igor Susemihl. He stated that Igor, the Russian Orthodox Metropolitan from Vienna, was currently residing in Munich, where he had a chapel with a few Russian Orthodox members. In his statement Trofimoff referred to his aristocratic Russian background, telling how he found his way to Paris, immigrated to the United States with the help of a Quaker family, enlisted in the U. S. Army in 1948. and served, either as a soldier or civilian, with the U. S. Army ever since. He then gave the names of his five wives and dates of marriage, concluding his statement with:

> Prior to my interrogation I have been advised of my rights as the accused. Especially pointed out was that I do not have to provide a statement concerning the matter and at any time may contact a defense attorney of my choice. I am announcing that I have understood the advice. I am deciding as follows: I can be asked questions. I will then each time decide whether I want to respond.[13]

Buchbender began by asking Trofimoff if it were true that he was an agent of the KGB.

"I categorically and absolutely deny that," he replied. "What is correct is that for 45 years I have worked against these people."[14] He explained the operation of and his responsibilities in the JIC, and when asked again about being recruited by the KGB, issued another categorical denial: "At no time have I ever been recruited by anyone for the Soviet Intelligence service or for any other intelligence service from the Soviet Union or the Warsaw Pact."[15]

Asked if he knew a person named Ikar, he said "no," but when asked to tell about any contacts with Igor Susemihl, he did admit and explain his relationship with Igor Susemihl, stating that he visited his foster brother every time he was in Munich.

"Mr. Trofimoff, have you received money from Igor Susemihl?"[16] Buchbender asked.

"Yes, I had asked him several times to lend me money in order to be able to meet my obligations in connection with my children. The amount came to a few thousand marks each time.

"Susemihl had also lend [sic] me money in connection with the purchase of a home in the 80s, since I was no longer able to pay my interest based on the declining dollar value.

"Four years after the purchase I had to sell the house . . . I have returned the money borrowed from Igor every time. At present I am no longer indebted to him."[17]

Buchbender asked, "Did you in 1969 have the opportunity to transfer to other units of the MI in order to climb up the military career ladder?"[18]

"I was offered to become the advisor to the battalion commander. It would have afforded me the opportunity to advance one step in my career path. My salary would have increased as well. I was even offered this position twice. I declined this offer both times for I was happy here in Nuremberg . . . I would have had to move to Munich."[19]

Asked about his cameras, he described three different ones. "I am also in possession of a tripod which I have not used in years. I have probably stored it somewhere in the basement . . . I do not own any other flash devices or lamps to illuminate the object to be photographed."[20]

Buchbender then asked, "Mr. Trofimoff, don't you believe it is time that you admitted to being this agent 'Anteiy' [sic]."[21]

"I am neither the agent 'Anteiy' [sic] nor any other agent. I have neither worked for the KGB nor any other intelligence service."[22]

Trofimoff admitted to Buchbender that, on occasion, he had visited Igor's home overnight carrying with him an unlocked briefcase containing classified documents he was taking to the JIC. "I myself have never shown the contents of my briefcase to Igor . . . I also cannot imagine that Igor in secret went into my briefcase and looked at the documents."[23]

When Buchbender asked for details of Trofimoff's reunion with Susemihl, he replied that sometime in 1963 Igor called him at his Frankfurt apartment from the airport, offering to meet during a layover, and that they talked for about 45 minutes before Igor continued his flight. Some time later his foster brother called again, this time from Munich, and Trofimoff visited him there. "Thereafter, I visited Susemihl approximately once a year in Munich."[24]

Referring to the loans made by Igor, Buchbender asked, "Mr. Trofimoff, where did this money come from and what has Susemihl asked of you in return? Did Igor Susemihl maintain contacts to the former USSR and does he maintain contacts today?"[25]

"I don't know where Susemihl took the money from. He never asked for considerations such as in the form of information regarding the U. S. Army, my coworkers and superiors, or in form of information I have access to . . . in the past he had traveled to Moscow several times, particularly, according to what he told me, for religious synods."[26]

With his last question for the day, Buchbender was persistent. "Is it not so that you are telling the untruth and that in reality Igor Susemihl, for information provided from your working area with the U. S. Army, has provided you with a compensation?"[27]

Again, Trofimoff denied the allegation. "It is not true that I gave Igor any information and he paid me with money. I have only borrowed money from him and later returned it."[28]

At 5:05 p. m. Buchbender told Trofimoff he would be held overnight and taken to the Karlsruhe Federal Supreme Court the next day.

The next morning, before departing for Karlsruhe, Buchbender had more questions.

"Mr. Trofimoff, have you during the past received presents from Igor Susemihl and, if yes, what type of presents were they?"[29]

When Trofimoff replied that he had no memory of any presents, Buchbender said, "Mr. Trofimoff, found in your residence were . . . "[30]

Trofimoff interrupted to say, "Excuse me, I take everything back. Located at my residence are small Russian boxes, varnished jewelry boxes, specifically four or five. I have received those from Igor Susemihl as presents."[31]

"Mr. Trofimoff, yesterday during the search in Munich we found in the possession of Igor Susemihl an intelligence aiding device, more specifically, a container in the shape of a screwdriver. This confirms the findings by investigative authorities that accusations against you and Igor Susemihl are accurate. What is your comment?"[32]

"I would like to first be able to ask a legal advisor. I nevertheless like to state for the report that, if an intelligence aiding device was found with Igor Susemihl, one should not inevitably conclude my

*Hollow screwdriver found by German agents in Susemihl's apartment,
December 14, 1994. (U.S. Justice Dept.)*

participation. I have nothing to do with the entire matter."[33]

Trofimoff writes that he was told by the German agents that his
and Igor's statements ". . . were absolutely identical and had only one
difference, namely the amount of money I claimed to have received
from him as a loan, and the amount he stated to have given me."[34]

Trofimoff writes:

> In the morning, while still in the office of the BKA, my
> boss, the commander of the 18th Military Intelligence
> Battalion, entered and informed me officially that my
> security clearance had been suspended . . . I was
> placed on administrative leave immediately, and my
> approved retirement under the early retirement pro-
> gram with the accompanying bonus check of $25,000
> had been withdrawn . . . Later that morning, a team of
> BKA agents drove me to Karlsruhe to be presented to
> a superior court judge as required by German law.[35]

As Trofimoff was arrested in Nuremberg, Bernard Zeitler and other
BKA agents arrived at Igor Susemihl's home in Munich to arrest him
and search his apartment. Igor was in bed when Agent Zeitler and his
team arrived, and his housekeeper, Gudula Walker, answered the
doorbell. When the agents identified themselves, Mrs. Walker asked

them to enter and went to Igor's bedroom to tell him that BKA officers wanted to speak with him.

When Susemihl appeared, Zeitler advised him he was accused of espionage, presented a search warrant, and advised him that he was allowed to make a statement.

In his brief statement, Igor says that he agreed to the searches, and "immediately offered to be available for an appropriate questioning at the Bavarian State Office of Criminal Investigation (LKA) in Munich. I state that I have understood the instructions. I want to give a statement in this matter; I waive the presence of an attorney."[36]

The interrogation began at approximately 7:30 a. m., with Zeitler first asking about Mrs. Walker.

Susemihl described his relationship with Gudula, concluding with, "Since we had become the proverbial very good friends, in the meantime, she moved in with me . . . I want to emphasize here, that we are neither engaged, related, nor related by marriage."[37]

Zeitler then went to the heart of the matter. "Mr. Susemihl, you are accused of having been active for several years as an agent, first for a Soviet and afterwards for a Russian intelligence service . . . you are also accused of having introduced George Trofimoff, who is being charged separately, at the beginning of the sixties, to your intelligence handlers. What is your position on this?"[38]

"I state that at no time ever have I been an agent for either the Soviet or the Russian Intelligence service . . . This accusation does not correspond to the facts."[39]

Igor then embarked on a lengthy monologue covering his relationship with his foster brother, "little Georgi" Trofimoff, his early education and military service, and the beginning of his theological studies which resulted in his being ordained a deacon. Married in 1940, he had a son Nikolaus in 1941, was ordained a priest in 1945, and immigrated with his family to Australia in 1948. Interested in visiting the roots of the Russian Orthodox Church in Moscow, he received an invitation to visit the Moscow patriarchy in 1956.[40]

"Mr. Susemihl," asked Zeitler, "on the basis of the current investigation and the circumstances in Moscow described by you, one must go on the presumption that you were introduced to the KGB during this visit."[41]

"That I cannot confirm. Years later, it did become clear to me that this patriarchy in Moscow had been controlled extensively by the KGB. Never, at any time, was I ever asked to participate in intelligence work or in espionage activities."[42]

"Mr. Susemihl, according to current information, you did introduce George Trofimoff to the former KGB. The reason for this was Mr. Trofimoff's financial difficulty. In order to help him at least a little with his financial problems, you advised him to deliver some 'secret documents' to the KGB. What is your position on this?"[43]

"I did not request secret documents from Trofimoff, nor did I receive or pass them on to anybody. I have nothing else to say about that."[44]

"What kind of trips did you undertake to the East Bloc countries?"[45] Zeitler asked.

Igor replied that, as a member of various international religious organizations, he attended conferences in several Eastern Bloc countries and East Germany. In 1957 he decided to follow the leadership of the Moscow patriarchy and received different assignments until the beginning of 1963. "I received the instruction from the foreign office of the Moscow patriarchy to open a parish in West Germany. I decided on Munich . . . Since that time I have lived in Munich, except for brief interruptions. I was named archbishop to Vienna and Austria approximately 20 years ago. It was during this time that I went to Vienna very often."[46]

"Mr. Susemihl, did you also have contacts with members of the Soviet Embassy in Vienna?"[47]

He answered "yes," explaining that since the church was on Embassy grounds, he was always in contact with the ambassador and traveled to Moscow frequently. "In this context I had to report, above all, to the foreign office of the Moscow patriarchy concerning my church work in Germany and in Austria."[48]

Zeitler produced a picture, which Susemihl identified as Alexander Blagow, head of the consular section of the Russian embassy in Vienna. Igor confirmed that Blagow obtained his (Igor's) entry visas to Russia and obtained cigarettes and tea for him from the United Nations offices in Vienna.[49]

"Mr. Susemihl, Alexander Blagow is a known member of the Russian successor service to the KGB. It seems unbelievable when you state that your contacts with him had been solely restricted to the occasions described by you . . . it is much more likely to go by the presumption that these contacts were of an intelligence nature. Please comment."[50]

"I state again that I have had no intelligence contacts whatsoever with a Russian intelligence service."[51]

Zeitler asked, "Mr. Susemihl, according to existing information, your cover name with the Russian intelligence service is 'Ikar.' Please comment."[52]

"This is my pet name, which I have been called since childhood, but that only by my parents . . . as a small child I was not able to speak my first name 'Igor' correctly. I made 'Ikar' out of it."[53]

"What can you tell me about the name Antey?"[54] Zeitler asked.

"I never heard this name. If I am told that this is the cover name of Trofimoff, then I can only state that this name is unknown to me."[55]

"What was your relationship to George Trofimoff after the second World War?"[56]

Igor generally confirmed what Trofimoff had reported regarding their reunion in Frankfurt. After that, he said, they met frequently at his (Igor's) home whenever Trofimoff traveled to Munich on business. "Trofimoff confessed to me that he was in financial difficulties because of the excessive furniture purchases by his first German wife."[57]

"Mr. Susemihl, did you do anything on your part to eliminate the debts of George Trofimoff?"[58]

"I did not do anything regarding this matter. But I lent him money twice, once DM 500 and once DM 600. After a lengthy time period he did pay this money back to me. Never, at any time did I make cash gifts to him."[59]

This last statement of Igor's was a major discrepancy in the testimony of the two foster brothers, and Zeitler wasted no time in capitalizing on the conflicting stories.

"Mr. Susemihl, George Trofimoff, who is being prosecuted separately, stated today during the interrogation that he borrowed amounts between 1,000 and 5,000 DM from you on more than three dozen occasions since 1969 . . . Considering the situation, one must presume that these payments were a reward for intelligence activities. What is your position on this?"[60]

"That description, as given by George Trofimoff, is not correct . . . I only lent him money twice, once 500 and once 600 DM . . . I could have never lent him amounts between 1,000 and 5,000 DM because I never could have spared that much money."[61]

The interrogation ended at 5:00 p. m. when Zeitler informed Igor that he would be held overnight and brought before the Federal Supreme Court in Karlsruhe the next day.

Initially in Karlsruhe, neither Trofimoff nor Igor was told of the other's presence. Trofimoff appeared before Supreme Court Judge Dr. Bernd Dieter Bode at 2:50 p. m. George's attorney, Karlheinz Linle, and BKA agent Buchbender were present.[62]

Judge Bode explained Trofimoff's rights and gave him the right to make a statement.

"I am prepared to give additional statements concerning the case. I am entirely refuting the accusation of having been a KGB agent. I do not know who can claim such a thing and for what reason."[63]

While his statement was limited primarily to his relationship with Igor, one comment suggests a potential conflict with his foster brother: "My former wife Marion had seen Igor two or three times . . . He did not like Marion."[64]

To a question regarding money received from Igor, Trofimoff replied, "He repeatedly loaned me money which I always paid back regularly."[65] He said that on some occasions, his foster brother borrowed money from a bank to loan to him, and on those occasions he paid the interest Igor owed the bank. Regarding the frequency of the loans, he retracted his previous estimate of some three dozen loans:

"If I stated yesterday that Igor loaned me money about three dozen times, after contemplating, I wish to retract my words. It was not that often. It was 10 to 12 times at the most. The amounts were between 1,000 and 5,000 marks on the average. Once, he loaned me 10,000 marks when I had to pay a penalty in the amount of 14,000 marks for premature redemption of a mortgage . . .

"Igor never handed me the money amounts in one sum, but paid in installments. And besides, he always got the money back that I had borrowed. Igor had money in the bank and picked it up himself . . . I suspect that Igor probably had church funds at his disposal."[66]

Regarding his financial situation, he said that he was gradually decreasing his debts. "Presently I still have two outstanding loans, one about $6,000 and another about $8,000."[67]

He told the judge that a $28,000 down payment on his Florida home ". . . has already been made to a bank in Florida; my wife paid $10,000, which she had received from an inheritance."[68] (Jutta told the author privately, after the trial, that she paid the entire amount with her share of her mother's estate, which her mother gave her in advance.)

Despite his continuing protestations of his close relationship with, and high admiration for, his "big brother," Trofimoff apparently decided to distance himself from Igor as he volunteered an amendment to a previous statement regarding his handling of classified documents: "I have carried interviews of targets that had been questioned which sometimes added up to entire books . . . During my stay in Munich, I almost always spent the night at Igor's and brought these records, which were in my unlocked briefcase, into Igor's house, meaning from Friday till Sunday afternoon. I do not know whether Igor, during that time period, examined these records. However, I do not believe so."[69]

The investigation, which began at 2:50 p. m., was interrupted at 5:55 p. m. until it resumed at 10:40 p. m. when Trofimoff appeared jointly with Susemihl before the Federal Judge.

Igor's appearance before Judge Bode began at 6:35 p. m., with agent Zeitler attending. [70]

After his rights were explained, the priest declined the offer of counsel and began his statement. It soon became clear that he had become disenchanted with his "little brother."

Igor related that at his reunion with Trofimoff after the war in Frankfurt, "He was at first very reserved and unfriendly."[71] Their next meeting, Igor said, was in Bad Homburg, about half a year later. After Trofimoff's transfer to Nuremberg, ". . . we met quite often, whenever he visited his Munich headquarters. He would visit me during those times and sometimes spend the night. He arrived carrying a suitcase or briefcase; however, I never saw the contents. He visited me around three to four times a year. We talked, ate together. I was angry because he drank my whiskey . . . I never received written documents from Trofimoff from his work . . . I only knew that he worked in the intelligence field for the U. S. Army. However, I knew no details, and also did not ask questions."[72]

Concerning the KGB and the Russian Orthodox Church, Igor said, "I personally never had any contact with the Soviet intelligence service. However, I assume that from the ranks of the clergy, there must have been persons working for the KGB. I am very certain of that. The KGB was everywhere, also in the church."[73]

As he continued with his statement, Igor launched more barbs at Trofimoff. "After Trofimoff had moved to Nuremberg, I loaned him money twice. It had to do with his move; his wife had purchased new furniture. I can no longer remember the exact amount that I loaned him. Both amounts were under 1,000 marks. He paid back the money much later and after having been reminded. It is not true

that I loaned him money after he purchased the house and encountered problems with the interest rates. It was very difficult for me to
comprehend at that time how it had been possible for him to
acquire the house at all. In accordance with Marion's wish, he purchased the house by using credit from a German bank. She was a
very young, lively girl whom he had met in the red light district.
She was working for a dermatologist and she gave Trofimoff a run
for his money, he bought her a fur coat, among other things."[74]

The judge called attention to Trofimoff's statement that Igor had
allegedly loaned him much larger sums before, and the priest
replied, "This is an outright lie. I neither withdrew money from the
bank to give to Trofimoff, nor did I take out credit at the bank for
him. I have never ever taken out bank credit. Also, I never have had
money to the extent that I could have or wanted to loan him."[75]

Regarding the screwdriver taken from his home, Igor said, "This
is my screwdriver. I used it very seldom. I never realized that it
could be unscrewed that way. I absolutely deny that it has been
used as a means of transporting items of intelligence value. I never
knew that there was a chamber to conceal things and that it could
be opened. When I purchased the home, a number of tools
remained behind. I do not know whether the screwdriver can be
counted to the tools that had been left behind. However, I did not
purchase it."[76]

After Igor's interrogation, both Trofimoff and Susemihl were
brought before Judge Bode at 10:40 p. m. for his decision.

After the judge's interrogation, both Buchbender and Zeitler
asked the judge to issue arrest warrants. Each agent emphasized
that the defendants were "strongly suspected" of carrying out intelligence activities, and that the "strong suspicion" rested on classified
information presented by a reliable source, a U. S. military official.

In addition to the "strong suspicion" allegation, Buchbender
argued that: "Investigations show the accused was recruited by the
'separately prosecuted' Susemihl . . . The urgent suspicion is based
on information by a source of a U. S. Army office . . . the intelligence
connection of the accused to the Russian secret service has lasted to
the present time . . . Reason for arrest is the danger of the defendant
taking flight."[78]

Trofimoff's legal counsel requested that an arrest warrant not be
issued on grounds that: "He had doubts concerning the "strong
suspicion . . . it is not adequately known what information was to

have been delivered."[79]

In addition to the "strong suspicion" allegation, Zeitler's arguments included: " . . . the accused is strongly suspected of carrying out intelligence activities for the KGB . . . under the cover name of 'Ikar' . . . In 1969 he won over the accused Trofimoff . . . Reason for arrest is the danger of the defendant's fleeing."[80]

Igor, not represented by counsel, asked to have the request for an arrest warrant dismissed as it was just before Christmas and his coming Christmas services would have to be canceled. He offered to deposit money as security, stating that he would not take flight since "I have a very strong, personal relationship with Gudula Walker."[81]

The Court's Decision[82]

It was almost midnight that evening when Dr. Bode issued his decision:

> The requests of the Federal Attorney General at the Federal Supreme Court of Justice for the issue of arrest warrants against the accused George Trofimoff and Igor Susemihl are
>
> **rejected.**
> <u>Reasons:</u>
> There is no current strong suspicion against both accused that they conducted secret service like spy activities within the time of the statute of limitations . . . As the limitation of action was interrupted the first time on Dec. 12, 1994, by the decree of search directions, the criminal actions of the accused would have had to continue after Dec. 12, 1989. This is not substantiated . . . The accuracy of the source reports has been confirmed in many details by the pre-investigations of the Federal Intelligence Service, but their tactical time is so far back that additional evidence is necessary to justify the strong suspicion also for the period thereafter, especially within the statute of limitations. This is missing . . . Strong suspicion in the sense of the requests for warrant of arrest is therefore not given. Therefore the requests have to be rejected.[83]

Dr. Bode, Judge at the Federal Supreme Court of Justice, signed the rejection on 12/16/94.

Thus, even though German investigators had developed sufficient evidence to support the charges that both Trofimoff and Igor had previously committed espionage, Judge Bode concluded that there was no evidence to show that their espionage activities occurred within the five-year period covered by the German statute of limitations. Judge Bode rejected the requests for arrests made by agents Buchbender and Zeitler, ordered the charges dropped, and both accused men were released.

Jutta was devastated by her husband's arrest. "I had no knowledge of any spying activities by George," she told the author. "I was completely surprised by his arrest and as soon as he got home that morning I asked that he tell me truthfully what had happened. He said, 'I swear on my mother's and father's graves that I did nothing.' "[84]

Trofimoff is a very convincing individual, and Jutta believed what he told her. "If I had any doubt that he was telling me the truth," she said, "I would have divorced him on the spot."[85] While she was concerned with the loss of Trofimoff's retirement bonus, her faith in her husband convinced her that, even with the loss of the bonus, their new, eagerly anticipated life in America would be secure. At that time, however, she was unaware of other unpleasant surprises that lurked in their future.

Chapter
8

A NEW START

> We rarely find a man who can say he has lived happy, and
> content with his life can retire from the
> world like a satisfied guest.
>
> —Horace (65-8 B. C.),
> *Satires. Book I, i, Line 117*

Trofimoff's original request for retirement from Civil Service was approved on October 21, 1994, with the retirement date established as December 31.[1] A separation incentive payment of $25,000, to be made upon his retirement, was also approved but was canceled on December 23. The reason stated on the cancellation notice was "Canceled per Direction of Organizational Commander."[2] With the stunning news that his retirement package, to include his bonus payment, had been withdrawn as a result of his arrest by the German agents, his immediate dilemma was whether he should, or should not, contest the decision and fight for his retirement bonus. His thoughts on the matter were revealed during his videotaped interview with FBI Agent Dimitry Droujinsky.

> The thing is, I could go to court. I could fight it. But you see what happens when you're a civilian employee . . . When you are under court procedures your file is flagged. That means your pay stops . . . My baggage was packed. I had ready, orders already to go back . . . And all that would have been suspended . . . I took an American lawyer in Frankfurt . . . since this was a classified matter he would have to have special permis-

sion from the government to get all the information. And for that he needed a clearance, and it would take anywhere from three to six months to get the clearance. And then it would take a year or two to get it through court. And I said to myself, meanwhile how am I going to live? . . . so I decided I'm not going to, because I could not win. There's one thing that was against me: that I had contact with a suspected agent.[3]

Later, as Trofimoff and Jutta discussed the pros and cons of their move to America, Jutta recalls that he said to her, "Let's go to America and start a new beginning." She later told the author, "If I had not believed what he swore to me after his hearing in Germany, I would have left him—but since he convinced me that he did nothing wrong, I agreed to stay with him and make the move to Florida."[4]

With the loss of Trofimoff's retirement bonus, they were desperate for money to make the down payment on their house. "My mother had a will," Jutta said, "so I went to my sister and my mother to ask if I could have my share of the inheritance in advance. They both agreed, so my mother gave me my share in cash. That is how we obtained the money for the down payment."[5]

For assistance in resolving his dilemma and insuring that his Civil Service retirement proceeded as scheduled and that his retirement pay remained intact, Trofimoff engaged Robert J. Fiore, an American attorney residing in Frankfurt, Germany. Mr. Fiore, in an e-mail to the author, said:

Mr. Trofimoff retained me to assure that his retirement was quickly and properly processed . . . Although I was not involved in the German case I did inform Mr. Trofimoff that there was no statute of limitations in the United States on espionage and that he could be subject to a Federal warrant in the United States at any time after he arrives (in the United States). I recall George saying 'you mean the FBI could knock on my door at any time during the rest of my life?' and I said, yes, and you have read about such cases.

George could have remained here and been untouchable. As the husband of a German citizen, he would have been entitled to a residence permit and the United States Government would have sent him

Entrance to Indian River Colony Club where George and Jutta purchased a home in 1995. (Author's collection)

The Trofimoff home on Patriot Drive in Indian River Colony Club outside Melbourne, Florida. (Author's collection)

his retirement check every month. He would not have been extradited due to the statute of limitations . . . one other item I did not feel I should lay on George, espionage carries the death penalty in the United States. Germany will not extradite on a charge carrying the death penalty.[6]

So, the mystery of why Trofimoff decided to return to the United States, even with this dire warning from his attorney, is still not explained. Possible explanations for his decision could be:

- He was convinced that the case was closed for good and that the United States would never reopen and pursue it after he returned to the United States.
- More likely, his great ego and arrogance made him believe that even if the FBI did pursue the case, they would never be able to prove his guilt.
- Or, he is, in fact, innocent of the charges levied against him.

For whatever reason, Trofimoff decided to return to the United States. "I officially retired from the Civil Service on March 4, 1995," he writes. "We left our rented house in Nuremberg and moved with a few bags and our cat 'Struppi' to my mother-in-law's house near Bad Kissingen, where we remained until 28 May, 1995."[7]

The Trofimoffs flew to Florida and moved into their "dream house" on the first day of June. Their furniture and other possessions arrived the same day, and they began to organize their new home. "We soon discovered that the house did not have some of the essentials required by law in Germany, but not mandatory in Florida. We had to spend considerable amounts of money."[8]

Trofimoff's love of the good life again surfaced as he spared no expense in improving their home, financing the improvements with readily available credit cards. An extensive lightning arrestor system and an intruder alarm system were installed, and new furniture and hurricane shutters were purchased. Trofimoff, who loved to work outdoors, supplemented the community-provided landscaping with additional palms and other native Florida trees and plants until the house became a tropical paradise.

Jutta tried, without success, to keep her husband's spending in check. "In Germany," she said, "you cannot run up large credit card debts. The amount due must be paid at the end of each month, but here in America, George was able to increase his credit card debts without any limit. I think that we must have spent from thirty to forty thousand dollars on the house, charging the amounts to credit cards . . . he had to take out a second mortgage to satisfy the credit card debts."[9]

In the meantime, even as the debts mounted, the Trofimoffs were, in his words, "the happiest couple imaginable."[10] They plunged into the social life of the IRCC, enjoying the many amenities available to members. "We played lots of tennis, splashed around in our own pool and spa, and enjoyed the overall comradeship and friendship of our neighbors and members of the IRCC . . . we visited some of the locally renown local restaurants and clubs, and joined the Patrick Air Force Base Officer's Club on the beach."[11] Their lovely home was situated on a prime lot, backed up by a small lake and an undeveloped area where all types of waterfowl provided continuous entertainment. "It was a wonderful life," he writes, "marred only by the fact that we had plunged a little too deeply into the desired items for our home."[12]

Serious financial problems began almost immediately. Trofimoff acknowledged that his reckless spending on the new home resulted in an onerous load of high-interest debt. ". . . we had therefore acquired considerable debts, especially on the so-readily available credit cards. I have to admit that I was the person responsible for getting us into this hole. Jutta kept cautioning me, but I just didn't want to listen to reason, and thought to be smart enough to get us out of this dilemma. I took out a second mortgage on the house, which temporarily relieved the burden . . . but only temporarily."[13]

The financial problems were compounded when Trofimoff, still in love with fine automobiles, was lured to a local Chrysler dealer with a flyer received through the mail. "I went with him," Jutta told me, "and immediately knew he had made up his mind to buy a new Chrysler. I tried to talk him out of it. I told him we didn't need a new car, but I couldn't stop him."[14] Jutta remembers that their older, serviceable car was fully paid for, but the trade for the fully-loaded, elegant Chrysler required monthly payments in excess of $600, adding another burden to their rapidly-increasing load of debt.

Trofimoff's foster brother Igor and his housekeeper visited the Trofimoffs in their Florida home in late or 1996 or early 1997. "I told him about my troubles with the second mortgage," Trofimoff writes, "and he promised to 'look into it' upon his return to Munich. At Easter time in 1997, Igor told me on the phone that he asked his main office, the Patriarchat in Moscow, for permission to disburse such a

The supermarket in Melbourne, Florida where Trofimoff took a job bagging groceries in a futile attempt to get out of debt.

large amount of $42,000 from his special account or as advance on his salary, and that he expected no difficulties."[15] (Trofimoff told the author privately on several occasions that he expected to receive an inheritance from his brother, but even after Igor died the money never materialized and the financial problems continued to escalate.)

Trofimoff did not introduce the author and his wife to his foster brother, and they were unaware of Igor's visit until several months later. Jutta remembers that the visit was somewhat strained as Trofimoff and Igor got into a rather violent argument at one time, and Igor threatened to leave early. She was not fully aware what they were arguing over, but says that part of their argument was petty, involving the brothers' memories of childhood events. She knew that Trofimoff told Igor of his financial problems and was aware that Igor telephoned his foster brother after his visit to tell him that he would receive some money. "George told me that Igor said it will take time as the money must be sent through church channels."[16]

When asked what she thought of Igor, Jutta said, "I didn't like him. He was distant, and I could never get close to him."[17]

Realizing his dire financial predicament, Trofimoff tried for some time to find a job, but at his age in Florida, that was a formidable, almost impossible task. Finally, he decided to take a job bagging groceries at a local super market. "It will take me a long time," he confided to the author during one of the evening card sessions, "but eventually I will work the debt off. Please don't tell my friends here about my debt, but tell them that I am working only because I can no longer play tennis and I need to get out and mingle with people. It is too boring for me to stay at home every day while Jutta is enjoying tennis with her friends."[18] Even though Trofimoff bared his soul while telling of the problems of his huge debt, neither the author nor his wife ever had the slightest inkling of the real problems he was facing.

While the Trofimoffs continued to enjoy their life in Florida, even as they plunged deeper and deeper into debt, they were completely oblivious to the storm that was gathering on the near horizon—a storm that would begin early in the morning on July 10, 1997—one that would leave their wonderful life in their "dream house" in shambles.

Chapter
9

LETTERS, TELEPHONE CALLS AND VIDEOTAPES

Oh, what a tangled web we weave,
When first we practise to deceive!
—Sir Walter Scott, 1771-1832
Marmion, Canto VI, Stanza 17

Trofimoff's problems went back decades, but they became infinitely worse in July of 1997 when the FBI gave Germain Salazar a special assignment. Salazar, born in Columbia, South America, immigrated to the United States in 1961 and enlisted in the U. S. Air Force. In the Air Force, he was given undercover counter-intelligence assignments, working, at times, with the FBI. He retired in Orlando, Florida, in 1985, continuing similar work as a civilian.

Early in the morning on July 10, 1997, an FBI agent drove Salazar, a short, nondescript individual, to the Indian River Colony Club, in Melbourne, Florida. While IRCC is a gated and guarded community, guards are instructed to allow Federal and local officers to enter the community with no questions asked. On that morning the FBI driver had no trouble gaining access, and he drove Salazar to within two blocks of Trofimoff's home on Patriot Drive. Salazar was dressed informally in a sport shirt, shorts and sneakers to attract as little attention as possible. He continued on foot to Trofimoff's residence. (The irony of a retired U. S. Army Colonel, accused of spying for the Soviets and residing on Patriot Drive, did not escape the attention of the media.) When Salazar rang the doorbell at about 7:00 a. m., Trofimoff, clad in pajamas, opened the door.

> 10 . VII . 1997
>
> Dear Friend
>
> We urgently need to meet with you to discuss a developing situation of your past cooperation with us. This situation is serious to all of us. Please use public telephone to call trusted friend who will wait at 407.752.9136 at 10 oclock a.m. or at 11 oclock as backup, today. Do not use your home telephone to call or discuss this with somebody. Do not forget to destroy this letter after you make telephone call.
>
> Your friends

The hand-written letter delivered by Germain Salazar, working for the FBI to Trofimoff's home on 10 July 1997. (U.S. Justice Dept.)

Trofimoff describes that event: "And as always in life, out of the clear blue sky, the troubles began. In August 1997," (He had a rare lapse of memory in citing the month. The delivery was in July, rather than August.) "a strange message was delivered by a total stranger to my door . . . It was referring to my past activities in Germany with an oblique reference to my arrest. It was signed 'Your Friends.'

"That same evening, I received a phone call from a representative of the Russian Embassy in Washington, who offered financial assistance if I would consent to explain 'a few things' in my past life in Germany. I told him that I had no past and that I did not want to have anything to do with him or 'friends,' and to please leave me alone."[1]

Salazar described the event:

> Their (the FBI's) request was to personally deliver an envelope addressed to Colonel Von Trofimoff.[2] I went to his home . . . there was a housing project for officers, a very selective community . . . I was driven . . . By, uh,

an FBI agent . . . I was dropped off a couple of blocks
(away) since I knew already the address . . . I knocked
on the door . . . The gentleman was . . . say a six-two,
six-three, figure, uh, a very corpulent, robust individual. And I wanted to make sure that that was the person I looked for, so I said, 'Colonel Von Trofimoff?'
And he says, 'Yes.' And I said, 'uh, I am tasked with
delivering you this personally—this envelope.'

So he says, 'do you live in here?'

And I said, oh, no. I said, I could never afford to . . .

I left, and was picked up by the same agent again
and driven out of the community.[3]

The letter was worded and written in a style of handwriting to
make it appear that a European wrote it. The writer of the letter was
FBI Special Agent Dimitry N. Droujinsky, a specialist in "False Flag"
operations (i. e., operations in which an undercover agent assumes
the identity of someone else in order to obtain a confession or information from a suspect). For the next three years, Droujinsky would be
in almost continual contact with Trofimoff—by telephone, letter, and
face-to-face meetings, posing as a member of the Russian Embassy in
Washington, D. C.

Droujinsky was born in Jerusalem in 1939 of Russian parents. He
immigrated to America in 1959 and joined the U. S. Marines, becoming a U. S. citizen in 1963. In the Marine Corps, he was assigned to
intelligence duties, and after an honorable discharge, he attended college, studying modern languages. He is fluent in French, Russian,
Arabic, and English and is able to speak other languages. After college
he became a special agent for the FBI and retired after 31 years of service. For 30 years of that time, he specialized in foreign counterintelligence operations and participated in many "False Flag" operations.
Retired, he still works in similar roles when needed.

In late 1996 or early 1997, FBI Special Agent Anthony "Tony"
Wagoner approached Droujinsky and asked for his assistance in the
Trofimoff case. Droujinsky began his involvement in the case by writ-
ing the first letter to Trofimoff.

After reading the letter, Trofimoff writes, "I was baffled . . . I did not
want any trouble—my past experience during my arrest in Germany
was the cause of that, and I did not want our idyllic retired life disturbed . . . I was retired and did not want to have anything to do with
any authorities. I ignored the letter . . . and destroyed it."[4]

When Trofimoff did not respond, Special Agent Droujinsky called him and introduced himself as Igor Galkin from the Russian Embassy in Washington. Droujinsky told Trofimoff that there was an urgent matter concerning a "mutual" project that should be discussed. This call was a long one, lasting at least 30 minutes. Igor described the unexpected disappearance of an analyst with sensitive material, voicing concerns of his Washington office that the missing analyst might be dealing with German authorities. Droujinsky offered protection for Trofimoff, emphasizing that there was a high possibility that the missing analyst would cause problems.

Trofimoff, who from the beginning of the conversation steadfastly denied knowledge of any "mutual project," revealed his rising concern in his response: ". . .Well can you, can you imagine what my life would look like if I get in contact with anybody whatsoever? . . .Well the best thing for me to avoid the problem is to avoid meeting anybody, and you know if and when the problem arises, I will have to take care of it myself. This is the United States and it's not that easy to, ah, bamboozle people in the United States."[5]

Droujinsky continued to pressure Trofimoff, emphasizing that they had contacted him out of concern for his safety, offering protection.

". . . the best, the best protection for me is nobody gets in touch with me for anything at any time,"[6] Trofimoff responded.

Throughout the conversation, Trofimoff repeatedly asked to be left alone, saying, "Igor, please tell whoever it is that I'm not worried and that I'm definitely going to swear, and I can swear on a stack of Bibles that I was not involved in anything . . . I don't want any help . . . I just don't want anything. I want to be left alone. And if I'm in any kind of trouble I got out of it before and I'll get out of it again."[7]

When the agent asked Trofimoff if he could help with some current problems, his reply was in the form of a question:

"So in what way am I supposed to help? I can't help. Listen I'm completely out of touch with everything . . . I don't want to get back in. I hated my last few years in the service. I don't want any part of it anymore."[8]

Trofimoff's notes generally agree with what he said in the recorded conversation with Droujinsky. "I firmly declined to help in any way, denying any participation in 'mutual activities.' I firmly and repeatedly refused any need for help, or assistance of any sort, and demanded 'no contacts' for the future . . . For a moment I thought it to be some kind of a trap, but I couldn't figure out by whom and why."[9]

Droujinsky made no further attempt to contact Trofimoff until September 24, 1997, when an undated letter with no postage appeared in George's mailbox. This letter was designed to heighten Trofimoff's concerns.

```
Dear Friend,


Please read this letter very attentively. We understand your concerns

regarding our Washington colleauges contact with you on July 10 but it is

imperative you must be made aware of the important problem that exists

to our former mutual project and even more to your own well being.

It is unfortunate, that since the contact conditions have become

worsened. The departed analyst of what we spoke was for many years     .

responsible for our projects in Germany and the projects of our former

associates there that had been turned over to us. The analyst also destro

our information storeage systems and took microfiches of work production

files containing original materials provided and photographs and taped

records of meetings of our officers and contacts.It is obvious this

developement is of great importance because the publicity of these inter-

actions cannot be acceptable. Our superiors have directed it is the

priority to resolve this. For our part we will continue diligent

evaluation of your situation. Please for your part be especially alert

to all developments and if you believe you are in need of assistance of

any kind please contact us. Because of this situation we have special con

methods. We have reliable arrangements for direct forwarding of mail to

a designate location. Be sureto print "Forward As Directed" in the bottom

left corner of the envelope and address to "ASL International Mailing

Service, 1929 18 Street NW., #1134, Washington D.C., 20009"




                              With Best Regards

                              Your Friends
```

A copy of the letter mailed to Trofimoff on 24 September 1997. (U.S. Justice Dept.)

"This letter increased my feeling of some kind of a trap," George's notes say, "but I couldn't define the reason for it, nor could I discover the source. This letter, exactly like the first one, was written in a 'stilted' style, deliberately creating the impression that it was written by probably a Russian with possibly a background of intelligence activities."[10]

Trofimoff did not respond, and in late November, 1997, another letter arrived, attempting to escalate the problems described in the first letters. Again, the letter was worded in a style to make it appear that a person of European origin had drafted it. Referring to much apprehension at higher levels, the letter asked Trofimoff to give assistance in rebuilding the files taken by the missing analyst.

The letter forwarded negatives of classified document cover sheets, along with a device for reading the film. Trofimoff was asked to provide any comments/observations he could make to help in restoring the missing files, and was asked if it might be possible that his fingerprints could be on any of the film negatives he had transmitted to the Soviets. Trofimoff was told he was in a unique position to give insights on rebuilding the files to help not only him, but also others who were involved and in danger because of the defection of the analyst. Told to use the Washington, D. C. address given in the previous letter, he was to sign any correspondence with "FRANZ." To insure telephonic identification of parties in case of an emergency, the letter provided a question that would be asked by a caller, and the correct response for Trofimoff when he answered the call. In closing, the letter offered help with finances and documentation he might need (presumably, if he had a need to leave the United States) and cautioned him to destroy the letter, but to make a note of the instructions.

"I was completely baffled by this letter," Trofimoff writes. "I did not want to have anything to do with it, especially because of the enclosed photos of SECRET documents, which are certainly not readily available to the general public, thus hinting at some kind of connection to officialdom . . . (I) destroyed the letter and the enclosed negatives by cutting them into tiny pieces, burning them and flushing the ashes down the toilet."[11]

With no response from Trofimoff, Droujinsky contacted him again on February 4, 1998, in a call that lasted considerably longer than the July 1997 conversation. Trofimoff continued to plead his ignorance of the situation, but the FBI agent displayed his skill in keeping him on the phone, as Trofimoff repeatedly insisted that he knew nothing. "I, I don't know what you want from me . . . I think this is all a big mistake . . . "[12]

Droujinsky told Trofimoff he was instructed to make a follow-up call because of the items sent with the November letter, and asked if he had looked at the film in the package.

"Yeah, I looked at it real quickly . . . And I destroyed it immediately."[13]

Droujinsky pointed out that a missing analyst not only destroyed some records, but also took some items from the files with him. Trofimoff's help was needed in reconstructing the files.

Trofimoff insisted that the items could not have come from him. "The, the these things that I saw, ah, that you showed me, I have never seen those in my life. I cannot remember having ever seen them . . . So now you're putting me on the spot again, in a spot where anything can happen. Someone is going to wind up and start this thing all over again. Now believe me, I'm too old to wind up in jail sometime."[14]

Droujinsky again introduced the matter of financial help. "Oh, by the way, also ah, George, ah, there is some good news, ah, you'll be happy to hear that our records of your financial payments and the payments we made to you have been found. And this is of great importance you understand because, ah, we know that they were not taken away . . . some people, ah, some higher-ups in my organization, they're wondering . . . is there reluctance on your side to assist . . . because you need money, ah, because I was told that if you need money again we can give you financial assistance and we can do it in a very secure manner you know."[15]

Trofimoff continued to refuse assistance and became more concerned.

"Are you, are you trying to ruin my life? . . . how do I know that you're not recording everything we're talking about?"[16]

With Droujinsky's insistence that Trofimoff's assistance was important, and his assurances that mutual trust was necessary, Trofimoff began to become more comfortable and trusting, and made a telling comment: "Igor, I've been in this business for a long, long time and I just want out of it. Honestly, . . . if I could help you I would be happy to help but I can't help you."[17]

Droujinsky continued to press for a meeting, pointing out that Trofimoff was in a good situation since he was cleared in the German Courts and was living in America as a free man. Trofimoff was still worried. "Well I'm not under suspicion now, but if I'm gonna meet with you, I'm sure as hell gonna be under suspicion . . . I won't be (a

Dear friend,

In our last letter we advised of keeping alert to developements. You must be aware now of unfortunate situation of three friends of our former colleagues on October 4 in this city. This is direct in its relation to the problem we discussed in prior contacts. And this is what is known only on the surface. There exists much apprehension at levels above. It is known those unfriendly to us will use these situations for detrimental political and economic results. There exists also fear in the service our higher levels will consent to act preemptively to avoid sanctions or fall to unfriendly pressure to expose past cooperations and not protect our valued friends.

The total priority is now to rebuild the operational measures files of the missing analyst and prevent more exposures. Should we not succeed we will not be capable to control decisions by the higher levels.

Some operational measures of course if uncovered will make for worst repercussions than compared to others. This is what makes this contact of such importance and the decision for this unusual step to be approved.

It has been instructed to ask assistance from you, to most important to determine your security, and to be certain to not miss any friend who should be alerted. From your past professional specialty and most recently your unfortunate experience in Europe, you have unique position to provide insight what cannot be obtained from outside of this.

First-just now discoveries have uncovered shards of microfiche and other materials this analyst attempted to destroy at his departure. These are being reassembled using dates and types of information to compare with what is remaining of past records.

Second-first pages of these informations have been put on film negatives for your review. A 2X magnifier is provided for use. The negatives contain a page or describe this information. To assist to recall all are numbered at bottom with total pages also. All notations and numbers are eliminated for preventing tracing.

Our need is this-
1. During questions used in your situation in Europe was there any indicators this missing analyst was source of information leak that was cause of your problem.

2. What comments and observations about the information on the film negatives can you give to help us rebuild these records.

3. Is there risk to you from tracing of these or any other materials. Could fingerprints or other methods be traced back to you.

After review please promptly send your conclusions. For security reasons your response should be signed "FRANZ". Include listing of the Document number of the page or described information and next to it the comment or observation to the address given before-

                              "ASL International Mailing Service
                               1929 18 Street NW, #1134
                               Washington, DC. 20009

        FORWARD AS DIRECTED"

We believe it is now important to provide to you a sign if we discover an emergency exists. If so you will receive a telephone call on the exact hour. Strictly follow these terms-

Caller- "Hallo. Is this (your first name only). Karl Workman speaking. I was told that I could obtain from you collections from the composer Franz Lehar."

Your Anser- "Obviously I was recommended to you by mistake. Because I sold my collections several years ago."

In any case please be especially alert to any suspicious activities. Meanwhile we are ready to prepare documentation and financial assistance is for your use if necessary. You should contact us at the reliable address given before if any possible problem is noticed. Be certain to sign the name "FRANZ".

Please understand it is very difficult to communicate in this way you have instructed what is needed to be accomplished for our mutual interests.

You are reminded to destroy this letter but make a note of the instructions. Do not use a personal computer to respond. We wish you well and eagerly await your response.

To assist to read film negatives
Press side push buttons to use the lens.
Press another time to expose lightbulb.
Hold film negatives up to indirect light source or window.

A copy of the letter mailed to Trofimoff in late November 1997. (U.S. Justice Dept.)

free man) much longer if this continues."[18]

Clearly, Trofimoff was under pressure, and tiring of the discussion, he wanted to end it. When the agent continued to press for verification that the documents in the November letter were delivered by him, Trofimoff said, "I don't, I don't think your record is right. I really don't and honestly please, please Igor. I got to cut it out now, I have to go. I have an appointment."[19]

"Well, okay George . . .You know, the, Moscow will be very, very disappointed but you know because over the years . . . I was told that you were helped and you were treated very well and now you don't want to reciprocate and . . . help us a little bit."[20]

"Too much time has gone by and I've been hurt pretty badly and I'm very sick right now and, ah, ah just, I just don't want to fight any problems . . . I'm sorry, I'm very sorry, tell them that I'm sorry but I'm just too old and too sick to do anything. Okay?"[21]

"Well I guess I'll have to report that but they'll be very, very disappointed . . . they're very serious about this, there are many people we need to help, you know."[22]

Trofimoff still had not agreed to a meeting, and realizing that he was making no progress, Droujinsky thanked Trofimoff again for talking with him and the conversation ended.

Trofimoff writes about Droujinsky's last words:

> This last statement sort of reminded me of the fact that my brother, Igor, had helped me financially over a period of many years and had just recently promised to help again. Could it be that his main office, the Patriar- chat in Moscow, was actually investigating the possibility of rendering financial help if I could prove to have rendered some 'assistance' in the past? . . . I did not know what to think or believe, but the idea of possible financial assistance took root and did not let go of me any more.[23]

After the February conversation, another letter was sent in August in an effort to escalate the situation and make George more concerned with his safety.

The letter was followed up with another call from Droujinsky on August 26, 1998, and as in previous conversations, Trofimoff refused to offer any assistance. Speaking in Russian, he said, "Guys, how come you won't just leave me alone, huh?"[24]

Droujinsky asked Trofimoff to speak in English, and said he had

```
Dear Friend,

        Please read this intently for this contains information which in
the base is great importance to you.  It is now thought to be more grave
problem because was recently determined that one past officer who met
you in Austria may be a collaborator with the German service.  This officer
"Anatoliy" is possible cause of part of your past problem with German
authorities.  Photograph of Anatoliy is here to assist you.

        Other situations now present in Germany that possibly caused by this
officer.  It is partly mentioned in this article.  You should be alert and
not be misled by their propaganda try to hide the seriousness.

        We would like to stress again you take careful attention if you must
contact your brother.

        For your protection this exchange must take place should contact occur
by someone different than our colleague from our most recent conversations.----

        Us:  Didn't we meet while sking in Zurich.
        Your Answer:  No, I always do sking in Austria.

        Please destroy this after your review.




                                        Best Regards,

                                        Your Friends
```

A copy of the note sent to Trofimoff on 6 August 1998. (U.S. Justice Dept.)

been directed to speak with him regarding the last letter. He asked Trofimoff if he had received it, and asked about a picture that had been sent with it.

"Yes, I have . . . but I destroyed it (the letter) five minutes later . . . I looked at it (the picture) very, very thoroughly. But you must understand my position. Jesus, I'm retired. I'm living here. I got my last few years. I don't want to get involved. I don't want to wind up in jail. Can you understand that?"[25]

"Of course, of course. And that's what we're trying to help you prevent from happening."[26]

"I'm, I'm with you, you know?" Trofimoff said. And, in Russian: "I, I . . . for me, it's my motherland, yes?"[27]

Droujinsky again asked Trofimoff to speak in English, and he responded, "A few words in Russian are always good . . . Everybody knows that I'm fluent Russian, that I was born in a Russian family, that I went to a Russian school. I am proud of it."[28]

As the conversation continued, Trofimoff's responses and his tone of voice indicated that he was becoming more comfortable with his responses and less adamant in his denials.

Referring to the young girl, Marion, that Trofimoff had married, Droujinsky asked if it was possible that she knew anything that could "expose us," and when Trofimoff assured him that she knew nothing, Droujinsky asked if she was aware of any payments made to Trofimoff.

"No, she was only aware of the fact that I borrowed money from Igor whenever I needed it."[29]

Droujinsky then addressed Trofimoff's relationship with his current wife, Jutta, asking him if she knew anything about their relationship.

"Oh, no, no, she knows a little about it, of course . . . But, only on the periphery . . . Well, believe me, I can trust her with my life . . . I assure you, you don't have anything to worry about on this end."[30]

Trofimoff's comments were beginning to indicate his acknowledgment of his involvement with the activities Droujinsky was describing, but he was still concerned and leery of the overall situation. In Russian, he said, "Igor, I'm afraid. I'm afraid . . . How can I not be afraid?"[31]

Droujinsky returned to English. "George, as I explained to you before, and I have to reiterate now, is, you know, if there were any chance that there'd be danger for you . . . we, we would have an idea about it, and then we would not be in contact with you. So, believe us. We want to protect you very much and, as we want to protect ourselves. You understand that?"[32]

Droujinsky then focused his attention to finances, asking Trofimoff if he had put any money into a bank in Germany or elsewhere, or if he had kept all the money and spent it.

"I have no money in any bank anywhere . . . Igor, believe me, I have no money whatsoever . . . All that money? That was all spent. Every bit of it . . . I don't have a single extra dime. I live off my retirement pay, you know, my pension. And that's all I have. I don't have a single dime to my name."[33]

Droujinsky asked if Igor told Trofimoff about the "concealment device" or screwdriver found in his house, and if he (Trofimoff) had ever kept anything like that.

"Yes, he did . . . we never used it . . . Who am I? Am I stupid?"[24]

The agent again mentioned a picture Trofimoff had been asked to identify, that of Anatoliy.

"Now, uh, I have one thing also that my superiors have a concern about. We believe that Anatoliy is the cause of this problem. You know, that you, the problem you had in Germany . . . Because he's a very angry person, uh, George, you know? Uh, between you and me, he did not feel that his work was appreciated, you know?"[35]

Trofimoff responded, "The only thing is, . . . I have never seen this man in my life. He might've, he might've known about my relationship with Igor . . . and may have drawn conclusions out of that. But I've never seen him, and I'll swear to this until I die."[36]

Droujinsky then asked Trofimoff if he remembered a meeting that took place in the Salzburg area, and if the picture sent to Trofimoff was the person he met with.

While Trofimoff denied that he had met with the person pictured, he began to be more candid and offered some identifications. When asked if he remembered whom he met, he said, "God, I don't remember now anymore . . . the first one was Nikolay. I remember him."[37]

Droujinsky again asked Trofimoff if he was in need of funds.

"Igorek," (Trofimoff used the familiar form of Igor), "there's no way, you know, uh, it's a silly question. Everybody here in America can always use money . . . I am, I am very deep in debt. I am living in a fairly nice house, and I have a nice car, and that's all. And I have a pension, and I have to live with this pension. So any additional money, what the hell, where am I going to get it from, you know? . . . How can I prove where I got it from? . . . I don't want to get involved, and the main thing is I can't help you . . . if I could help, if I could do something for you . . . maybe I could because, after all, we are now allies, right?"[38]

Then, in Russian, he said, "It's my Motherland. Understand that. No matter what it's like, it is my Motherland. Even though I've never been there, it's my Motherland."[39]

Droujinsky again asked Trofimoff if he would agree to meet with him.

"Well, Igor . . . We'll have, we'll have to make some kind of arrangement . . . what I would like, if, if anything like that, I'd much rather have you just come here, right here . . . I mean right here in my house . . . it's much better than anywhere else."[40]

Droujinsky responded that he had been in Florida twice before, and was willing to meet with Trofimoff at his home, or wherever he wanted.

Trofimoff was still cautiously afraid, "Igor, I don't trust these things. You have to be careful. You are being followed, you know, too. Don't forget that . . . I'd hate like hell to wind up in jail for the rest of my life."[41]

"And, uh, like I said, if my superiors decide that I should have a meeting with you," Droujinsky said, "then I'll, of course, notify you ahead of time, and then we'll make arrangements, and I'll come to see you."[42]

The conversation ended with Trofimoff asking Droujinsky to make sure that his people understood that they didn't have to worry about him in any way. Droujinsky promised him in turn that he would assure "his people" that Trofimoff would do "everything for the motherland."

Trofimoff's notes were written long after his arrest in June 2000 and do not necessarily reflect what his thoughts were during the time he was receiving the letters and telephone calls from Agent Droujinsky. What they do reveal are the thoughts that began the development of the defense he used during his trial. He thought perhaps there was some connection between the letters and telephone calls and his brother's statement that he would try to get funds from the Moscow Patriarchat to relieve his financial problems.

"I phoned my brother in Munich," he writes, "and cautiously asked him about it (the 'connection' referred to above) by referring to my second mortgage. He (Igor) confirmed the fact that he had asked for permission to disburse such a loan, but that it would take some time to process because of 'Red Tape.' He explained to me that the Patriarchat had created a special fund for Russian refugees abroad when they needed financial help to establish themselves in their new homes, and that he had used this fund on many occasions in the past, without having to ask for permission. This sum of $42,000, however, was too large and needed approval from the main office.

"It seemed to me that I was beginning to understand all of these contacts with my friend Galkin (Droujinsky) who appeared to me as a possible representative of the Church with the Cultural Attaché in the Washington Embassy. I was still wondering about the connection with intelligence activities, but when you need financial help as badly as I needed it at that time, you disregard all the threatening signs, and see only the part, which you want to see!! It was at this time that I began to consider a possible person-to-person meeting . . . my conversation with Galkin had become more friendly and cooperative. As I had become convinced that he was probably doing the investigation for the Patriarchat, I decided to find out more about it, and try to appear to want to help . . . Galkin kept insisting on a personal contact with me, and I finally agreed, although, as I told him, I would have preferred to have it at my house. We agreed in principle, but no date was set."[43]

Trofimoff's notes elaborate on the defense he was beginning to develop for his trial: "I decided to cooperate and 'play the game.' I decided to assure him and convince him that I did love 'my Motherland' and that I really did something for 'my country.' "[44]

With the conclusion of this conversation, thirteen months after Salazar delivered the first letter to Trofimoff, Droujinsky had, with letters, telephone calls and infinite patience, converted Trofimoff from a doubting, fearful and uncooperative individual who "knew nothing" about the activities the agent described, to a friendly and unsuspecting subject freely admitting his past involvement with the Soviets, and one who was perfectly willing to meet with the agent at a yet-to-be-determined time and place.

The web had been woven, and the trap would soon be set.

Droujinsky made no contact with Trofimoff until February 18, 1999, when he called.

"George, I have some very good news, very important news, also . . . my superiors have approved my travel to meet with you soon, and the final arrangements are being made right now, and I'm calling to make the date. Can you meet me on Wednesday next

The hotel in Melbourne, Florida where Trofimoff met with undercover FBI agents in February of 1999. (Author's collection)

week, February twenty-fourth?"[45]

Trofimoff was ready to meet, and asked what time the meeting would be held. He was still leery, however, asking why Droujinsky still wanted to meet.

"Well, George, I'll explain to you everything and hopefully this will be the last time that we get in contact, but we need to resolve some things . . . So that's why we need to meet and resolve it . . . do you know the Comfort Inn on Wickham Road?"[46]

When Trofimoff acknowledged that he was familiar with the Comfort Inn, Droujinsky gave details for the meeting:

> . . . go there on Wednesday, on the twenty-fourth at 10 a. m., go to the lobby . . . as you enter, walk to the left, and across from the elevators, there are a few telephones on the wall . . . I will begin calling you there at 10 a. m. on that date, and when we get connected, you say 'hello' and I will say 'Is this George?' and you say 'yes' and then I'll identify myself. And then I'll tell you exactly where to meet me . . . .[47]

Trofimoff was still wary and suspicious. "Igor, Igor, I don't like that arrangement. Listen. I don't want to go into that Inn. I don't want to answer any phones out there. I would much rather meet you and then take you home, and bring you here."[48]

Droujinsky finally convinced Trofimoff that for security reasons it was better to meet in a public place. Trofimoff had to report to his job at 11:00 a. m. for bagging groceries, and since it was estimated that the meeting would take some two hours, they agreed to meet at eight o'clock in the morning.

Agent Droujinsky, a master of "False Flag" operations, had successfully convinced the cautious and suspicious Trofimoff that a meeting with "Igor" was a safe thing for him to do.

After the trial, Assistant U. S. Attorney Terry Furr said, "Droujinsky's work was masterful. This guy is the finest undercover agent I've ever seen. There's no one even close to him . . . He's an artist like Beethoven."[49]

Trofimoff arrived at the hotel at 8:00 a. m. on the morning of February 24. Droujinsky met him in the lobby and escorted him to his room, which had been carefully bugged. To capture anything significant that might be said on the way to his room, the agent was wearing a "wire."

From the beginning, Trofimoff was wary and suspicious. In the lobby, before entering the elevator, he asked, "Are you alone? . . . Completely alone?"[50]

In the hotel room, regardless of assurances that they were alone, Trofimoff was still worried, as he asked repeatedly if Droujinsky was "bugged."

Droujinsky assured Trofimoff that he did not have to worry about anything, as he had rented the room with no connection to "his" country.

Satisfied with Droujinsky's assurances, Trofimoff became comfortable and at ease. Casually dressed and in good humor, he told of his young life in Berlin and his relationship with his foster brother, at first speaking almost entirely in Russian. During the entire meeting he was animated and smiling, continuously gesturing with his arms and hands. Asked about his current job, Trofimoff responded in English, explaining that he was packing groceries as a part-time job because he needed extra income.

The conversation turned to Trofimoff's arrest by German authorities, and Trofimoff said, "They arrested me and Igor at the same time, at six o'clock in the morning. Him in Munich, and me in Nuremberg . . . ten people just walked right in, showed me their papers and . . . they took the house, they took it apart. I had nothing!"[51]

Trofimoff confirmed he had stopped working for the KGB six years prior to his arrest . . . "I'm glad we stopped, because, uh, your headquarters didn't want to take a chance . . ."[52]

On the subject of cameras, Trofimoff related how at first he used a Minox purchased at the KGB's request, but later returned it to his foster brother because it was limited to 16 pictures per roll. Using that camera, he would need 30 to 40 rolls at a time, and buying that much film at one time was too dangerous. He was given a larger double-frame camera, which allowed him to photograph as many as 72 documents on a single roll of regular film.

Trofimoff told how, after his arrest by the German officials, he was relieved of all duties, his security clearance was suspended, and his early retirement bonus, which he said was to have been about $25,000, was canceled. He decided not to fight the loss of his bonus, as he feared the loss of his retirement pension if he did so. His bags were packed, he had orders to return to the United States, he believed that his retirement pension was safe, and legal action to preserve the bonus would take time.

"Everything would be suspended," he said, "so I decided I'm not going to, because I could not win. There's one thing that was against me: that I had contact with a suspected agent . . . which was Igor . . . And the moment you have contact with a foreign agent, regardless of what country, you are immediately suspended from intelligence duties."[53]

Trofimoff then spent several minutes describing his relationship with his foster brother, Igor, before the discussion returned to his decision to not fight the loss of his bonus.

". . . I never reported that I saw him (Igor) . . . I knew if I report it and they start checking it, I lose my job, right there and then, so I never reported it. They could have gotten me on that."[54]

While he was now speaking freely, Trofimoff was still cautious and asked Droujinsky to confirm, again, that the meeting was not being recorded.

Apparently satisfied with Droujinsky's denial of any recording, Trofimoff resumed his cooperative attitude and, in response to the agent's questions, he began to recall memories of the agent Anatoliy. Droujinsky produced a map of Austria, asking Trofimoff to pinpoint the location of his contact with that agent.

"I had one contact, one single contact in Austria . . . that was my last contact. That was a very big guy . . . Maybe he was Anatoliy."[55]

Trofimoff was still leery and suspicious, as, in Russian, he again asked Droujinsky to give his word that he was not working for the Americans. When the agent again strongly denied that any taping was taking place, Trofimoff continued with his concerns, still speaking in Russian.

"Yes I know. You tell me that you came specially from the Embassy. But if you are filming all of this and then give it to the Americans . . . then you already have everything in my own words."[56]

After studying the map for some time, Trofimoff selected the village of St. Johann, Austria, as the place he met with Anatoliy, where, he said, there were two churches across the street from each other. He then described the recognition "parole," the question and answer by which agents identify each other.

". . . the question was, is this such-and-such church, and I said no, it's not this one, this one is across the street. This is how he knew who I was, so . . . first we meet, then, you know, they check and all that. And then a second man came up, and he took my package and he left."[57]

When asked if his package contained documents or films, he said that he never had documents, but that he always gave films.

Droujinsky then asked why this man wanted to meet with him (Trofimoff).

"Well, to see me, to tell me how good everything was, and he gave me some money, to be honest about it, and uh . . . that was it! . . . That was the last time."[58]

Droujinsky questioned Trofimoff regarding what Marion, his fourth wife, and Jutta, his current wife, knew about his activities.

Regarding Jutta, Trofimoff told the agent that she knew he was getting money from his foster brother, but that she knew nothing else.

"So she didn't know about your operational work?"[59]

Trofimoff's response again revealed that he was not hiding his involvement with the Russians:

"No, no. Not at all . . . after I was arrested she started thinking about it, and she says 'where there's smoke there's fire!' But she knows absolutely nothing about it and she had absolutely nothing to do with it. And the only thing she knows is that I met Igor on several occasions, and uh, that uh, he gave me money."[60]

When Trofimoff said that the previous wife, Marion, knew nothing, Droujinsky expressed his satisfaction that, for the two wives (Jutta and Marion); there was nothing to worry about.

Regarding the conflict between what he and his foster brother told the German agents about money he received from Susemihl, Trofimoff said:

> Now, I think that this is the only place where we possibly made a mistake, but I think I know why that happened, but I, because I think Igor was worried about having so much money. Because he was in Germany and he had to pay German taxes. And if he had too much money, the Germans would get him on tax evasion. And I think this is why he claimed that he only gave me two-three thousand marks, and I said he gave me five or ten thousand marks, you know, and this is the only discrepancy we had . . . I'm sure that's the reason.
>
> The only people that got me in trouble were my children because when they were interrogated (by the German agents) they claimed that I was spending money right and left and that I had girl friends and all this, which in a way wasn't true at all. Because, what

they forgot is that most of the money that I got was for
them . . . they were trying to get even with me because
I didn't remarry their mother.

And what they forgot is . . . Nicole went to college
in New York, Hofstra University, which is a very
good, private university . . . It's in Long Island. It was
$12,000 a year. $6,000 per semester, plus I gave her a
hundred dollars . . .

I was paying for it, this is what I needed the money
for. It wasn't for me. I didn't need any money . . . I did-
n't gamble, I didn't go to whorehouses. I did have girlfriends, but never lived with one! The girlfriends you
know, I had one here and uh, but these were girls, all
working girls, all normal secretaries and whatnot.

. . . like I said I didn't throw money around . . . Sure
I'd go to a good restaurant once in a while, but I mean,
and like I said, I did make good money, but what was
wrong with that?

The agent continued to explore how Trofimoff spent his money,
and Trofimoff related what he told the German agents after his arrest:

. . . I said, so okay, so, I have a car, I had, uh I love to
have a sports car, I always had a Corvette. Corvette is
an expensive car. But, I said, look at me, I buy the
Corvette like every other American, I pay one-fourth
down and then I make monthly payments for the next
three years. And if you check my cars and my records,
I said, you can check, yes, I did drive a Corvette, but I
paid for it. Monthly payments, like anybody else, like
every German who buys a Mercedes or a BMW. So, I
have no money in the bank. I have nothing but debt,
like I have today. My whole life was nothing but
debts.[62]

Cameras and photographic equipment were the next topics.
Trofimoff related how German officials took three cameras when he
was arrested and later returned all of them. One, an Olympic double-
frame he received from his KGB contact, was the one he used to photograph two pages at once. When photographing documents with this
camera, he used a tripod.

" . . . But they never found the tripod," he said. "And it was standing right there. It wasn't standing, it was collapsed. It was laying in

the corner in one of the shelves . . . Thank God for that. They didn't take that one. And I destroyed that."[63]

Droujinsky asked him why he said "Thank God for that."

"Because . . . I had a, a gadget on it, that you could turn the camera around, upside down . . . which you normally can't do on a tripod . . . And I, I threw that away, far away, you know, in another country."[64]

Droujinsky then asked about two gooseneck lamps that were in his basement. Trofimoff replied that he told the German agents that he needed the lamps for his detailed work in making tiny model ships. When Droujinsky asked him if he used them for copying documents, he readily replied, "Yes."

Time was running out for this session, and when the discussion turned to scheduling the next meeting, Trofimoff again revealed his concerns and suspicions.

"Anyway, I am very suspicious, I mean, I have to be very careful." Then, speaking in Russian, he continued: "Igor, believe me, all this time I'm afraid. I'm still afraid . . . When I spent that night in that German prison, I thought, my God, what have I done with my life? For almost 50 years I served . . . first in the Army, then in the Department of the Army, and then I end my life sitting in a prison somewhere for something I did, on the whole, for my children. I did not get anything out of it. And now, if something happens now, everything, everything will be, pardon the expression, f____d up."[65]

Trofimoff was worried about the film he used, and the documents he had photographed. "I was worried about the rolls. My fingerprints were on them . . . .The Germans told me . . . that there was a whole library. It's true. When you come right down to it, I must have taken . . . photographed, I don't know, 50 books, 60 books, 70 books, maybe more. So there was a, probably a whole lot."[66]

Droujinsky produced photographs of KGB officers for Trofimoff to identify. He remembered one, Volodya, whom he met once, then a second time, when he delivered rolls of film.

> . . . like I said, that's the only time I gave him the rolls, there were usually 10, 12, 15. Packaged well, uh, prepared. And that was maybe once a year, maybe . . . normally I gave the rolls to Igor . . . and he took them directly to Moscow . . . I didn't request special payments. Never. I just told Igor that, 'Igor, I got so many debts, could you try and get me a little more money?[67]

Responding to Droujinsky's question, Trofimoff confirmed that his money came only through Igor.

The agent produced more pictures of KGB officers, asking Trofimoff to identify them and point out on a map where he had met with them. Some identifications had been made when Trofimoff announced that he had to leave and report for work. When Droujinsky asked if Trofimoff could meet again on the next day. Trofimoff replied that he could not, but that he could meet later that same afternoon at five o'clock.

That evening, after Trofimoff digressed in Russian for several minutes talking about meetings with KGB officers in Austria, Droujinsky had more photographs for him to identify. This process continued for some time, with Trofimoff recognizing a few of the pictures. One he had met at "the very first original get-together . . . 'cause that's when Igor told me they would like to meet me . . . "[68]

"So Igor's the one who sort of started you," said Droujinsky.[69]

"He was the one that was doing the whole thing. . . My meetings were perfectly open. . . The ones in Austria, that was a different story . . . Now we took special precautions on those. I was watching, you know, my rear view mirror."[70]

Droujinsky noted that "dry cleaning yourself" (a procedure whereby an agent going to a meeting insures that he is not being observed or followed) was correct procedure. Trofimoff recalled occasions when he delivered packages of sealed film containers and later received money taped in envelopes. He recalled the last meeting he ever had, when he met a senior, older officer and handed over a package of sealed film containers, receiving an envelope with money.

After viewing several other pictures. Trofimoff tentatively recognized some of them. "But they still look (like) passport pictures . . . You know, like I show you a picture of me, and you look at it and say maybe it's him and maybe it's not him."[71]

When asked if his last meeting was in 1987, Trofimoff said that he didn't know whether it was in 1987 or 1988, but he believed that it was in 1988, because that was when he met his wife (Jutta).

Droujinsky then asked when Trofimoff started working for the Soviets. His reply described how he started his espionage career, providing information to the Soviets through his foster brother, Igor, the Russian Orthodox priest.

> . . . it must have been '70. But it was very informal . . .
> There were no photographs, there was just talking . . .

He would ask me something and I would tell him
something . . . verbal information . . . he had a few
questions about current events . . . first, it was just a
conversation between the two of us . . .[72]

When asked whom he was giving the information
to, he replied to Igor . . . He was traveling between the
Soviet Union and Germany . . . and he was an
Australian citizen . . . he would ask my opinion on this
and that . . . then, he would maybe ask me, well, what
does your unit think about it . . . Or what does the
American government think about it?[73]

When Droujinsky asked Trofimoff if Igor's questions made him
suspicious, his answer described the beginning of a classic KGB
recruitment:

No, not in the beginning . . . I said, I needed money.
And I told him my wife bought some furniture and I
can't pay for it, I don't know how to get the money.
And he says, I tell you what, I'll loan it to you . . . So
he gave me, I think 5,000 marks and then, it wasn't
enough, because I needed more, and about three or
four weeks later I said to him, 'You gotta help me one
more time, and I'll give it back to you when I have a
chance.' . . . And that was the end of it. Then he talked
to me a couple times. Always like this. And then he
says, 'Well, you know, I'll tell you what. You don't
owe me any money . . . And if you need some more, I
can get you some more . . . don't worry about it. You're
going to have to have a few things, this and that.' And
this is how it started.[74]

Trofimoff displayed his true nature as he continued, speaking in
Russian. "And actually, I tell you. In my soul I'm Russian, I'm not an
American . . . I was never an American, it's just . . . help for the
Motherland . . . I said many times that I was doing it for the
Motherland, not for the Bolsheviks, not for, not for the Communists." [75]
Trofimoff began to ramble in Russian, repeating details about his fos-
ter brother, his early life, and his family history.

Droujinsky wanted to get back on track with subjects he wanted to
discuss. When he asked if they could come back to these points later,
Trofimoff replied, "Well, it's so that you know me a little better . . .
who I am . . . and why I was doing all this."[76]

Trofimoff's comments provide an insight into his thinking and rationalization for his actions. In his confused, convoluted logic and sociopathic thinking, he concluded that since he had no access to, and thus could not provide any information on, American forces, it was harmless to the United States if he gave the KGB only that information concerning what U. S. forces knew about the Soviets and their allies. He did not consider the effect on U. S. and NATO forces if hostilities commenced and the Soviets knew everything that their enemies knew about their own forces.

"Of course, the money helped," Trofimoff said in Russian. "I told them at the time, that foremost I am doing it for the Motherland. . . . And secondly, I told them as far as the Americans are concerned, don't ask me. Because in the first place I know little, almost nothing, and in the second place I don't want that, I don't want to be a traitor . . . I considered that it would be good if you knew what we know about you. Of course, some may say that is also treason. In my opinion I was never a traitor, because I never gave anything American to anybody."[77]

Droujinsky, speaking in Russian, again asked Trofimoff to speak in English.

Trofimoff returned to English. "I didn't know any American positions, any American organizations, I didn't know any of that. I didn't know any American operational plans . . . But I had a questionnaire . . . what they wanted to know about your forces."[78]

Trofimoff told Droujinsky that his work for the KGB ceased in 1987 when his brother told him to stop his photography, and that for the time being, they didn't want anything. However, George continued his photography of classified documents, accumulating some 25 rolls of exposed and repackaged film. Each roll, Trofimoff said, contained pictures of 72 pages.

Trofimoff told how he packaged the exposed film, always in the original package, pasted closed so that it looked like it had never been opened.

Even though he had been told to stop his activity, Trofimoff said that he delivered the 25 rolls to Igor, and later asked him how the Soviets liked the package.

"Then, maybe three months later, or four months later he told me, 'This was excellent, it was very, very good.' And that was it . . . from then on, nothing . . . he told me to stop . . . he told me to destroy the camera . . . so I smashed it with a hammer . . . and I threw it in the garbage, far away."[79]

When Droujinsky asked Trofimoff if Igor had told him why he wanted his activities stopped, Trofimoff replied that Igor said they (Soviets) were worried about possible contacts. They wanted nothing more and wanted a complete stop to his activities.

After producing several more pictures of agents for Trofimoff to review, Droujinsky questioned him regarding additional meetings that had been held and then shifted the discussion to payments Trofimoff received from the Soviets.

Trofimoff said his payments were based on a standard amount of $7,000 per month, paid in used Deutsche Marks. He often asked for more, when financial difficulties arose. One such request arose from his need for a down payment on his house.

"They helped me, they helped me, they gave me the money to pay the down payment for the house . . . about 90,000 marks . . . about 40,000 dollars . . . Just one lump sum."[80]

Trofimoff said that the deal offered by the bank was a very good one, and he asked Igor for help. "So he went to his contact in Moscow and he told him this. And they gave him 90,000 marks."[81]

As the value of the dollar sank vs. the soaring German mark, Trofimoff needed more assistance in making payments on the house.

" . . . the dollar went down, and again it went down, and they helped me once, and they helped me twice, and they helped me three times. Then I couldn't hold it anymore. And I told them I'm selling the house. And I sold the house at a loss. I didn't make any. I didn't get any of my money back, it was all gone . . . I had no money in the bank. I had no house. I had nothing but debts."[82]

When Droujinsky told Trofimoff that some of the information he had provided went directly to Ustinov, the Minister of Defense, Trofimoff replied that his brother, Igor, had given him that news.

"Yes, I got a medal, you know . . . Red, red banner. I don't know what number it was."[83]

Droujinsky produced some classified documents. "So, I'm going to show you some copies of documents. Now we don't know if they, if you, uh, gave them or not, uh, we don't know . . ."[84]

"Now you're putting the rope around my neck."[85]

As more documents were displayed, Trofimoff confirmed they were documents the JIC would have had on file, but he never specifically acknowledged that any one document came from his office.

". . . but if you ask me now, have I seen this? Maybe," he said, "if I

The Order of the Red Banner medal that Trofimoff claimed to have been awarded. (U.S. Justice Dept.)

had it, then you got it . . . But it's not necessary that it came from me. You might have also gotten it from someone else, because this thing was given to everybody."[86]

Later, referring to the documents he had displayed, Droujinsky asked Trofimoff to identify which of these documents could have come from his JIC.

Trofimoff could not contain himself as his ego and arrogance took control. "Let's put it this way: If I had 'em, I gave 'em all. But I want you to know one thing—that I had so many of these. It was hundreds!

It was not one, or two, or three. I only had one safe to save documents in. And it had so much stuff in it."[87]

Droujinsky then asked Trofimoff about his procedures for destroying documents.

"Before I destroyed it, I would put it on the side . . . I took it home with me. Then next morning I brought it, and I said, 'Okay, now let's go burn it.' That way there wasn't even a trace that I had it."[88]

Droujinsky displayed cover sheets from many SECRET order of battle documents on Russian and Warsaw Pact Forces and Russian Chemical and Biological Warfare information, asking Trofimoff if he was sure that they were documents he had photographed.

"At that time it was a gold mine!" Trofimoff answered. "All of them . . . Because, like I said, there were hundreds . . . And there were thousands of pages . . . I gave them all. There wasn't a document that I, that I had you didn't get."[89]

Even with his treachery against the United States, Trofimoff did reveal some compassion for others. When Igor questioned him at length in an attempt to discover if Trofimoff had passed to the KGB names of important sources that had been interviewed at the JIC, he replied, ". . . I didn't know the names . . . besides, I'll be honest with you, Igor. I didn't . . . maybe this is a weakness, but I did not want to get individuals into trouble . . . I thought to myself, well, these guys, they left the Soviet Union because they hated it, they didn't like it, they didn't want it, okay. Why? It's not my reason to ask, but I don't want them to get into trouble. So, I thought that it wouldn't be fair if I gave them away to you. But most of all, that was one consideration, and the second consideration was definitely security. I was worried about showing (their names). Because then they could say, okay, this guy came over, he was interrogated by Nuremberg JIC . . ."[90]

Igor turned to photography. Trofimoff explained that some books had 400 to 600 pages in loose-leaf binders, relatively easy to copy. Others were stapled and more difficult. When Droujinsky asked if he photographed everything, Trofimoff described his photography methods:

"They were usually between 400 and 600 pages. They were stapled. I'd pull the staples out. Then I had to be careful. I had to change films. I had to listen whether my wife would come home."[91] He explained the care he exercised with stapled books, removing the staples carefully and replacing them in exactly the same holes. (His wife Alexa was not living with him regularly, and he worked in the basement when she was absent, using the gooseneck lamps and the double-frame camera.)

Droujinsky asked Trofimoff if he had any trouble removing the books from the office and taking them back.

"I was scared every time."[92]

Trofimoff confirmed that he carried a briefcase every day, to work and back.

"I used to bring my lunch in my briefcase. And I'd take home the mail . . . they didn't have authority to stop me . . ."[93]

The discussion returned to photography.

Trofimoff had prepared a piece of white board with marks so he could line up the page to be photographed, using his tripod to hold the camera.

"That's great," Droujinsky said. "And the lighting came from those two lamps? . . . You did not use a flash on them?"[94]

Trofimoff replied that it would have been impossible to use a flash, and that with two 100-watt light bulbs, a flash was not necessary.

The JIC prepared reports of interviews, called Information Intelligence Reports (IIRs), and Trofimoff recalls in his notes that he was careful with them. "I told him (Droujinsky) about the contents and classification of such reports and further explained that I had never furnished such reports because they identified my JIC as the originator."[95]

"I couldn't . . . afford to take those . . . because if you get those, you would know where they came from . . . I did give them some. I had one or two important sources, and they gave me some pretty good information, and what I did, I neutralized the report with a copying machine . . . I just made a copy of the original. Then I took it to my desk and when nobody was there, I cut it out . . . I'd cut off half the page, and just leave the information on there. Not where it came from, no nothing, just the information itself."[96]

Trofimoff steered the conversation to his financial problems. He told the agent that he was worried about keeping his house, and that if he died a "normal" death, he didn't know how his wife would manage. "I have life insurance, okay? I have accident insurance. If I die in an accident, she gets $300,000, no problem. If I die a normal death, only $60,000 . . . If I could get rid of my second mortgage . . .

"So, I've paid now four years on my second mortgage, and out of those four years I've paid, per month, almost $1,000 . . . that's $48,000. And do you know how far my loan went down? $600 . . . This is what

(a) mortgage does, you know? . . . and if I could pay off the $32,000 now, . . . I wouldn't pay any more interest. You can pay it off any time . . . if you have the money."[97]

Droujinsky told Trofimoff that he would report the situation to his superiors to see if any help could be arranged.

"Well, then, please don't misunderstand me. I'm not asking for anything," Trofimoff said. "I just want you to know, I want you to know that this is what it is. And this is why I'm working now."[98]

Droujinsky then asked Trofimoff if he would like to obtain some false documentation for him and his wife in case "something" happened.

"Igor, what can happen to me? What would I do in Russia?" Trofimoff reverted to Russian. "I'm 72, 73 years old. What . . . what would I do there? What, divorce my wife? That's impossible. I love her too much." Then, back to English, "That's the first one that has really been good to me . . . She's not going to go, Igor, no, thank you . . . I would like in the future, maybe sometimes, to go there to visit St. Petersburg . . ."[99]

"Okay, anyway, we're just offering it to you."

"Yeah, all in the future."

Droujinsky said. "Okay, now, I want to give you something . . . a post office box address and number. Uh, this is just, just in case something comes up. Let's say you notice somebody's watching you, or whatever, you know, and, and you want to notify us. So, this is a clean box, you know, nothing to do with the Embassy or Russia or anything like that, you know. It's an American name. It's a post office box. So you can write to us, uh . . . This is a phone number . . . I have a recording machine you know. So, if you need to talk to us, you can call me, and it's a clean number. No, no connection to the Embassy . . . And so, if you send us a letter, and you can send it in, you know, just innocuous, how do you say? Innocuous? . . and then sign it 'Franz.' "[100]

Droujinsky probed to discover if Trofimoff had worked with others and asked him if he had any assistants, accomplices, or partners.

"Igor, I'm not an idiot!" (in Russian). Then, he returned to English. "The moment you have a partner, that's two of you. You cannot vouch for him."[101]

Trofimoff asked Droujinsky to visit him at his home, but the agent politely declined, for security reasons.

"Who in hell is going to see you?" asked Trofimoff. "The gatekeeper? Nobody stops me . . . My neighbor's on a cruise . . . There's no one to see us . . . and my wife is in Germany."[102]

Trofimoff still wanted to make the point that he needed financial help. "Tell those guys that they could help me . . . I don't know how, but, uh, maybe they can find some way."[103]

Droujinsky promised that he would take Trofimoff's request to his superiors, and that perhaps something could be arranged.

During the rest of the meeting they discussed how they could communicate later, with Trofimoff assuring Droujinsky he was willing to talk more if additional information was needed. He reverted to Russian in saying good-bye. "Once more, all the best. Don't forget me."[104]

Droujinsky bade his goodbye, also speaking in Russian.

In each of these two three-hour sessions, the skill of Droujinsky, posing as Igor Galkin, manifested itself in converting Trofimoff from a fearful, nontrusting individual who would not discuss his past or admit any involvement in espionage activities to a willing and verbose individual disclosing details of his espionage activities over almost 25 years. The web had been woven with consummate skill, and now, with Trofimoff indicating his need for, and interest in, obtaining financial support from the Soviets, Droujinsky's next task was to offer an incentive sufficient to draw the unsuspecting Trofimoff into a baited trap.

Trofimoff sent the author (through Jutta) many pages of hand-written notes containing his comments on the videotaped meetings with Droujinsky. Clearly, as he wrote these notes, he had access to the transcripts of the videotapes, as his comments are annotated with reference to numbered pages in the transcripts. His comments repeat over and over that everything he said during the meetings with Droujinsky comprises one completely fabricated story, and that he gave this false information to the FBI agent (whom he says he thought was a representative of the Russian Orthodox Church) in order to receive cash payments to help resolve his financial problems. His defense during his trial was based solely on this premise—that all he said on the tapes was a lie.

After the meetings, Droujinsky made no effort to contact Trofimoff. During the trial the prosecution noted that prior to the Melbourne meetings, Droujinsky initiated all contacts, but after the meetings, Trofimoff initiated each contact. He had been swept into Droujinsky's web.

On August 12, 1999, an envelope arrived at the Alexandria,

Virginia address given to Trofimoff by Droujinsky. Inside was a single sheet of paper, hand-printed, with a cryptic message:

"Need help! Please call! Franz."

Trofimoff was rising to the bait offered by Droujinsky.

Trofimoff, in his notes, says, "After my brother Igor died in Munich, I used the 'emergency address' in Alexandria and sent a letter with the word 'HELP.' I did not know what else to do, as my brother had previously informed me that he had requested permission from his Patriarchat to give me money for the second mortgage . . . I thought that Galkin could look into it . . . I still basically believed that he was connected with the Patriarchat."[105]

Droujinsky called on August 13, and Trofimoff told him that, with Jutta away, he could talk freely. He said that his foster brother, the priest, had died. "He, he was going to help me a little bit, you know, financially . . . He promised to help me, and then, uh, he died, and now I'm sitting here without the help I was hoping to get . . . You know, I called him on his birthday . . . And he said, okay, George, I didn't know uh how bad off you were . . . I'm gonna try and help you. And then a week later he died."[106]

Droujinsky told Trofimoff he had submitted a report about Trofimoff's financial needs, but had not received an answer. He asked Trofimoff how he could explain having extra money.

Trofimoff replied that there was no problem, as his brother just died and he could say that he got the money from him (Igor) before he died.

Droujinsky then asked Trofimoff how he could explain the money to his wife.

Again, Trofimoff was sure that there was no problem, as Jutta knew that he had asked Igor for help.

Droujinsky wanted to know how much money Igor had promised to give him, and Trofimoff replied simply that he had asked his foster brother for thirty thousand dollars.

Droujinsky then ended the conversation. "I'll relay this to my superiors and I think they're also planning on something for you . . . And I'll call you and let you know the results."[107]

On August 31, Trofimoff called to leave another message, saying that he had an important matter to discuss. Droujinsky returned the call on September 9 and asked Trofimoff what he needed.

"It's just that uh, I'm going to lose my house, if I don't get a little help . . . I need the money to make the payments, the second mortgage

A copy of Trofimoff's hand written note to Droujinsky asking for help.
(U.S. Justice Dept.)

payments . . . That's all I need. It's just to get rid of that second mortgage."[108]

When asked the size of the second mortgage, Trofimoff told
Droujinsky that while the total amount was $43,000, if he could get
some of that amount he possibly could help himself for the remainder.

Droujinsky explained that delays had occurred in getting approval
for the money, but assured Trofimoff that he expected good news very
soon.

The second mortgage is "not a million dollars," Trofimoff said.
"But to me, it's a catastrophe. Because, if I lose this house, I lose everything. We have no money at all. I have no money."[109]

Droujinsky said that he was sure help would be forthcoming, but
that the world political situation was causing delays and imposing
temporary restrictions on his ability to travel and bring money to
Trofimoff.

Trofimoff hoped that it would not take too long, noting that the
banks have no compassion whatever, and would take the house away
from him. Droujinsky said that no one wanted Trofimoff to lose his
home, and asked if he could give an idea of how much time he had.

Trofimoff replied that they (he and Jutta) were "scraping the bottom," and asked that help arrive before the end of the year.

"George, I want to mention one more thing for you . . . when the money . . . has been approved and we get it here . . . I'll have to come, to travel to meet with you, to give it to you, you know . . . And will it be possible for you to come to Tampa to meet me?"[110]

When Trofimoff replied that he could come to Tampa on a day's notice, Droujinsky told him that when he had the money, he would call to arrange a meeting.

After a month passed with no news, Trofimoff left another message on October 1, renewing his call for help. Droujinsky returned the call on November 4. He told Trofimoff that they needed more time, and that Trofimoff must be able to talk to him without Jutta being there.

When Trofimoff said that Jutta was absent and he could talk freely, Droujinsky introduced the subject of Mrs. Walker, the housemate of Trofimoff's foster brother in Munich. He wanted to know how much Mrs. Walker knew about the priest's finances and his relationship with Trofimoff. "Now," he asked, "did she know the priest, uh, that he gave you money from us?"[111]

Trofimoff explained that she never saw him receive money from the priest, that he and Igor never discussed their business in front of her, and that he never passed anything to Igor in her presence. "We were much too careful . . . she didn't know too much about his finances . . . He always kept that away from her."[112]

Droujinsky wanted to know how Trofimoff would handle the receipt of a large sum of cash, as he understood that a report had to be made for amounts larger than $10,000.

Trofimoff had done his homework. "Well, I looked into this, you know . . . if you have constantly, like every month or so you have fifty thousand dollars . . . then they start being suspicious . . . but if you come in one time, and let's say deposit $20,000, there's absolutely no question about it . . . And if you go through the mortgage company, that's different all together. They have nothing to do with the bank."[113]

Next, Droujinsky wanted to discuss the payments Trofimoff had received from the Russians over the years. "Now, can you please help us with this, George," he asked. "We have recovered many receipts of payments made to you."[114]

Trofimoff replied that they could not have receipts as he had never signed one. Droujinsky replied that he had not meant that Trofimoff signed the receipts, but that their agents had to have receipts that they had made the payments.

Droujinsky asked Trofimoff to give, to the best of his memory, a total of all of the types of payments that he had received to assist in reconciling payment records of agents who had made the payments. When Trofimoff had a problem trying to recall a total figure, Droujinsky asked him if he could give a good guess. "Well, George, what do you, what would you say may be the maximum amount? Just approximate. Can you give me some kind of amount?"[115]

"It was all in D-marks for one thing . . . if you take everything put together, it may be four thousand a month."[116]

"Four . . . so four thousand . . . that would be forty-eight thousand per year approximately," said Droujinsky. "And times twenty years . . . nine hundred sixty thousand marks, approximately? Just, I'm making in my mind. Does that sound right?"[117]

"Yeah, it could be . . . something like that . . . I had three children going to college. That's what got me into all this trouble."[118]

Droujinsky discussed the financial aid that Trofimoff was requesting. There were delays, he said, because there was confusion on the amount. ". . . the first request was for thirty thousand, but then it was forty-three thousand, and they had to start all over again, you know. You understand?"[119]

Trofimoff responded that he would be happy with thirty thousand.

However, Droujinsky had more to add to his anxiety level: ". . . the European Department initially responded, uh, unexpectedly to this additional request for more money . . . They responded that you have been paid very adequately for the materials that you provided during your period of cooperation."[120]

"Igor, I never said that I didn't. And I never asked for more money. Remember you said, 'We want to help you.' So I said, okay . . . I am helping. If you can help me, then please that's the only thing with which you can help."[121]

The pitch of Trofimoff's voice rose to a whine as he repeated the story of his lost retirement bonus, the costs of his lawyer in Germany, and other expenses he had encountered.

"So this is why I asked, if you can help, please do. But if you cannot, just tell me . . . I am not forcing anybody, I'm not . . . you know, I'm not saying that I was unhappy. I never said that I wasn't paid adequately. I certainly was . . . I just need some help, just one-time help." [122]

Droujinsky said that he was sorry that this second request was to cause so many problems, since he was just trying to help.

"Send them, send them a telex," said Trofimoff. "Tell 'em that this is not true. That I only wanted the thirty, but, and this, and this is just a one time thing. Never again, you know . . . In fact, if you remember, I didn't want to have anything to do with anything anymore . . . I'm completely out of it. It's been too long and, frankly, I'm so close to dying anyway, and I would like to die in such a way that my wife can have . . ." He broke into Russian. "I'm absolutely not requesting anything. I just said if you can help me, help me by giving me money only . . . I don't need anything else. I'm always agreeable. If I may be able to help you somehow. If it is necessary for us to see each other again, or something . . . Fine."[123]

Droujinsky again asked Trofimoff to return to English. "Unfortunately," he said, "the Center has directed that until your request for payment is resolved in the current international . . . tensions between, uh, my country and this country here . . . are eased . . .the payment will be delayed a little bit . . ."[124]

Trofimoff pleaded that if help was not forthcoming, everything he did in his life was "going up in smoke."

Droujinsky asked for Jutta's work schedule to determine the best times for calling, as he preferred to talk with Trofimoff when he was alone. He asked if either he or his wife were planning any trips in the near future.

Trofimoff replied that Jutta was planning to visit her mother in Germany and was leaving on November 17, returning on November 26. He said that if Droujinsky wanted to meet with him, the time of Jutta's absence would be a good opportunity for a meeting.

Trofimoff continued his attempts to impress "Igor" with his loyalty to the Russians. ". . . in all these years . . . I have never said a bad word, I have always done my duty. And even when I was really with my pants down, when they arrested me and all that . . . I kept integrity and honor and everything put together."[125]

When Droujinsky told Trofimoff that he was happy that he had a new and good life in America, Trofimoff replied that his new, good life would continue only if he received the financial help he was requesting. Without the help, his life would be terrible.

Droujinsky told Trofimoff he would report to his superiors, and he would be in touch as soon as he heard anything. Again, with no promises made, the conversation ended.

Droujinsky called Trofimoff on December 8, and his news was dire. He explained that deteriorating relations between the two countries resulted in orders to hold up any payments or travel and that the situation was out of his control. He was very sorry to say that they could not help him at that time.

In Russian, Trofimoff blurted out, "Well, there's nothing left for me to do except put a bullet in my forehead."[126] He was frantic, as, returning to English, he repeated over and over again his desperate situation. "Well, Igor, when you needed me, you know, you called me many, many times. And now all of a sudden when I need you, you don't call me anymore, and now you call me that you're not going to do anything, so . . . It's okay. It's, uh, I'm used to it."[127]

The tone of Trofimoff's voice again became desperate. "I have no place to go. I have absolutely no recourse, other than killing myself. I got really absolutely nothing else to live for . . . Thank you very much for calling . . . And you have a Happy New Year."[128]

Trofimoff left another message for Droujinsky on January 19, 2000, saying he had some news to discuss. His call was returned on January 21.

"Well," Trofimoff said, "the news is that I was offered to have my, uh, first mortgage renewed . . . But I need twenty-three thousand dollars . . . So, if you can see anyway to help me, that would help me for the rest of my life and I don't have to worry about it."[129]

Droujinsky asked if that figure was instead of the figure that had been discussed before.

"Yeah. Just twenty-three thousand . . . they (the bank) said, 'Okay, you sign a new first mortgage, and if you pay twenty-three thousand dollars off, we'll uh do it. The whole thing.' " Trofimoff's voice became very high-pitched. ". . . It has to be paid off by twenty-five February, at the very latest . . . Please, Igor, try everything you can . . .Save my life. Please." And, in Russian, pleading, "I am completely alone now . . . If you don't help, no one can help me."[130]

Droujinsky said that he would report Trofimoff's message. He hoped that he would soon have good news.

Trofimoff writes in his notes: "I called again a few days later and left a message saying, 'Have you forgotten your promise?'

Galkin returned the call on February 23, promising help after the elections in Russia."[131]

In that call, which would be a very short discussion, Droujinsky said, " . . . George, I just want to . . . tell you that I have, uh, what is called good news for you."[132] He told Trofimoff that the temporary problems should be resolved with the election of the new Soviet president in the next month. His superiors were asking Trofimoff to be patient a little while longer. He promised to call soon to provide the time and place of a meeting.

On February 29, Trofimoff notes he left another message with Droujinsky but did not receive a return call until May 10.[133] When Trofimoff answered the telephone and realized the agent was calling, he immediately started speaking in Russian, telling Droujinsky that he thought he had been forgotten.

"No, no. We did not forget you, George. Listen, George, I have good news for you . . . everything has been approved . . . And we're finalizing the last of the details. And can I meet you in Tampa on June 14. Okay? . . . I will call you about one week before that . . . to tell you exactly what time and place."[134]

"Oh, Igor, you're, uh, saving my life . . . I was ready to put a bullet in my head." Trofimoff was beside himself, speaking in Russian. "Wonderful . . . I thank you very much . . . Bye bye."[135]

Trofimoff writes of his excitement over the news: "Immediately after this call, full of enthusiasm, I told my wife that my brother Igor had come through with his help, even from the grave, and that we would be able to reduce our debts considerably."[136]

On June 2 Droujinsky called again to give the details of the meeting. He gave Trofimoff directions to the Tampa Airport Hilton Hotel, asking Trofimoff to meet him in the lobby at 11:00 a. m. on Wednesday, June 14.

After he was satisfied that Trofimoff had written the directions down correctly, Droujinsky asked how he planned to explain his absence to Jutta. When Trofimoff told him that he planned to take her with him, he said, "Uh, we would prefer that she not come with you. It's much better this way. Okay? So maybe you can think of some reason that you have to go there. She doesn't know that you're coming to meet me, does she?"[137]

Trofimoff acknowledged that Jutta knew he was going to meet "somebody." Droujinsky again asked him not to bring her.

Apparently because he did not want to cause problems, Trofimoff said he would comply with the agent's desires.

So, after almost three years, Droujinsky's elaborately planned web was complete, the bait was in place, and all that remained to be done was to spring the trap when Trofimoff appeared at the Hilton on June 14.

Chapter
10

TROFIMOFF'S ARREST IN THE UNITED STATES AND PRE-TRIAL CONFINEMENT

When Fortune smiles, I smile to think
How quickly she will frown.
—Robert Southwell (1561-1595),
I Envy Not Their Hap

The Trofimoffs were in a festive mood as they traveled to Tampa on June 13, 2000. Disregarding Agent Droujinsky's admonitions, Trofimoff decided to take Jutta with him to the meeting. After all, he had waited a long time for this money, and he had told Jutta it was his inheritance from his brother, Igor. Characteristically, it was no surprise that he wanted her presence. His ego demanded that she (or someone) be with him to share in his good fortune and congratulate him for his accomplishment.

After the trial, the author asked a knowledgeable FBI agent for the rationale of Droujinsky's insistence that Trofimoff attend the Tampa meeting by himself. In reply, the agent said, "It is much cleaner if a third party is not involved. I have seen people faint in situations like this—then an ambulance and medical personnel must be called. Then, sometimes the third party interferes with the arrest. It would have been much better if he had flown over. We would not have been involved with his car, and he would have gone through the airport's metal detector so we would have known he was unarmed. While we didn't expect Trofimoff to come to the meeting armed, we never know what to expect in these situations." When asked how the car would have been handled if Trofimoff had driven to the meeting alone, the agent replied, "It would have been impounded, searched, and later returned to his wife."[1]

The couple planned to spend the night in Tampa, have a nice meal, and enjoy the windfall that Trofimoff had expected for so long. He writes, "On 13 June we went to Tampa, stayed overnight in a hotel, and proceeded to the Hilton as arranged for ten o'clock in the morning."[2] Arriving at the Tampa airport an hour early, they entered the Hilton's parking lot and Trofimoff left Jutta in the car to attend his meeting. It seemed strange that Jutta did not accompany her husband into the hotel. The Florida heat in June is oppressive, and sitting in an automobile can be very unpleasant. Jutta maintains it was her choice to wait for Trofimoff in their car. "I was driving, and I couldn't find a parking space, so I let George out to go by himself. I had no desire to go with him."[3] Neither she nor Trofimoff realized they had been under FBI surveillance from the time they arrived at the hotel's parking lot.

Trofimoff writes:

> I walked confidently to the entrance where I sat on a bench for a few minutes. Trofimoff writes. At exactly ten o'clock, several men approached me from all sides, and one of them, after identifying himself as an FBI agent, arrested me for 'alleged espionage activities against the United States.' This was probably the worst moment of my life, and I was too shocked to be able to think clearly, except pointing to our car and telling the agents that my wife was waiting for me there. I was informed of my rights ... When handcuffs were placed on my hands behind my back, and shackles on my feet, I really felt that the end of the world had arrived.
>
> My immediate concern, however, was my wife Jutta, sitting in the car and observing the whole procedure. What was she going to think of me, and what was she going to do when I was not allowed to go home with her? A money problem was one thing, but charges of espionage were something altogether different, and I was certain that I would be detained at

least overnight. Well, the FBI agents herded me to a
van and seated me in the rear. Two agents went to my
wife and started talking to her. That is the last I saw of
her that day and for the next week.[4]

The agent who identified himself and arrested Trofimoff was
Special FBI Agent Anthony Wagoner. During the trial, he testified:

I walked out of the hotel. George Trofimoff was seated on a bench just outside the door . . . I walked up
from behind him. I called his name, identified myself
. . . told him he was under arrest for conspiracy to
commit espionage against the United States . . . I gave
him his rights . . . I asked him if he understood those
rights, and he said, 'yes, sir' . . . I told him we were

I-4 Westbound to
I 275 Southbound Exit 22

Right on LoisAve drive North
about $\frac{1}{2}$ mile. Hilton on RightSide

After 9 Jun 1-888-502-6512
or (202) 783-1869

*Trofimoff's hand-written direction's to the meeting in Tampa,
14 June, 2000. (U.S. Justice Dept.)*

> going to get into a van and then go to the FBI Office in
> Tampa . . . Special Agent Joe Navarro and Special
> Agent George Quinlan were to my immediate side. In
> the van, Mr. Trofimoff was asking questions, 'what's
> this all about?' I explained to him that he had been
> indicted by a Federal Grand Jury for conspiracy to
> commit espionage . . . he asked about his wife. I told
> him that two agents were with his wife . . . they would
> take care of her.[5]

Agent Wagoner testified that during the ride to the courthouse he
asked Trofimoff why he was at the Hilton Hotel. "He said he was at
the hotel because he had received a call from a man by the name of
Igor . . . he said this Igor told him that he represented Susemihl
(Trofimoff's foster brother) and that this Igor had money from
Susemihl to give to him . . . he said it was around twenty thousand
dollars."[6]

Trofimoff writes:

> I was taken to the FBI office . . . and finger-printed for
> about an hour-and-a-half . . . I was again thoroughly
> searched, my wallet was taken, and everything inside,
> including $111.00 which I never saw nor heard of
> again, was placed in a large envelope.
>
> I was taken, again in shackles, to the Courthouse
> where I was given a copy of my indictment and then
> given a preliminary bond hearing, which was then
> postponed for a few days for lack of a defense attor-
> ney at my side.[7]

Taken to the Hillsborough County jail, Trofimoff writes that he was
taken to a "general population" cell until the next day. "I was interviewed by someone from 'Classification' who decided that I should
be placed in 'protective custody,' supposedly because of my 'high
profile' case, which could entice someone crazy to murder me."[8] He
was then moved to a wing in the jail reserved for inmates requiring
maximum security where he remained in solitary confinement, 'for
his safety,' for the next seven weeks.

As the FBI agents arrested Trofimoff in Tampa, other agents
swarmed into the Indian River Colony Club to go through his home.
The security guard who was on duty at that time told the author that
a Suburban with FBI agents arrived at the gate. One showed his
badge, asking him to admit seven following cars. The bar was raised

and they all proceeded through the gate. Later the guard went with the community General Manager to the Trofimoff house to see what was going on. They found that the agents had the house surrounded and would not let anyone get near to it.

The residents at IRCC are very supportive of each other, as demonstrated by retired Navy Captain John Calloway, who lived nearby. Calloway, a 1946 graduate of the U. S. Naval Academy, was very friendly with the Trofimoffs. As he drove past their home on June 14, he noticed the cars and several individuals milling around the house. The garage door was open. When Calloway saw an individual climbing up a ladder into the attic, he immediately stopped and asked the agent for identification, and wanted to know who he was and why he was there. When an agent showed his badge and told him that he was there on official business, Calloway proceeded to his own home.

Jutta in a later conversation related her version of the story. In Tampa, when Trofimoff was arrested, she, waiting in their car, could not believe her eyes as she saw her husband, handcuffed and shackled, placed in a waiting van and whisked away. Almost immediately, FBI agents approached her, saying that her husband had been arrested. They asked her to accompany them to a room in the hotel, where she was interrogated for some two hours. When her interrogation was complete, they were satisfied she was innocent and had no part in Trofimoff's activities. She was asked if she wanted to go to the Courthouse to view the indictment proceedings, but she declined that offer, as "I just wanted to get home."[9]   Released to return to Melbourne, she remembers that when she was told she was free to go, a door opened into an adjoining room where she saw other agents with what she thought were cameras and recorders, so she assumed her interrogation had been recorded.

After her release, Jutta says there was no offer from the FBI to assist her in returning to Melbourne. "I was given instructions to reach Interstate 4 (the route to Melbourne), and then I had to drive home by myself (more than 100 miles) in a state of shock. I don't remember anything about that drive. I have no idea how fast I was driving, and I was very happy to get home without an accident or being stopped by the police."[10]

After the trial, the author queried an FBI representative on this point. He said, "I am quite sure that the female agent present at the time offered to have someone drive her home, but she (Jutta) thought she could handle the drive back. Perhaps she was so distraught at the time that she does not recall that the offer was made."[11] This individual also maintained that Jutta's interview was not recorded.

When Jutta arrived at the entrance to IRCC, a throng of reporters and TV cameramen was waiting. Trofimoff's arrest made national (and international) news, and it didn't take long for representatives of all major networks and newspapers to gather at the entrance to garner whatever information and pictures became available. After making her way through the crowd, she drove to their home on Patriot Drive where she encountered more reporters. IRCC is gated, but the back gate, near Trofimoff's home, is not manned. (Residents open the gates with a "clicker.") It was easy for reporters to park their cars outside and proceed on foot to Trofimoff's house. When Jutta arrived, she immediately called IRCC security personnel who promptly ejected the interloping reporters.

In her home, the FBI search crew was still present. They had gone through the house, taking any and everything that could possibly be used as evidence. All of Trofimoff's personal items were taken, including pictures, photo albums, financial records, income tax returns, etc. In addition, many of Jutta's personal items, to include an album with pictures of her daughter and grandchildren, a camera, and even her passport had all been confiscated. At first, the agents refused to return her passport but relented when she threatened to call the German Consulate. "It was good that I arrived before the FBI left," she said. "It would have been very difficult to obtain my passport later."[12]

When the agents departed, the house was in complete disarray. Everything had been opened, and there had been no attempt to put anything back in order. The agents had gone through the attic storage in the garage, opening suitcases, ripping the linings out. Boxes of Christmas decorations had been opened and their contents were strewn around, with many ornaments shattered. It was several days before Jutta was able to get her home in some semblance of order. It is interesting that the FBI searchers, thorough as they were, failed in their search to notice an electric paper shredder that Trofimoff kept in plain sight in his garage.

In May 2000, the author and his wife attended his 50th reunion at West Point. Returning to Florida, they stopped to visit friends in Hilton Head, South Carolina. Arriving at Hilton Head on Wednesday, June 14, they were watching the late afternoon TV news when, unbelievably, Trofimoff appeared, handcuffed, striding across the screen.

Everyone watched, dumbfounded, listening as the reporter described Trofimoff being led away by FBI agents in Tampa, Florida, after his arrest for espionage. The reporter went on to say that Trofimoff was the most senior member of the U. S. armed forces ever to be charged with that serious crime.

All were transfixed as they watched and heard the announcer continue, telling how Trofimoff had been arrested that morning in Tampa, where he was lured by the FBI with the promise of receiving a large sum in payment for his alleged former spying activities. The report concluded with the announcer stating that Trofimoff was arraigned in Federal court and was presently held in a Tampa jail. His wife, who was with him, the announcer reported, was not charged and had returned to her home in Melbourne, Florida.

Everyone's first reaction to the news was disbelief, but as more facts regarding the arrest were revealed, many emotions bubbled up from inside, to include complete surprise, sadness, disappointment and betrayal. With these mixed emotions, one could not help feeling sympathy for Trofimoff, but, at the same time, one had to conclude that if Trofimoff was, in fact, guilty of these extraordinary charges he would deserve any penalty the court might mete out. While the afternoon's news certainly did not look good for the author's "perfect neighbor," he vowed to keep an open mind until more details were available.

Doris, the author's wife, decided to call Jutta immediately. She reached for a phone and soon was talking to a frantic Jutta, who had just arrived after a long drive from Tampa. Sobbing that she desperately needed support, she pleaded for a return to Florida as soon as possible. Her first words were that her husband's arrest was a complete surprise. Doris assured her that we would return as soon as possible.

Returning to IRCC the next day, the author and his wife found Jutta still in a state of shock. Between sobs, she began to relate her experiences of the last two days.

Trofimoff had told her that his brother's long-promised money had arrived in Tampa, and she described how they drove to the hotel at the Tampa airport to get it. She was driving and stayed in the car, looking for a parking space. In just a few minutes she observed her husband, in shackles, being led to a van and driven away. Soon, FBI agents arrived to tell her that Trofimoff had been arrested. When she asked why, they told her that he was charged with espionage.

"They asked me to go with them to a room in the hotel and for about two hours they asked me a lot of questions. Finally, they said they were convinced I was not involved and told me I could return to IRCC. I was half-crazy driving home and don't remember how fast I was driving. I was lucky to get home without an accident. It took me one and a half hours to get home. Don't ask me how fast I was driving—I don't remember anything. All I could think of on the way was home . . . home . . . home."

"The front entrance to IRCC was full of reporters and TV cameras," she continued, "and when I got home the FBI was still there, going through everything. They had my passport and would not return it until I threatened to call the German consulate. When they finally left, they took all of George's papers and pictures, and many of my personal things. Everything in the house was left torn apart and I still haven't cleaned up the mess they left."

Over the weekend, Jutta began to regain her composure and the crowds of reporters dispersed. Trofimoff's bail bond hearing was scheduled for Tuesday morning, June 20, in Tampa. Jutta was in no condition to make that drive alone, and the author and his wife told her that they would drive her to the hearing.

On the way to the hearing, Jutta repeated her belief that Trofimoff was innocent. Married to him only a short time when he was arrested by German authorities in 1994, she believed his protestations, at that time, that he was innocent. After moving to America, she had no inkling that he was the subject of an intensive FBI investigation. Further, he had not told her about the telephone calls and letters he received from Droujinsky, which began in 1997. Her dénouement would not be long arriving.

Trofimoff had insufficient resources to pay for an attorney so the court appointed Daniel Hernandez, a Tampa-based attorney, as his counsel. Before the bail hearing began, the author asked Hernandez if his services were pro bono. "No," he answered, "I'm being paid by the court, not as much as I would be paid on a private case, but adequately." Then, addressing Jutta, he said, "I can assure you, Mrs. Trofimoff, that I will give my absolute best in the defense of your husband."[13]

It was a shock to see Trofimoff at the hearing. Wearing an orange jumpsuit, with handcuffs on his wrists and manacles on his feet, he wore a sad and resigned expression. Although he sat at a table only a few feet away, it seemed as if he was already in a different world. The author and his wife, Doris, somehow knew that they would never again enjoy a pleasant dinner and evening of cards with their neighbors. Earlier, Doris had said that she wanted to go to the hearing, as that might be the last chance she'd have to see Trofimoff.

At the hearing, the Federal prosecutor, Terry Furr, spent more than an hour detailing the 32 specific criminal acts contained in the indictment entered by Donna Bucella, U. S. Attorney for the Middle District of Florida. Furr's presentation was more like an opening statement in a trial than a bail hearing. He desperately wanted to insure that Trofimoff would not be granted bail. He was successful since the presiding U. S. Magistrate Judge Mark Pizzo took little time to deny Hernandez' request to release his client. Judge Pizzo agreed with Furr that Trofimoff would probably attempt to flee if released, as he considered the weight of the evidence in the case to be significant.

Jutta was visibly shaken while Furr told of the two three-hour videotapes in which Trofimoff described in detail his espionage activities during the some 25 years he was assigned to the Nuremberg JIC. When those tapes were made, she was in Germany with her daughter who had just given birth to her second baby, and she had no warning of what she would hear on that fateful day in Tampa. Certainly, she did not expect to hear about her husband's videotaped clandestine meetings with Agent Droujinsky. When asked if she knew about those meetings, Jutta, dumbfounded, could only shake her head. Jutta later told how, in a telephone discussion with Trofimoff a few days after the bail hearing, had the audacity to tell her that he would probably have never attended the meetings if she had not been in Germany visiting her mother, daughter, and grandchildren.

At the conclusion of the hearing, Trofimoff rose and faced Jutta, who also stood. As Trofimoff reached out to her, his jailor pulled him away, allowing no physical contact. Trofimoff and Jutta would not see each other in person again until his trial, 12 months later.

Outside the courthouse, a large contingent of reporters with cameras was waiting. The author and his wife took Jutta's arms and forced their way through the crowd, repeating "No comment" to the never-ending questions. During the drive back to Melbourne, Jutta was a mental wreck because of the devastating information she received during the hearing. Repeatedly, she wondered aloud how her husband could have hurt her so deeply.

Trofimoff must have been very distraught at the time of the hearing, but he was even more upset than imagined. He told Jutta a few

Political cartoon in Florida Today, *18 June 2000.*

days later in a telephone call that that his experience was extremely degrading, and that he felt like an animal when he came to the court-room that day. He was aroused at four a. m., and a short time later, was driven the three short blocks to the courthouse, chained together with some 30 other prisoners.

The next twelve months were a nightmare for both Jutta and her husband. Trofimoff could make collect telephone calls to her, but the only personal communication they had was when Jutta drove to the Tampa jail for a visit. Each visit, scheduled in advance, was strictly limited to one hour. Face-to-face contact was not allowed, and they communicated through computer monitors and microphones.

Jutta was now alone, faced with the knowledge that her husband was, apparently, not the same man she believed she had married several years before. Her struggle with that dilemma would continue for many months. Devastated by the revelations of the last few days, the author, with strong feelings of betrayal, was determined to discover as much as possible about the events preceding Trofimoff's arrest and imprisonment.

Trofimoff lost the fine life he was accustomed to lead and was forced to live in a world he never knew existed. The wonderful life style he had become accustomed to was gone; he was placed in an alien environment, forced to coexist with an unsavory group. "They were all accused of various crimes," he writes, "ranging from murder, to burglary, bank robbery, and drug offenses . . . We had all become a number, not a person . . .I will never forget the misery and the despair found in such an environment . . . One thing has to be stated at this time. Life in a county jail is not a vacation, and is definitely not something to look forward to. Overall, it's tough and takes a lot to get used to!"[14] Trofimoff's ability as a survivor would be sorely tested during the next 12 months.

Soon after his arrest Trofimoff told the author (through Jutta) that he wanted his life story told and that he would be given exclusive rights to write it. As soon as his prison life was somewhat settled, he began to write and forward page after page concerning details of his early life. At first, the pages were hand-written. Later they were printed after Trofimoff received computer lessons. It was impressive that he was able to pull so many facts from his memory —names, dates, and places—all without any notes.

Jutta's life was drastically changed for the worse. While she would not face the physical hardships and privations experienced by her husband, the mental anguish and financial problems to be

The Morgan Street Jail, Tampa, Florida where Trofimoff was held pending trial. (Author's collection)

encountered would be almost as hard for her to bear as the conditions he faced.

IRCC was a community of retired officers and widows of all U. S. armed services. The residents, as a group, were understandably outraged that a member of their community was charged with espionage. However, the attitude of some residents toward Jutta, who had been declared by the FBI to be innocent of any of Trofimoff's activities, was hard to understand. She received several threatening telephone calls, and rumors were rampant, referring to "the spy's wife." Her once idyllic life was rapidly unraveling. She had to rely on the support of a few close friends who understood her situation and provided assistance and support in those difficult times.

Jutta's financial problems were dire. Trofimoff, in satiating his lust for the high life, had taken out a second mortgage on their home and had amassed so much credit card debt that he had been hard-pressed to pay the interest on the debt, much less pay off any principle. In addition to the second mortgage and credit card debts, large monthly payments were required for a new Chrysler he had impetuously purchased. At the time of his arrest, the value of the Chrysler was less than the amount owed to the finance company.

Initially, Jutta tried to make the credit card payments. All records had been confiscated during the FBI's search and it was difficult to develop a clear picture of the debts her husband had amassed. She soon realized that, with the financial problems she had inherited, she needed professional help, and she engaged a local attorney for assistance. On his advice and with his assistance, she stopped all credit card payments, notified the finance company that she wanted to surrender the Chrysler, and initiated bankruptcy proceedings. At the bankruptcy hearing, not one of the credit card companies appeared, and the entire debt was erased. (Trofimoff's total credit card debt to three different companies totaled some $80,000.)

Ironically, had Trofimoff filed for bankruptcy instead of trying to obtain some $23,000 (a fraction of his credit card debt) from those he thought to be Russian "friends," he would never have been involved with Droujinsky, would not have been coerced into attending the videotaped meetings, and would still be living peacefully at IRCC.

Knowledgeable FBI and Department of Justice sources assured the author that, without the videotapes, the government would not have been able to prosecute the case. Of course, knowing Trofimoff's personality, his ego would never have allowed him to embarrass himself before his friends and neighbors by filing for bankruptcy.

Even though Trofimoff's civil service and military retirement pay was still being deposited to their joint account, Jutta soon realized that she could not continue the payments on her home. She wanted to stay in the United States as long as possible, at least until after the trial was completed. She had no way of knowing if those retirement checks would continue. She had no other income, and when the basic mortgage on the house was added to the amount due on the second mortgage, the total exceeded the price she could expect to sell the house for. She made the difficult decision to default on the mortgages and move to less expensive quarters in a nearby apartment complex.

When she moved to America with her husband, Jutta brought many items of her own personal property, such as sets of beautiful dishes, silverware, table linens, and other valuable items. Aware that the government might at any time confiscate their property, she decided to pack her most valuable items and return them to her family in Germany. Neighbors helped her pack those items and arrange for their shipment to her mother. She made arrangements with a local auction house to dispose of the larger furniture items, which she would not be able to ship to Germany or take with her to a new apartment.

Throughout the remainder of 2001, Jutta lived in her small apartment and made periodic visits to the several Florida state jails in which Trofimoff was held. During the year, the pressures she faced began to have an effect, not only on her, but also on their cat. As soon as her husband was arrested, Jutta told the author and his wife that their cat seemed to know that something was wrong. She cried a lot and huddled closely to Jutta whenever she was at home. After Jutta moved to her smaller apartment the cat's condition steadily worsened. She wouldn't eat and started losing her hair until, finally, Jutta called the author to say that she had died. "Of loneliness," Jutta maintained. She seemed to be a direct victim of Trofimoff's imprisonment.

The uncertainty of the trial's date was another unnerving factor. First scheduled to be held shortly after Trofimoff's arrest in June 2000, it was delayed and rescheduled several times during the year. Everyone began to wonder if it would ever be held.

At times Jutta was convinced that her husband was completely innocent, and at other times, she was more realistic. "Whatever happens to George will be his doing, not mine," she once said. "I have to start planning my own life."[15] She also noticed a difference in her tennis game. A good player, she thoroughly enjoyed the sport, but she once mentioned that her game was getting much more aggressive. "I don't know why," she said, "but today, before I realized it, I tried to hit a ball directly at my opponent. I have never been that aggressive, and I wouldn't have done that before."[16]

While Jutta waited for the trial to commence, she slowly adjusted to the realization that George might never be free. However, she retained her compassion for his personal circumstances and maintained her loyalty to him. "If I don't visit him, no one else will," she said. "He desperately needs someone to give him support, and if I ever stop my visits to him, it will probably signal his end." Her life was in disarray, and would never be the same as it was before her husband's arrest.

Chapter

11

THE PROSECUTION

And then it started like a guilty thing
Upon a fearful summons.
—William Shakespeare (1564–1616)
Hamlet, Act 1, Sc.1, Line 148

Trofimoff's trial for espionage began on Monday, June 4, 2001, in the Sam E. Gibbons U. S. Courthouse in Tampa, Florida, with selection of the jury and reading of the charges. U. S. District Judge Susan C. Bucklew presided. Bucklew, a diminutive lady with short gray hair, kept the court in good humor throughout the trial with her ready wit and keen sense of humor. Even so, she made it clear to everyone present that it was her court; she exercised firm but polite control over the proceedings.

Greg Kehoe, a former federal prosecutor, underscored the trial's importance. "It is unusual for these cases to go to trial, When the government proceeds in these cases, they usually have an extremely strong case . . . they are very selective."[1]

Representing the Government were Assistant U. S. Attorney Terry Furr from Tampa and Laura Ingersoll, Senior Trial Attorney of the Internal Security Section of the Department of Justice in Washington, D. C. Furr, a large, imposing dark-haired individual, was clearly driven by his intense desire to obtain Trofimoff's conviction. His favorite posture was to lean forward from his podium, his hands reaching out to grasp each edge. During the trial he was in constant motion, moving from the podium to his seat at an adjoining table to retrieve notes he referred to as he presented his case.

Laura Ingersoll, an attractive lady considerably shorter than Furr,

was an experienced and energetic prosecutor who also exhibited an
intense desire to secure Trofimoff's conviction. As the trial progressed,
it became clear to all that she and Furr had spent many hours together preparing their case.

Sitting at the government's table during much of the trial were FBI
Special Agents Joe Navarro from the Tampa FBI office and Anthony
(Tony) Wagoner from Washington, D. C. Each played a major role in
the FBI investigation, one that covered more than seven years. During
the early stages, Wagoner was in charge of the European phase, and
in 1995 when Trofimoff moved to Florida, Navarro assumed control.

Trofimoff's counsel was Daniel Hernandez, a court-appointed
attorney from Tampa. Shorter in stature than his opponent, Terry Furr,
Hernandez was of medium build with a large shock of black hair
tinged with gray. In his defense of Trofimoff, Hernandez tried hard,
but in the final analysis, he could not compete with the juggernaut of
witnesses, evidence, and high technology brought to bear by Furr and
Ingersoll.

The first day was spent almost entirely on jury selection. Judge
Bucklew and Hernandez questioned each of the 52 prospective jurors
in depth. At the end of their questioning, sixteen jurors, eight men and
eight women, were selected. The judge told the jurors that, at the end
of the trial, she would distribute written instructions regarding the
law that applies to the case; in the meantime, she would give preliminary and general instructions:

> It will be your duty to find from the evidence what the
> facts of this case are. You, and you alone, are the
> judges of those facts. You will then have to apply the
> facts, as you decide them, to the law as I give it to you.
> And you must follow the law that I will give you,
> whether you agree with that law or not.
>
> Nothing that I say during the course of this trial is
> intended to indicate to you that I prefer one verdict
> over another. It's up to you, as jurors, to decide what
> a proper verdict is . . .[2]

The judge continued to give further detailed instructions, and
when she was finished she asked the Federal Prosecutor to read the
Indictment. The judge had a few more comments for the jurors, and
before declaring a recess, she asked Furr for a list of witnesses scheduled for the next day.

When deliberations began on Tuesday, June 5, the judge reported that one of the jurors was involved in an early morning automobile accident and would be unable to be in court before the following day. Rather than delay the start of the trial, she decided to proceed with the remaining fifteen jurors. All 15 remained present for the entire trial, which would last for almost four weeks.

The judge asked the jurors if they had read, heard, or seen anything overnight that would adversely affect their ability to serve as objective, unbiased jurors. She cautioned them that during the entire trial they should not expose themselves to information regarding the case from outside sources. They were to consider only the evidence presented to them during the trial. (These questions and instructions were repeated at the beginning of each day for the duration of the trial.) She further stressed that they should not consider as fact anything they had heard the previous day when the government's specifications were read, or anything said during the opening arguments of each side.

Furr assumed his favorite posture and leaned forward, extending his arms to either side of the podium in front of him as he paused for effect, his eyes roving over the members of the jury. Beginning his opening arguments deliberately and slowly, he gave a preview of

The Sam M. Gibbons United States Courthouse in Tampa, Florida. (Author's collection)

what the jurors would hear during the presentation of the government's case. "When I say those words 'spying' or 'espionage,' . . . it probably conjures up some images in your mind. And I want you to forget what you've seen on TV, or what you've seen at the movies . . . Because what you're going to hear in here, what you're going to see in the way of evidence, is going to be real."[3]

Furr's summary, including the background of the U. S. Cold War with Russia, was a spy story worthy of the likes of a John Le Carré thriller. During his presentation the jury focused intently on his every word. Later in the trial their interest would at times falter, but at the beginning, they seemed to grasp the importance of the case and were attentive to everything Furr had to say. Most took extensive notes.

Trofimoff, several pounds lighter than when he was arrested a year before, nodded and smiled to the author and Jutta as he entered the court room and took his seat. During the opening arguments he was alert, listening carefully to Furr's words. At his bail bond hearing a year before, he was in shackles and wore an orange prisoner's jump suit, but this day he had no chains. He wore a gray pinstripe suit, a white shirt, and a maroon tie. Occasionally he turned to view the jampacked courtroom (all spectator seats were filled) to smile and mouth a few words to Jutta. Always near but unobtrusive was a plain-clothed marshal, Trofimoff's guard and escort to and from the courtroom.[4]

"You're going to hear about a person," Furr began, ". . . now dead, named Igor Susemihl . . . essentially the lifelong friend, almost brother of the defendant . . . Susemihl became a member of the clergy of the Russian Orthodox Church . . . he was called a Metropolitan . . . you will hear it's the equivalent of a Cardinal . . . He was also a KGB agent . . . He recruited the defendant to commit espionage."[5] Furr further alleged that Igor received films depicting classified documents from Trofimoff and passed them on to Moscow, later paying Trofimoff for his services. Furr maintained that Trofimoff kept his relationship with Igor a secret in violation of U. S. regulations.

Furr continued to tell how, when an undercover FBI agent, posing as a member of the Russian Embassy in Washington, contacted Trofimoff by letter and telephone. Trofimoff was first leery and frightened, refusing to acknowledge and speak of his espionage activities. However, with repeated calls and persuasion by the FBI agent, Trofimoff became less concerned and finally agreed to meet the agent in a Melbourne hotel. During two videotaped meetings, Furr said,

Trofimoff gave details of his spying, telling how he photographed several volumes—possibly as many as 50,000 pages of classified information. (So much information, in fact, that he didn't even bother to read many of the documents he was copying), and passed the exposed film to his foster brother.

Furr's detailed comments on Trofimoff's self-destruction were illuminating, but he pointed out for the jury that Trofimoff himself voiced the most damning revelation. "He (Trofimoff) makes it very, very clear in the tapes that he doesn't think of himself as American. He says he never has. He's Russian. And he said he did it for the motherland."[6]

Furr told the jury that they would hear from a Marine, who was stationed in Moscow as a young man, was recruited by the Soviets, and later convicted of espionage, he continued:

> You're also going to hear about another former KGB officer. His name was Vasily Mitrokhin. He was a KGB archivist . . . for years he smuggled out scraps of paper, notes of paper that said what was in the files.
>
> You're also going to hear from a another former very high-ranking member of the KGB. He was engaged in counterintelligence . . . he personally met with the defendant in Bad Ischl, Austria . . . He'll identify him (Trofimoff) . . . And he will tell you that Trofimoff was a major spy for the KGB.[8]
>
> Finally, you'll hear from the former Commander of the United States Army in Europe—a retired four-star general . . . he's going to tell you strategically what this hemorrhage meant to the United States.[9]

In summary, Furr told the jurors that the testimony of the witnesses in the case would be compelling and urged them to listen carefully, as it was a very important case.

After a morning recess, Hernandez rose to deliver his opening argument. He echoed the judge's instructions, reminding the jury that nothing said by himself or Furr should be considered facts and that their decisions should be based only on what they hear from the witnesses. He further explained:

> I believe the evidence in this case is going to show that Mr. Trofimoff is an American patriot and not a spy for the Soviet Union . . . he has never asked what his country could do for him. He has always asked what he could do for his country.[10]

Hernandez dismissed as inconsequential all of the government's evidence except the secretly recorded six-hour meeting. He acknowledged the critical nature of that meeting and the videotapes, but he maintained that the tapes merely portrayed two people lying to each other.

> I believe the evidence will show, ladies and gentlemen, that this video contains an attempt by two people trying to deceive the other, each for their own particular purposes.[11]

> Let me make it clear, ladies and gentlemen, that Mr. Trofimoff categorically denies the charges. He categorically denies working for the KGB or the Soviets or the Communists. He denies ever betraying his country . . . Specifically, he categorically denies that he has ever maintained or used any names like Antey, Markiz, and Konsul . . . the allegations in the indictment.[12]

> . . . in fact, ladies and gentlemen, I believe the evidence will show the fact is that this was an outrageous act by the Government enticing a 73-year-old financially troubled man with blatant, blatant promises of substantial money in order for him to give information.[13]

Hernandez told the jury that during the trial they would see a performance rivaling a Steven Spielberg production, one involving many government officials and state-of-the-art electronics.[14]

> On this side of the courtroom it's Danny Hernandez and George Trofimoff. And I suspect that the Government in this case will—will come at Mr. Trofimoff with a force (he pointed to the four individuals sitting at the prosecutor's table) of a Goliath.

> But keep in mind, ladies and gentlemen, that David against Goliath prevailed with a slingshot and a rock. Mr. Trofimoff (pointing to Trofimoff) has his slingshot and his rock. His slingshot is his innocence, and his rock is the truth . . . He will slay Goliath! I believe that when you've heard all of the evidence, the lack of evidence and the conflict in evidence, the only just verdict in this case would be a verdict of not guilty.[15]

With opening arguments completed, the prosecution began to present its case in a history-making trial that was to set records; it was the first time that so many KGB agents, spy masters, and FBI agents testified in a U. S. courtroom; that U. S. prosecutors used classified documents as evidence in open court while keeping them secret and out of public view; and that U. S. prosecutors capitalized on the work of former KGB archivist Vasili Mitrokhin.[16]

As Furr and Ingersoll unfurled their case, it was clear from the beginning that a considerable part of the government's effort would be devoted to education of the jury. It was a relatively young panel; the average juror's age was estimated to be no more than 40 years. Several of the jurors would have little (or no) recollection of the world situation and the U. S.-Russian Cold War that existed in the 1970s. They would have little knowledge of the KGB's organization, methods of operation, and the conflicts existing between the United States and Russia during those hectic years. It was also unlikely that any of them had a full understanding how documents become classified, or the significance of, and the control and security requirements for, different categories of classified information.

To successfully prosecute their case, the government representatives planned to educate the jury on these points. The prosecutors accomplished this by calling many "expert" witnesses: individuals who described the procedures for classifying sensitive information and the requirements for filing and safeguarding them; special agents from U. S. intelligence agencies to tell of anti-KGB operations they had been involved in; a young Marine convicted of espionage to demonstrate the insidious nature of the KGB's recruiting procedures; and even a KGB officer who, after being disenchanted with his own government, was convicted in Russia for treason and, after release, moved to the United States and became a U. S. citizen. One reporter said to the author that it was like a Tom Clancy novel. Even the court's bailiff, a grizzled veteran of many cases, said that with all the witnesses, the case reminded him of a James Bond movie.

Former Federal prosecutor Greg Kehoe was quoted as saying, "The first thing I would do is put on evidence of the terrain, of the antagonistic position we were in. Give some historical context . . . explain the relationship between the United States and the Soviet Union."[17]

Terry Furr and Laura Ingersoll planned to do just that, but they first introduced a witness to paint a verbal picture of Trofimoff and his background and to document his military and civil service history.

Special Agent Gary S. Pepper, a specialist in foreign counterintelligence activity from the U. S. Army Intelligence and Security Command at Fort Meade, Maryland, had been the senior agent in charge of the European phase of the army's investigation of Trofimoff in Nuremberg, Germany. He presented documents from Trofimoff's personnel file depicting his entire service record from his enlistment in the U. S. Army in 1948 up to the time of his arrest by German authorities in December 1994 when his security clearance was withdrawn and he was placed on administrative leave.

Pepper gave a brief summary of Trofimoff's personal life, beginning with his birth in Berlin in 1927, his travels through Europe to Paris, his immigration to America in 1947, his enlistment in the U. S. Army in 1948, and his duty assignments as a member of the U. S. Army and later as a civil service employee. Pepper was in Nuremberg when Trofimoff was arrested, and he personally inventoried the classified documents stored in the JIC. He presented a list of those documents to give the jury an overview of the types of classified documents Trofimoff had access to, displaying interior and exterior photographs of the JIC.

Furr called as his next witness Mike Moschetti of Sierra Vista, Arizona. Moschetti, a 22-year veteran of the U. S. Army, had been an interrogator, a subordinate of Trofimoff at the JIC during the years 1979-1985. Moschetti described Trofimoff as "a wonderful boss," who had the complete trust of all members of the U. S. Army element. Shown a floor diagram of the JIC, he pointed to Trofimoff's office and the immediately adjacent vault where all the classified documents were stored. He testified that no one kept track of the classified documents and that he was not aware of any log for their control. " . . . The whole atmosphere . . . was complete trust . . .. Our security was trust."[18] He stated that external security was the responsibility of the Germans, and that one had to be "buzzed in" and "buzzed out" by German personnel whenever entering or leaving the JIC.

Moschetti was still on the stand as the trial resumed on Wednesday, June 6, and Furr asked him if German guards ever searched his belongings when he left or entered the JIC. He answered with a decisive "No," and when Furr asked him if Trofimoff carried an attaché case regularly, he testified, "Yes, he did. He carried a bag every single day."[19]

Moschetti described the workday as 8:00 a. m. to 4:00 p. m., emphasizing that all classified materials and working papers had to be secured and everyone out of the building no later than 4:00 p. m. He said the Germans had no access to the Army's vault, which had to be securely locked (two doors) before the Army personnel cleared the building. At that time an internal electronic warning system, controlled by the Germans, was activated.

Regarding the work habits of his boss, he said that Trofimoff left early sometimes, but often was the last to leave. " . . .He was a great boss to work for . . . if there was anything we personally had to take care of, Mr. Trofimoff would say . . . 'go home—and I'll lock up.' "[20]

Furr asked him about Trofimoff's fourth wife, Marion.

"She was a young woman, very attractive, considerably younger than Mr. Trofimoff, very nicely dressed . . . long, honey blond kind of hair . . . younger than George."[21]

Furr then asked Moschetti how George treated Marion, and whether he spent much money on her.

"He referred to her always with a German term of affection, like 'little mouse,' he obviously cared very much about her and—you know, and treated her almost like a little girl sometimes . . . he bought a lot of very nice clothing for her. He bought a lot of collectibles, the type of things from Franklin Mint."[22]

Furr's final question asked Moschetti if he could have taken documents in and out of the JIC.

"I would have had no problem with it whatsoever. There were no checks whatever."[23]

When Furr's questioning was complete, Hernandez began his cross-examination, asking if there was anything unusual about the way George treated his wife.

Moschetti's answer drew smiles from the jury. ". . . His wife was, I would estimate, about 30 years younger than he was . . . it was sort of one of those older gentlemen to a younger wife type of relationship . . . it was almost like a kept woman type (of) thing."[24]

In answering other questions, Moschetti revealed that in the JIC there were perhaps a total of thirty personnel, including some five or six members of the U. S. Army Element who were located on the second floor along with the U. S. Air Force Element. He was not aware of any internal security checks ever being made by German personnel, or of any security inspections made by any outside agency.

When Hernandez asked Moschetti if he had ever seen Trofimoff improperly handle classified documents, he replied, "No, I did not."[25]

Furr then called his next witness, Eugene Drozdza.

Drozda's testimony revealed that he was born in Poland and currently resided in Scotland. At the age of six, an orphan, he was sent to Siberia and was released some six years later when Stalin issued an amnesty for all Polish people. He arrived in the United States at the age of twelve and enlisted in the U. S. Army in 1950. He obtained his U. S. citizenship in 1954 and worked at the Nuremberg JIC as an interrogator on two separate assignments. After retiring from the Army in 1974, he received a U. S. Army Civil Service appointment and remained at the Nuremberg JIC until he was assigned to the Dusseldorf, Germany, JIC in 1987.

In response to Furr's questions, Drozdza described JIC interrogation procedures. He testified that permission was not required to remove classified documents from the JIC vault. "I don't recall of any log being present where we would be required to annotate our removal or bringing or returning the document . . . we would just go and just pull it out without anybody's permission."[26]

Furr asked if there was anything to keep Drozdza from taking classified documents out of the building.[27]

"If it was I who had wanted to take a document out of the building, I could do it easily without anybody knowing it."[28]

Asked if he had to have permission to take a document, Drozdza replied, "No, not at all. I didn't have to ask permission of anybody . . . I would just go and find it and use it, remove it."

Hernandez had not known what to expect from Trofimoff's two coworkers, but after their testimony he told the author privately that he didn't feel they had inflicted extensive damage to his case. He said that the most significant parts of their testimony were their descriptions of the poor document security at the JIC, and the disclosure that documents could be secretly removed with no interference from German personnel. Conversely, each individual stated that Trofimoff was a good boss, one he trusted completely. Hernandez considered that testimony to be a positive factor in establishing his client's honesty and respectability.

Having completed the discussion of Trofimoff's background and the description of the JIC and its operation, the government prosecutors turned to their next objective, the education of the jurors.

Herbert Briick, a senior official of the Central Intelligence Agency, was the prosecution's next witness. He described how the CIA, whose director reported directly to the President, is responsible for overseeing the entire U. S. intelligence community, and is the final authority in the determination of the level of classification assigned to sensitive documents.

The judge approved the government's request to designate Briick as an expert in classified material determination. She advised the jury that as an "expert" witness, Mr. Briick was to be treated as any other witness, except that he would be allowed to give his personal opinion on matters relating to his expertise.

In answer to a question, Briick discussed the basic definition of the three categories of classified material: release of CONFIDENTIAL information to unauthorized persons could cause damage to the United States; loss of SECRET information could cause serious damage; and loss of TOP SECRET information could cause grave damage.

When asked to describe the role that trust plays in the national security system, Briick replied, "Trust is the foundation of our ability to protect classified information."[29]

The next three government witnesses, one from the CIA and two from the Defense Intelligence Agency (DIA), described how critical classified information such as the Soviet's chemical warfare capability is integrated into National Intelligence Estimates and Intelligence Collection Requirements. Documents such as these, usually classified SECRET, list what is known of Soviet capabilities and what additional information is required by the various intelligence agencies. Copies were filed in the JIC and used by interrogators as guides in questioning sources. One witness testified, ". . . it represents all of our intelligence gaps, what we don't know about all these various subjects in all of these countries, and . . . why we are trying to collect this information . . . as a counter-intelligence officer, I would describe this as a gold mine."[30]

Retired Major General Charles F. Scanlon, a career U. S. Army intelligence officer, was the next witness to take the stand for the government. As a Colonel, General Scanlon was the Commanding Officer of the 66th Military Intelligence (MI) Group during the years 1978-1980. The 66th MI Group was responsible for several JICs situated along the West German border, including the one in Nuremberg.

Scanlon testified that during his military career, the primary threat to the United States was Russia. He stated that the U. S. Army's approach to dealing with this threat was to learn as much as possible about the posture of Soviet forces and defensive/offensive planning. "The systems of JICs helped in that effort. They were part of a larger intelligence-gathering effort that supported the U. S. Army in Europe in understanding what the military capabilities of the Russians and Warsaw Pact were."[31]

Furr showed Scanlon cover sheets of several classified documents and asked if they appeared to be the types of documents that were at the JIC. When Scanlon confirmed that the documents were the types that had been at the JIC, Furr asked him what harm would result if such documents fell into the hands of Soviets.

" . . . the simplest analogy that I can think of is the term 'devastating' . . . So, again it gives him (the enemy) that great potential advantage to win this deadly contest."[32]

Next, Dennis Butcher, a Senior Intelligence Officer from the DIA, was called. A civil service employee specializing in Russian forces, Butcher was approved by the judge as an expert witness in the analysis of Russian capabilities.

Furr introduced several classified documents listing Soviet forces and asked Butcher to comment on them. One such document defined the Soviet Order of Battle for the Southeastern Theater of Military Operations as of 1985. Furr asked Butcher to define "Order of Battle."

> What this document will contain is a comprehensive listing of the complete force structure of every unit and division within this region . . . The knowledge of a potential opponent's force structure, or his Order of Battle, is a fundamental element in making any judgment about the military capability of that force . . . In my opinion this would be absolutely critical information for any Soviet planner. It would give them an excellent insight into the exact and correct U. S. view of the Soviet forces . . . it's also an absolute gold mine from the viewpoint of the Soviet analyst.[33]

The final witness for the day was Stewart Wirtz, a Naval attaché and FBI Liaison Officer, stationed at the U. S. Embassy in Vienna, Austria. Wirtz described how he, at the request of the FBI, had traveled through several small villages in Austria, taking photographs, both aerial and ground-based. Photographs entered into evidence were of Am Stetten, Bad Ischl, Hallein, St. Johann, Zellam See, and the Russian Embassy in Vienna. As each photograph was viewed, specific landmarks were identified and pointed out. Laura Ingersoll conducted the questioning of Wirtz, but she gave no indication of the importance of, or reasons for, introducing the photographs. The court and the jury were left in suspense, but it would not be long before the reason for introducing the photographs would become clear.

As the trial reopened on Thursday, June 7, Furr announced that interpreters would be required for the next witnesses, who were members of the BKA or "German FBI." The BKA agents had participated in the investigation of the espionage activities of Trofimoff and Igor and their arrest and interrogation in 1994.

The witnesses described the events of December 14, 1994, when German authorities arrested Trofimoff and Susemihl simultaneously. The witnesses confirmed that both Trofimoff and Igor were questioned separately for the entire day and held overnight, with the interrogation resuming the next morning. Trofimoff and Igor each vigorously denied any involvement in espionage activities and freely admitted their acquaintance with each other, but only as foster brothers. Transcripts of the interrogations entered into evidence reveal that, on the second day, each appeared separately before Dr. Bernd Dieter Bode, Judge of the German Federal Supreme Court in Karlsruhe.[34,35]

Speaking in German, Norbert Buchbender, who had interrogated Trofimoff, testified that when he arrived at Trofimoff's house at 6:30 a. m. on December 14, 1994, Trofimoff was quiet and offered no objection to the search of his house.

Laura Ingersoll conducted the interrogation of Buchbender and asked him to state the objective of his interrogation.

"We wanted to find out if it was true that Mr. Trofimoff was actually doing espionage for the KGB and wanted to find out if he was really a spy."[36]

Buchbender testified that he read Trofimoff's rights to him and that he went of his own free will to the Nuremberg police station, where his interrogation continued. When Ingersoll asked him to identify Trofimoff, he pointed to him and described the clothes he was wearing.

Ingersoll asked Buchbender if Trofimoff talked about his financial relationship with Susemihl.

"He said that about three dozen times or so he borrowed money from Mr. Susemihl . . . He said it was something like between a thousand and five thousand Deutschmarks . . . Each time."[37]

Bernard Zeitler, a second BKA agent, interrogated Igor while Trofimoff's questioning by Buchbender was underway. While Trofimoff had been quiet and cooperative, Zeitler testified that the priest became very angry when his home was searched and he was taken away for questioning. Zeitler reported the discovery of a screwdriver with a hollowed-out compartment during the search of the apartment. He stated that Igor, as well as Trofimoff, denied any contact with KGB agents. One discrepancy between the statements of the two brothers arose when Igor admitted loaning Trofimoff approximately 1,000 marks, but on only two occasions.

On Friday, June 8, suspense was high in the courtroom as the government called two Cold War double agents, one who betrayed his country because of his convictions, and the other because of his love for a young, beautiful woman. The jury and all observers were spellbound as the amazing and intriguing stories of these two witnesses, one a veteran Russian KGB agent and the other a young American Marine, unfolded.

Boris Yuzhin, with a pleasant, father-like appearance, had a large shock of white hair and was fastidiously dressed. Born in eastern Siberia near the Chinese border, he attended college in the area of his birth, obtaining a degree in radio engineering. Speaking excellent English, he described how he was a Russian patriot and romantic, and he felt honored when he was approached by KGB agents and asked to join their agency. He jumped at the opportunity, even though, he said, his university superiors offered him a luxurious apartment and a salary eight times what his starting KGB pay would be.

"Well, as a patriot of my country . . . I was a typical product of the system, and naturally I was proud to be approached because they made it clear that it's not for everybody."[38]

When Furr asked him to describe the KGB, he replied, "Well, it's a tough question. It's a huge organization. It's like a state within a state . . . nobody knows for sure how many people work for the KGB."[39] Regarding its size, he said he could only guess, and gave his best estimate as at least one-and-a-half million individuals. Questioned about the KGB's relationship with the Russian Orthodox Church, he confirmed that the KGB had agents throughout the church.

Yuzhin said he loved his work from the start and was enrolled in the Red Banner Institute known as the "spy school," where for one year he received intensive training in all aspects of "tradecraft," as well as military training, concentrating on the United States. In answer to Furr's question, he defined "tradecraft."

"This is special spy equipment, like photo cameras, you know, like secret writings, things like that."[40]

His first overseas assignment (1975) was to the University of California, Berkeley. While his "cover" was as a journalism student, his mission as a double agent was to collect political, economic and military intelligence. He testified that during his training, he was told, "Boris, if you want to succeed in your mission against the Americans, you must learn to hate them. Just think for a while to hate Americans . . . So I was pretty sure that all Americans would be my enemies, you know, and I expected them to be hostile."[41]

He described how he began to question his belief in the Communist system.

"And this friendliness that I encountered came as a shock, real shock to me . . . I understood that my perception of this country was incorrect. And more, I realized that Americans were so patriotic that it was a hopeless, you know, idea to try to dissuade American politicians of the superiority of the Communist ideology in order to recruit them on an ideologic basis."[42]

After a brief recess, Furr began to question the basis of his beliefs.

"Yes, that's right. It was a long process . . . finally I came to the realization, you know, that all of my knowledge, all my ideological training were [sic] based on the entire lie . . . the entire system had been deceiving itself . . . I came to a conclusion that it would be better, rather than to be loyal to the system that had been lying for so long, to do something to change it . . . It was not an easy decision . . . it took me a lot of thought, but I was encouraged by Bolzarc's [sic] words who said, 'Only idiots don't change their convictions.' "[43]

He made contact with an American he suspected to be an FBI agent and described how, over time, he became a double agent and began feeding information about his country to the FBI in the hope that he would be able to change the Communist system.

He returned to Russia in 1976 where he was promoted to Major and in 1978 returned to San Francisco to resume his previous role, posing as a journalist for the Soviet news agency, Tass, playing "dirty tricks" to sabotage the careers of politicians disliked by the Kremlin.

In 1982 he returned to Russia and received a promotion to Lieutenant Colonel, but in 1986 he was arrested by the Soviets, charged with treason. He testified that his cover was blown by Aldrich Ames, but a fact not disclosed to the jury was that, just a few days prior to Yuzhin's testimony, Federal prosecutors in Virginia filed an affidavit accusing Robert Hanssen, an FBI agent charged with espionage, of betraying Yuzhin and two other senior KGB officers. The two others were executed, but Yuzhin was lucky. After almost a full year of interrogation, he was given a five-year sentence to a gulag in the northern part of Russia.

In 1992 President Boris Yeltsin, as part of a general amnesty for political prisoners, freed Yuzhin. ". . . for me, it was like a shock. Of course, I didn't expect even to—to survive all of these 15 years because conditions were terrible . . . I believe it was a political decision made by Yeltsin.[44] I didn't think I would survive," he said. Now an American citizen, he lives in the United States.

The next two witnesses were FBI agents who described operations during which American traitors were arrested while meeting with KGB agents. While neither of these operations had a direct bearing on the Trofimoff case, the KGB officers involved were identified and their pictures entered into evidence. Later, FBI Special Agent Droujinsky, during his videotaped meeting with Trofimoff, would present these pictures to Trofimoff for identification as individuals he did business with while at the Nuremberg JIC.

Next came the poignant and sad tale of Clayton Lonetree, a native Indian American, who was raised in an orphanage and joined the Marines in 1979 at the age of 17. He reenlisted in 1984 and was assigned to the Marine Corps Security Program, trained as an Embassy Guard, and sent to the American Embassy in Moscow. Tried and convicted of espionage, he was sentenced to a term of 30 years, which was later reduced to 15 years. He served a total of nine years and two months before being released. The government subpoenaed him to testify in the Trofimoff trial.

Lonetree, a nondrinking loner, testified that he never felt accepted as an equal by the other hard-drinking Marines stationed with him at the embassy. Soon he began to drink heavily to gain acceptance. Eventually, he noticed a pretty young Russian embassy employee, Violetta Sanni, and they began to exchange glances as they crossed paths during the day.

Furr asked if Lonetree was aware of the rules that did not allow fraternization with Russian employees. "Yes, there was a strict rule that we had to follow. We were not permitted to talk with any Soviet or other citizens of Communist countries."

Furr asked Lonetree to tell about Violetta. "She was a Russian . . . a clerical worker . . . She was . . . she did not look Soviet. She was very attractive."[46]

Clayton testified that he took occasional subway rides and lonely walks. One day, while sitting on a bench in a park, he saw her walking across the park. "I caught up to her, and I got on the same car in the subway as she did and—and we had a conversation . . . And we got off and had a little walk."[47]   Later, on another subway, he noticed Violetta sitting at the other end of the car. They exchanged glances and, "Suddenly," he said, "I found myself sitting next to her. She began to go with me on my walks, and soon we were having meetings on the subway."

Furr asked Lonetree if he was physically attracted to Violetta. He spoke softly with polite respect for Lonetree, as it was clear to all that the young Marine was extremely agitated and close to breaking down emotionally.

Lonetree testified that it was not long before Violetta took him to an apartment and introduced him to "Uncle Sasha."

Furr asked Lonetree if Uncle Sasha asked him questions about the embassy. "Over the next two or three months, did you—did you violate any rules regarding . . .the Embassy and bring some Embassy property . . . or something about the Embassy to him?"[48]

"Regrettably, yes. I did . . . I brought him floor plans of the American Embassy."[49]   Lonetree was visibly upset and needed a few seconds to compose himself.

Furr asked Lonetree if he ever considered reporting his activities to his superiors.

"I—I did try once. I—I went to the security officer's apartment building after the meeting and I had raised my hand to knock on his apartment door, but I—I just didn't knock."[50]   Lonetree was hooked and realized he was beyond salvation.

Embassy security guard assignments are limited to one year, and in the spring of 1986, Lonetree was transferred from Moscow to the U. S. Embassy in Vienna. He told Furr that before he left Moscow, Uncle Sasha gave him instructions for making another contact in Vienna. He was in Vienna only for a short time when Uncle Sasha appeared. This time, Sasha had money for Lonetree. At first, he refused to take it, but eventually he gave in and accepted his first payment of $500.

Lonetree's testimony resumed on Monday morning, June 11, as he told of a meeting in September 1986 when Uncle Sasha introduced him to "George," a new handler. Later, on December 12, he had a meeting with "George."

Lonetree testified that his new handler said to him, "Clayton, things are going to be different with me . . . I don't care about those things that Sasha wanted from you . . . that's not important."[51]

"George" immediately put more pressure on the young Marine, asking him to install listening devices inside the Embassy. He called for frequent meetings, normally in various churches in Vienna. Lonetree became more and more disturbed.

Furr asked, "After you finished the meeting on December 12, what was your—what was your state of mind as far as continuing with what you had been doing with Sasha?"[52]

"I was extremely conscious of what I had been doing. I was so far into this. I was depressed. I was violating my own principles of what I believe in. I wasn't living up to those standards. Finally I came forward and told somebody at the Embassy."[53] At this point, Lonetree broke down and began to sob.

Lonetree answered "no" when Furr asked if he ever saw "George" again.

To other questions from Furr, Lonetree testified that he had been convicted of espionage, receiving a sentence of 30 years, but was released after nine years and two months.

Lonetree's story is depressing: he is the only Marine ever convicted of espionage, but while his story was not directly related to Trofimoff's case, the jury was able to witness a vivid example of the insidious nature of KGB recruiting methods—another lesson in their education.

The entire court was eager to hear the next witness. The two three-hour videotapes had been a favorite subject of the press since Furr described them a year before in Trofimoff's bail bond hearing. Special Agent Dimitry Droujinsky orchestrated the effort to lure Trofimoff with letters and telephone calls to the meetings in a Melbourne hotel and subsequently to Tampa, where he expected to receive money but instead walked into the waiting arms of FBI agents. Everyone in the courtroom, observers, reporters, the jury, court employees, had been waiting a long time to hear and see Droujinsky, listen to the many telephone calls he made to Trofimoff, and watch the videotapes. There was an electric tension in the courtroom when Furr called his witness to the stand.

The full story of how Droujinsky lured Trofimoff to a Melbourne, Florida, hotel for two three-hour videotaped meetings is contained in Chapter 9, but listening to the recorded calls and watching the videotapes in the presence of the FBI agent added a deeper, more dramatic dimension to the matter.

When Special Agent Droujinsky was introduced to the court, his appearance added more suspense to the scene. He was an experienced "False Flag" operative, and the government was concerned with the possibility of compromising his identity. He wore what appeared to be a heavy toupee, a false mustache, and had heavy, horn-rimmed glasses, which were removed each time he read any document handed to him. His testimony lasted for almost four days as he exposed the jury to letters, telephone conversations, and six hours of videotapes. Before the recordings were played, each jury member received a thick volume containing transcripts of all calls so they could easily follow the conversations. All jurors took full advantage of the books, carefully following each call as the recordings were played. For the first time, jurors were able to hear Trofimoff's plaintive voice. It was a dramatic scene, the first of many to come, and the jury, as well as all spectators, was engrossed in this intriguing tale of agents and double agents.

One by one, the letters sent to Trofimoff were displayed and read to the jury, and the recordings of all telephone calls were played. The jury heard a worried and, at times, annoyed Trofimoff as he repeatedly stated his wishes to be left alone, steadfastly denying any knowledge of or involvement with the activities "Igor" spoke of.

On the tapes of the meetings, Trofimoff initially continued to reject all of Droujinsky's overtures, but as time passed, his mood and voice clearly became less stressful. He began to discuss his past activities more freely. The jury listened attentively as they heard Trofimoff's demeanor slowly change from a frightened and desperate tone to a calmer, more relaxed nature. Droujinsky's perseverance and skill were beginning to pay off. Trofimoff was on the verge of agreeing to a face-to-face meeting with the agent.

Furr, in interrogating Droujinsky, proceeded to draw from him details of the elaborate web he had constructed. After each letter was displayed and the following telephone conversations were played for the jury, Furr posed questions to Droujinsky to emphasize the more important and salient segments of Trofimoff's comments.

Referring to the telephone transcripts, Furr asked Droujinsky if, on page 8, he continued to try to get Trofimoff to meet with him. When the agent said, "Yes," Furr asked what Trofimoff's response was. " . . . he has been out of everything for too many years . . ."[54] Furr asked Droujinsky to explain what Trofimoff's response meant.

"Well, I understood that he has been cooperating with the KGB before, but now he's not doing it anymore."[55]

Hernandez objected to this response, and after a sidebar conference, the judge sustained the objection, but no objection could erase the perception that had been established in the minds of the jurors.

Everyone in the courtroom was engrossed with Droujinsky's skill in his "False Flag"operation recorded in the telephone transcripts as he complimented, cajoled, and slowly but surely convinced Trofimoff that he (Droujinsky) was, in fact, a KGB representative who was interested in protecting and helping Trofimoff. Droujinsky stressed that he needed Trofimoff's help in resurrecting damaged KGB files, and was willing to provide financial assistance in return. From a belligerent, suspicious and noncooperative introvert who would not talk and wanted nothing to do with Droujinsky's initial appeals, Trofimoff slowly evolved into a cooperative, trusting person who began to speak freely and finally agreed to meet with his new friend.

After playing the recording of the telephone call of February 18, 1999, which established the February 24 meeting in the Melbourne hotel, the tapes of the two three-hour meetings were introduced into evidence and played for the court. Again, the jurors were given thick volumes of transcripts to facilitate following the conversation while watching the video. While Trofimoff sat nonchalantly and seldom looked at the videotape, all jurors seemed to be mesmerized as the video depicted Trofimoff, sitting comfortably and sipping coffee, as he gave the most intimate details of his espionage activities over a 25 year period. As he spoke he gesticulated, arms waving, freely describing how he took classified documents from the JIC to his home, photographed them, and later delivered the undeveloped and repackaged boxes of exposed film to his foster brother, Igor, and, in other cases, to KGB officers. Full of pride and braggadocio, he exhibited no regret or excuses for his activities, as he boasted that he did it for the Motherland.

At the beginning, Trofimoff remained wary and suspicious, asking repeatedly if the agent was "wired" or if the meeting was being recorded. He was still cautious when, after discussing the cameras and film he used, Droujinsky asked him where he did his photography. Trofimoff smirked as Droujiinsky told Furr that Trofimoff would not tell him.

At this point the judge recessed the court for the day. After the jury cleared the courtroom, she requested comments on a motion from the press asking that the videotapes be released for public viewing. (Although the tapes were being shown in the courtroom, they had not yet been released to the press.)

The government was concerned that Droujinsky's identity would be compromised by release of the tapes and insisted on protecting him by disguising his voice and clouding his face wherever he appeared. Hernandez objected strenuously to any release of the tapes, arguing that, regardless of the judge's instructions to the jury, they could not be fully protected from the exposure that was sure to come when the tapes were released to the media.

The judge decided to withhold her decision until she could review the issues and arguments. "Let me think about it over the evening hours, and I'll enter an order in the morning."[56] The judge then declared recess at 5:00 p.m. to reconvene at 9:30 a.m. the next day.

The judge's first order of business on Tuesday, June 12, was to issue her order concerning the public release of the videotapes. "It's a balancing test . . . I guess I came down on the side of going ahead and providing it for two general reasons: . . . there is a presumption that if I instruct the jury not to watch anything, they will not watch it . . . The second thing is we've had the press in this courtroom throughout the trial . . . so the commentary is already there."[57] Her decision was to release the tapes with the restrictions imposed as requested by the government.

Playing of the videotapes resumed, and almost immediately, Trofimoff's concern when the meeting began was obvious to the jury, as they observed him asking Droujinsky if he was recording his entire history. Satisfied with Droujinsky's assurance, he became more comfortable and readily discussed topics such as his trips to Austria to meet KGB officers where he delivered undeveloped film and received cash in exchange. He also talked about his penchant for "the good life," which led to his money problems, and his use of the gooseneck lamps and tripod.

After the videotape of the first three hours was shown, Furr questioned Droujinsky at length to emphasize particularly significant points raised during the tape. Some of the more significant items he covered included Trofimoff's continuing concern and suspicion about possible recording of his comments and his statement regarding his method of transmitting classified documents. His repeated comment that he was "a professional" and his concern with the possibility that his fingerprints might be discovered on the rolls of film he delivered were also significant items. Other important points included his admission of having copied an entire library and that his payments generally came from his foster brother, Igor.

The second videotape was started late Tuesday afternoon, but before it was completed, the court recessed until the following morning.

Viewing of the second videotape resumed on Wednesday, June 13, with Trofimoff describing how his espionage career began with the financial assistance provided by his foster brother. After this video-tape was shown, Furr, questioning Droujinsky, emphasized the salient points of the taped meeting, including the KGB officers identified by Trofimoff and the Austrian villages where he met them and Igor Susemihl's recruitment of his foster brother. Other salient points included Trofimoff's boast that he had been awarded the Order of the Red Banner and his continuing concern when, after being shown cover sheets of classified documents and asked if he had passed them to the KGB, he accused Droujinsky of putting a rope around his neck.

After the videotape was completed, tapes of several ensuing tele-phone calls were played as the jurors followed the conversations in their books. Furr then discussed the calls with Droujinsky who con-firmed that, prior to the videotaped meetings, he had initiated each telephone discussion with Trofimoff, but after the meetings, Trofimoff initiated each contact.

The trial resumed on Thursday, June 14, with the playing of addi-tional telephone calls, and as the jury followed each call with their copy of the transcript, they could hear Trofimoff's calm request for help become a desperate plea for money as he threatened suicide if help was not received. Droujinsky had done a masterful job of prom-ising, delaying, and promising again and again until Trofimoff was frantic to receive any amount of money from the organization he had been led to believe was the KGB.

Finally, on May 10, 2000, almost three years after Germaine Salazar delivered Droujinsky's hand-written letter to Trofimoff's home, and after many extended telephone calls and six hours of videotaped meetings, Trofimoff's good friend, "Igorek," called him to say that funds were approved for payment, and a date was set for Trofimoff to travel to Tampa, Florida, to receive the money. His request for assis-tance, starting at more than $43,000, had dropped to a mere $23,000. Trofimoff was prepared to meet with "Igorek" for a relatively small amount, which would cover only a part of his larger debt. Special Agent Droujinsky had successfully completed another of his many "False Flag" operations. All that remained to be accomplished was to arrest Trofimoff when he arrived in Tampa. That task was to be carried out by FBI Special Agent Anthony Wagoner.

On Friday, June 15, FBI Special Agent Anthony Wagoner, a foreign counterintelligence specialist, was called as a witness for the prosecution. Wagoner's participation in the arrest of Trofimoff has been covered in Chapter 10 and will not be repeated here.

Hernandez' first big victory came after Wagoner's testimony when the government attempted to link the Trofimoff case to one of the most sensational U. S. spy cases ever: that of Aldrich Ames, the former head of counterintelligence in the CIA's Soviet branch. Ames, one of the most damaging spies in U. S. history, was considered responsible for the execution of at least 10 foreign agents who were spying for the United States. He was arrested in 1994, entered a plea of guilty, and was sentenced to prison for life without parole.

Two FBI agents were prepared to testify that a telephone number discovered in Ames' home was also found in an address book taken from Igor Susemihl's home when he was arrested in 1994.

Hernandez objected and asked for a sidebar, which lasted for some time. When the sidebar discussion was over, the judge dismissed the jury to explain the situation to the court. Judge Bucklew said that Hernandez maintained that linking the two cases would be unfairly prejudicial to his client, arguing that linking the two cases gave no evidence of espionage activity.

Judge Bucklew agreed with Hernandez. "I think I've got to come down on the side of Mr. Trofimoff . . . because I can see that it (allowing the two witnesses to testify) does have some relevance . . . but I think the unfair—or danger of unfair prejudice . . . outweighs any relevance . . . I just am concerned . . . I'm sustaining the objection."[58]

After the judge's explanation, the jury was recalled.

Time had arrived for another lesson for the jury—photography. David Davies from the FBI laboratories in Washington, D. C., took the stand. He was designated as an expert witness in espionage, tradecraft, cameras, and concealment devices. In response to questions, he described the various cameras used in spying activities, taking special pains to stand directly in front of the jury to exhibit an Olympus double-frame camera and demonstrate how it could be used to take pictures of two pages simultaneously.

In response to a question from Ingersoll, Davies confirmed that the Olympus could be mounted on a tripod and demonstrated how the tripod, with a special attachment, could hold the camera upside-down for photographing documents below it. He emphasized that a tripod without the special attachment could not be used in that manner.

Ingersoll then asked Davies to comment on lighting requirements in photographing documents.

"When you're going to illuminate the document, you basically want to illuminate it from both sides . . . If you had a single light bulb, what's going to happen is this side of the document is going to receive more light than this side . . . Standard illumination is two 100-watt light bulbs, one on each side."[59]

Ingersoll asked about the need for a marked frame to align the documents to be photographed.

"If you don't have that marked frame and you just put the paper down there, you're going to have to look through the view finder every time to make sure that you've got the entire document, you know, on your image."[60]

Asked to give an estimate of the film and time required to photograph a document of 400-500 pages. Davies replied, "Oh, probably eight rolls or so . . . Changing the film, it probably would take you a couple of hours to do it."[61]

Ingersoll read aloud what Trofimoff said about repackaging the film after taking pictures, and asked Davies if Trofimoff's description agreed with Davies' understanding of the practice of Soviet Intelligence Service agents. "That's a common practice, yes, ma'am."[62]

Special Agent Julian Koerner, a 29-year FBI veteran and head of the FBI's Tampa espionage unit, gave the next lesson to the jury. This time, it was a crash course on KGB recruitment procedures. The judge accepted him as an expert witness regarding Soviet Russian Intelligence Services, including the KGB and their recruitment and targeting of Americans.

Furr asked Koerner which organization the FBI generally sees as the largest threat to America, and without hesitation, Koerner replied that it was the KGB.

Furr asked, "What portions of the KGB do you as an investigator in this area run up against the most?"[63]

"The First Chief Directorate, which was the foreign intelligence gathering arm of the KGB. They're also responsible for counterintelligence outside of the Soviet Union."[64]

Furr then asked Koerner to describe the primary goal of the KGB's First Directorate.

"To spot Americans with access to information, to assess the

Americans, to attempt to develop a recruitment, and attempt to get intelligence against the Americans . . . to actually recruit and handle the Americans after they are recruited."[65]

Asked to describe the recruitment process, Koerner emphasized the difference between an agent (the person to be recruited or the non-professional informant) and the intelligence officer, who does the recruiting. He explained that recruitment was accomplished in three phases.

First, the officer identifies the needs of the target and begins an introductory phase during which a relationship is established and then moved from a professional relationship to a social or friendship level. Second, in the development phase, the officer moves the relationship to a personal level where questions are asked and requests for information are made. At first, innocent questions are asked or requests are made for innocuous, unclassified information. Finally, in the third phase, once an individual has passed classified information, rewards are tendered and the target agent has been fully recruited.

Once an agent is recruited, contact is maintained and periodic visits are made to the agent to "take his pulse," inquire of his welfare, identify any tensions or worries, pass on new techniques, give rewards, and insure that the agent knows the KGB is concerned with his welfare.

At the conclusion of Special Agent Koerner's testimony, Furr told the judge that while it was still early in the day, the government had run out of witnesses as a result of her recent ruling for the defense.

The judge released the jury and, after their departure, broached the subject of the report of the psychiatrist who had examined Trofimoff. Reports in the media had speculated that the report would conclude that Trofimoff's mental condition was such that he could have easily fabricated the entire story he related on the taped sessions in the Melbourne hotel.

Previously, Furr had asked to see the report before the psychiatrist appeared as a witness, but he had not yet been given that opportunity. The judge pointed out that Furr's request had two parts:

> The second part is to order that the Government get
> the results of any . . . tests bearing on the defendant's
> mental state . . . I don't think there's any doubt that
> the Government is entitled to the results of any cur-
> rent . . .tests . . . So, I'm going to grant the motion as it
> pertains to providing the Government with the results

of any current . . . tests. . . . As far as the second . . . I
need a little time to look at this . . . and it's all moot if
Mr. Hernandez isn't going to call him as a witness
anyway.[66]

Hernandez replied that his client did not want to undergo another
long examination, but that he would confer with him and would give
his response when court convened on Monday.

It seemed clear at this time that Hernandez would not call the doctor as a witness. In doing so, Trofimoff in all probability would be
forced to undergo another examination by a doctor selected by the
government, something he obviously did not want to do.

On Monday, June 18, before the jury was called, Hernandez
advised the judge that, after discussing the matter with his client, they
had agreed not to call the psychiatrist who had examined Trofimoff
earlier. Evidently it was decided that the agony of another long examination and the potential danger that might arise from another examination was enough to set aside any advantages that might accrue
from calling the psychiatrist.

The government then proceeded to call one of its more interesting
witnesses. His name? John Doe! After being sworn, the witness stated
he was unable to publicly state his real name, and the judge confirmed that the court was allowing him to testify under the pseudonym, "John Doe." A proper, dignified and well-dressed individual
with a large shock of white hair, "Doe" faced the jury and the court
with a friendly expression. In clipped, terse speech with a decidedly
British accent, he testified that he was a 30-year veteran of the British
Secret Intelligence Service (BSIS), which corresponds to the American
CIA. John Doe presented more the appearance of a benign father figure than what one would expect of a clandestine member of the
supersecret MI6.

Ingersoll asked Doe to define the BSIS.

Doe replied, "It's a British secret intelligence service, basically a
collector of information on events abroad, outside of the country . . .
The press likes to call it 'MI6' . . . That comes from the original cover
name of the organization . . . Military Intelligence Department Six."[67]
(Movie buffs remember "MI6" as the agency made famous by the
master fictional spy, James Bond.)

Doe identified himself as a specialist in Soviet/Russian affairs. He
had studied the Russian constitution to become thoroughly familiar
with the structure of the Russian government. He testified that he was

fluent in Russian, both in writing and speaking, and proceeded to spin a yarn that was to be the equal of any fictional spy story: the saga of Vasili Mitrokhin.

John Doe stated that Mitrokhin worked as an archivist for the KGB, with all KGB paperwork passing through him. When asked if the KGB kept detailed files, Doe answered, "The KGB was meticulous in record-keeping and kept everything for a very long time."[68]

His testimony covered Mitrokhin's activities during the period 1972 to 1984. Testifying for almost six hours, he brought some original papers and showed them to the jury. He described the different files maintained by the KGB and provided copies of files that made reference to the code names Markiz, Antey, Konsul, and Ikar. He testified that after Mitrokhin and his files arrived in England, he worked secretly with Mitrokhin for six years, translating and organizing the material.

"Mr. Doe," Ingersoll asked, "did you prepare in—in connection with your testimony here today a kind of a summary of some of those principal files? I'm showing you Government Exhibit 102. Is that the summary that you helped prepare for this purpose?"[69]

Doe answered, "Yes," and the summary of the Mitrokhin findings was entered into evidence. When the judge declared the court to be in recess until the next morning, Terry Furr's announcement that the prosecution's next witness would be Oleg Kalugin, a retired senior official of the KGB, caused a noticeable stir throughout the room.

On Tuesday, June 19, the court opened with more than 30 observers, the largest attendance to date. Everyone was in suspense, waiting to hear from the most famous of all the government witnesses, Oleg Kalugin.

A short, spry and energetic individual with thinning, dark hair, Kalugin bounded into the courtroom and approached the bar to be sworn. His face was square-jawed, and his dark, beady eyes swept over the entire room as he settled comfortably into his chair at the witness table. Speaking in perfect English with little accent, he related that he was born in Leningrad in 1934, the only child of a KGB official. He experienced little difficulty in attaining his ambition to become an agent of the KGB, he testified. After becoming a member of the KGB, his first assignment was attending a two-year intelligence school.

In 1958, as a Senior Lieutenant, he was assigned to the United States, with a cover as a Fulbright Scholar. He testified that his first mission was to learn as much as possible about the United States. He said that he advanced rapidly, and after several different assignments in the United States at the age of forty, he became a general, head of Directorate "K," reporting to the KGB's Chief of Intelligence. At the time of his appearance in the Trofimoff trial, he was a retired Major General and a resident of Maryland. Kalugin's book *The First Directorate*, describes his intelligence career with the KGB.[70]

When asked to describe the KGB record-keeping system, he testified that precise documentation is of prime importance to the KGB and that detailed records are kept of everything that transpires. He described two unique files maintained for each agent: the DOR file, which contains all records and documents relating to the handling of the agent, and the Working Production File, which keeps records of all materials obtained from the agent. "KGB officers always referred to the agents by their code name," he testified, "and agents never knew what their code names were."[71]

Furr asked if the real identity of an agent appeared in any of these files, and if so, who would have access.

"The first one contains both the real name and the code name," Kalugin said. "Access to those files, over many years, would have been limited to, at most, one-half dozen persons."[72]

Furr then produced a list of agent code names and asked Kalugin if he had prepared it.

"This is a list of valuable assets, only a fraction of the total. I personally wrote the list in late '73. At that time, agent Markiz was number 1."[73]

Answering Furr's question, Kalugin testified that he had access to all operational files, but that he could not review all operational files, nor could he meet with all agents.

"That would be impossible. I did review files of some of the most valuable agents."[74]

Furr asked if Kalugin reviewed the file of agent Markiz and asked if he knew the agent's real name.

"Yes, I did. His name was George Trofimoff."[75]

If anyone in the courtroom were dozing or inattentive at that time, Kalugin's revelation served as an immediate wakeup call.

Asked to tell the court what information he learned about Markiz, Kalugin stated that the agent, an employee of the U. S. Army's 66th Military Intelligence Group, had been recruited by a friend in Germany, a Russian Orthodox Priest, who was a KGB agent. "Markiz was handled by the KGB office in Berlin."[76]

Furr asked Kalugin if, as Chief of Directorate "K," he met with all agents.

> Again, that would have been impossible. However, we were expected to visit agents in the field occasionally, 'to look them in the eye.' I decided to meet with Markiz because he was one of our top agents . . . I met with him in Austria, the favorite place for KGB meetings.[77]

Furr asked if there were any particular issues or problems he wanted to discuss with Markiz. He replied:

> There were several things I wanted to discuss. First, Markiz had expressed great dissatisfaction with the money he was receiving, and from a review of his files, I thought that his productivity could be improved. I wanted to discuss some complaints we had received about Markiz from another source, and; finally, I was concerned with reports that Markiz planned to divorce his American wife and marry a young German nurse. I didn't want him to lose his U. S. security clearance from a marriage to a German.[78]

Kalugin went on to explain that the meeting with Markiz was not a regular operational meeting, but a special occasion during which he hoped to see if Markiz was trustworthy. He did not expect to receive any information at the meeting, nor did he plan to make any payment to the agent. He stated that the meeting took place on a promenade along the river in Bad Ischl.

Furr asked Kalugin how he recognized Trofimoff.

> I had been given a physical description—a big, tall, husky individual. I had seen his picture before the meeting. As we approached from opposite directions, I introduced myself as Oleg, and he responded that he was glad to meet me.

> He only knew he was going to meet a superior officer and didn't know my position. During our discussion, I asked if he was fully trusted by his superiors and his coworkers, and he assured me that he was trusted implicitly by all. Asked if there were any problems in getting material out, he reported no problems. He spoke excellent Russian.[79]

A rare moment of humor arose when Furr asked Kalugin if he mentioned Trofimoff's plan to marry the young German nurse.

"I discussed his plans to marry the young girl, trying to dissuade him. He said to me, 'When you're my age and feel the embrace of a young eighteen-year-old woman, you forget all about security.' I told him I understood that."[80]

With Kalugin's statement, the courtroom broke up and everyone, observers, the jury, and members of the court, snickered and grinned widely.

Kalugin told how he urged Trofimoff to improve his performance and look for more intelligence sources to include human sources. He testified that he was satisfied with the outcome of the meeting and that Trofimoff's financial rewards were increased.

"After the meeting I had no concerns with his honesty and integrity as a Soviet agent, working for us. During the next few years, the volume of material he provided showed a marked increase, and the quality improved significantly."[81]

When Furr asked if the documents provided by Trofimoff were valuable, Kalugin replied, "They revealed the extent of U. S. knowledge of Soviet forces . . . When we received the information from him, we took action with defensive measures. Since 1974, the quality improved significantly. One document, which listed CIA intelligence targets for 1978 to 1981, was very valuable and was sent to the Soviet Prime Minister. It was extremely helpful, and caused the Soviet military to make drastic changes."[82]

Furr asked Kalugin if he saw Trofimoff again after his meeting in Austria.

"Yes. In 1977 or 1978, I was in Yalta, the Crimea, and saw him there. He was invited to visit his country as a reward for his service. He was one hundred percent Russian, with some nobility in his background. He was staying in a resort hotel maintained for Soviet Armed Forces. It was a coincidence that both of us were there at the same time."[83]

Furr wanted to know how Trofimoff, an American, could have visited Russia.

"Visiting agents have a small piece of paper placed in their passport, authorizing entry. When they leave Russia, the paper is removed, and no record of the visit remains with the passport. I think he came from Vienna through Moscow, but I didn't make the arrangements."[84]

Asked if he could identify Trofimoff in the courtroom, Kalugin pointed to Trofimoff, saying, "He's wearing a light blue suit and a white shirt. He looks almost the same. He's lost some weight. He's older. But we all are."[85]

This was a major turning point in the entire trial, the first time a witness had specifically identified Trofimoff as Markiz, the KGB agent who had passed volumes of American secrets to the Soviets.

Furr asked Kalugin if he had ever met the priest involved with Trofimoff.

"In 1978 in Moscow, I invited him to my home. He did good work, particularly in recruiting Markiz. I wanted to thank him for what he had done."[86]

When asked if he was familiar with the Order of the Red Banner. Kalugin replied, "Yes. I have it. It is the highest military award for meritorious and dangerous service."[87]

Furr asked if the medal had ever been given to an agent working for Russia, and he responded that he had been involved in one example.

During the author's conversation with Kalugin in September 2002, he stated that while the example he cited during the trial was not an award of the medal to Trofimoff, he did confirm that Trofimoff did receive the medal. "After all," he said, "he deserved the award for the work he did for us."[88]

Furr asked Kalugin why he was transferred out of intelligence.

"I wrote a letter to Gorbachev, complaining about the Soviet system I became a public critic of the Soviet system and the KGB, was charged with leaking state secrets, and relieved of my duties because of insubordination. I could have landed in jail, but I was elected to Parliament and served there until the USSR's downfall . . . Now, I am a consultant to AT&T, and a permanent resident of the United States."[89]

Answering Furr's question, Kalugin confirmed that he had, in fact, described Trofimoff in his book without identifying him by name.[90]

Asked if he was appearing in the trial of his own free will, he replied, "I was given a subpoena . . . if I had been given a choice, I would not have come . . . but as an American resident, I had to abide by the law."[91]

After Kalugin's testimony, Special Agent Gary Pepper was recalled to give results of his research on Trofimoff's pension payments. He testified that during the year 2000, the civil service and military pensions paid to the defendant totaled almost $6,000 per month.

The day's last witness was retired four-star General Glen Otis, the Commanding General, U. S. Army, Europe, in 1983. Furr asked him to describe the extent of U. S. forces in Europe at that time. Otis, a small and slim West Point graduate (1953), testified that while the United States and NATO forces consisted of many thousands of troops, they were significantly outnumbered by Soviet Bloc forces. In the event of hostilities the knowledge of enemy deployments and plans would be of utmost importance.

"Our knowledge of his forces was critical to the way we laid out our defense plans. On the other hand, if he knew what we knew, it gave him an advantage because he could then change."[92]

With the testimony of General Otis, the government rested its case. The judge released the jury, placing the court in recess until Thursday morning.

After the jury cleared the courtroom, Hernandez entered a motion requesting acquittal of his client. The essence of his motion was that Trofimoff had, for a long period, been subjected to "outrageous government conduct"[93] with repeated offers of financial assistance from the special agent, posing as a representative of the KGB.

Hernandez continued his impassioned plea by alleging that the evidence against his client was inadequate. " . . . I submit that the evidence is insufficient to—to connect Antey, Konsul and Markiz to the defendant, and the court should grant a motion for judgment of acquittal."[94]

In response, the judge denied Hernandez' motion. "So, I have a hard time understanding how government—outrageous government conduct, should there have been any, should cause me to dismiss this indictment for a crime that occurred years ago. So, I would deny the motion."[95]

The judge then declared the court to be in recess until Thursday morning.

Chapter
12

THE TROFIMOFF
DEFENSE

Crimes are not to be measured by the issue of events,
but from the bad intentions of men.
—Marcus Tillius Cicero (106–43 B. C.,
Philippic. I, 14 (Quoted from the tragedian Accius)

Trofimoff's defense began when the court opened on Thursday, June 21, 2001. Hernandez called as his first witness Walter Burgreeff, a resident of Granada Hills, California. Burgreeff testified that he was born in Yugoslavia of Russian parents (his father served with the White Forces during the revolution). He arrived in the United States in December, 1949, obtained his citizenship in 1954, and was drafted into the U. S. Army in 1952. He first met Trofimoff during basic training, and they became good friends because of their similar backgrounds. Each of them had lost family members to the Communists, and they often discussed their parents.

Hernandez asked Burgreeff if he had had good reasons to avoid being drafted.

"Yes, all legal rights . . . because I was the only son and the only provider." (for his mother).[1]

Hernandez asked if he made any efforts to evade the draft.

"Oh, no, sir, on the contrary. It was a privilege."[2]

Hernandez spent time questioning Burgreeff, who confirmed that he and Trofimoff had known each other for some time, that they had similar backgrounds, and had remained close friends over the years.

Hernandez asked Burgreeff about Trofimoff's reputation at the JIC.

"Impeccable," he replied. "I know one thing, that our, you know, superiors and then his peers and my peers all had a great respect . . . I have never, never seen anything that was—could be criticized of his behavior."[3]

"Did you know his foster brother, Igor Susemihl?"

Burgreeff testified that he knew about Igor but had never met him. When Hernandez asked if Trofimoff tried to hide his relationship with Igor, he shook his negatively. "No sir, not at all."[4]

Laura Ingersoll conducted the cross-examination of Bugreeff. In answer to her first question, he testified that he was unaware that Trofimoff never revealed his relationship with Igor to the U. S. Army.

"Are you aware that Russian archives show that an officer of the 66th Military Intelligence in Germany during the late 60s through the 80s for over 20 years . . . turned over classified documents to the Soviets?"[5] Ingersoll asked.

Burgreeff shook his head, denying knowledge of Ingersoll's statement.

Ingersoll continued. "You said that George Trofimoff talked to you freely . . . and that he never hid anything . . . If you knew that for 20 years George Trofimoff . . . had taken classified documents home . . . secretly photographed them . . . and then sold that film to the KGB . . . if you knew that George Trofimoff had met with KGB officers . . . gave them classified U. S. information in exchange for money . . . if you knew that George Trofimoff told a man who he believed was a KGB Officer . . . in my soul I'm Russian, I'm not an American . . . would that change your opinion?"[6]

"Of course," he answered, nodding affirmatively.

The next defense witness was Arthur Farash who testified that he was an American citizen employed by the Washington State Patrol. He joined the U. S. Army in 1955 and retired in 1983.

Farash, after identifying Trofimoff, testified that after returning from Vietnam as a POW interrogator he was assigned to the Nuremberg JIC from November 1968 to October 1973. During that time Trofimoff was the civilian head of the U. S. Army element.

When asked about Trofimoff's reputation, Farash replied, "His reputation was impeccable . . . I had a very strong opinion of Mr. Trofimoff's character. He was a very strict, upstanding person . . . He was very fair with us, but on the other hand he was very strict . . . in some way he might have been considered a little arrogant . . ."[8]

Farash then described the physical layout of the JIC, internal procedures, and security systems. Responding to Hernandez' question, he testified that he had never seen Trofimoff remove documents from the JIC or engage in any suspicious behavior. In his cross-examination, Furr asked Farash if he watched others to see if they were taking items out of the JIC. When Farash shook his head and said, "No," Furr asked if he trusted the people he worked with at the JIC.

"Absolutely. As I say, we were soldiers, we had to trust each other."[9] Furr asked, "Would your opinion regarding Mr. Trofimoff be changed—would it be affected if you heard that for 20 or 25 years he sold classified information to the KGB?"[10]

"I would have to keep an open mind . . . If I knew he did it, it would be a different story."[11]

Testimony of the next defense witness provided one of the most explosive and sensational scenes of the entire trial.

Bernard (Bernie) Frenkel was born in Hanover, Germany, in 1925. He went underground in Holland to escape the Nazis, but was arrested by the Gestapo in 1942 and spent two years at Auschwitz. Short and overweight almost to the point of obesity, he related how, after his release from the prison camp, he came to America in 1949, was drafted into the army in 1950, and became a U. S. citizen in 1953. He was first assigned to the Nuremberg JIC from 1968 to 1971. After a tour in Korea and intelligence training in Arizona, he was reassigned to the JIC in 1981, where he remained until he retired in 1993.

Frenkel had nothing but good things to say about Trofimoff's reputation and character. He gave a detailed description of the JIC's physical layout, security system, and internal procedures for handling and safeguarding classified documents.

The fireworks began in cross-examination, when Furr asked Frenkel, ". . . if you knew that for 20 years George Trofimoff took classified documents out of the JIC, took them to his home where he secretly photographed them, then sold the film to the KGB . . . if Mr. Trofimoff met with a top KGB officer . . . and they talked about Mr. Trofimoff providing even more documents . . ."[12]

Before Furr could finish his question, Frenkel jumped to his feet, red-faced, and glowered at Furr. ". . . I tell you that I would say the officer, the KGB officer who told you is a liar." Still on his feet, he pointed a chubby finger at Furr, his beady eyes bulging with rage ". . . are you familiar with Mr. Trofimoff's background? Well, you tell me that the man whose entire family got killed by the Soviet Union is and will act as a spy for his country? I want to see some proof that he did it."[13]

Frenkel's indignation knew no boundaries as Furr continued with more questions. "This man you knew, the man you knew as George Trofimoff, would he have made a statement that in my heart I've never been an American, I'm a Russian and—when he's talking to someone he thinks is a KGB agent . . . he said he did it for the homeland."[14]

"I have never heard him make such a statement."[15]

The heated exchange subsided when Hernandez objected to one of Furr's statements as being argumentative. The judge drew some chuckles from the jury when she asked, "On which point?"

Before stepping down from the witness stand, Frenkel took one more swipe at Furr. "The prosecuting attorney, I think, should be very well aware that it is a very well-known fact that all officials who, in their contact or worked for the Russian Orthodox Church in the Soviet Union, or worked for the Protestant church, or the Catholic church, in any Warsaw Pact country, all were controlled by, and had contact with, the KGB or with the countries suspecting Intelligence Service. Otherwise, he couldn't hold the job. It's impossible."[16] With that comment, as he left the courtroom, he signaled a hearty thumbs-up to Trofimoff and grinned widely.

It was clear that Frenkel's loyalty to, and belief in, Trofimoff was unshaken. After his testimony, he told the author privately, "This is the worst and most flagrant example of a set-up rigged by the FBI that I ever hope to see. I still can't believe that George, with his many years of intelligence experience, was so stupid to go to that meeting in the hotel, but that certainly does not prove his guilt."[17]

While uncertainty revolved around the possibility of Trofimoff's taking the stand, prosecutors Terry Furr and Laura Ingersoll knew enough of his attitude and personality to have no doubt. During a break earlier in the trial, Furr said to the author, "The man is unbelievably arrogant."[18] Later, after the trial was over, Furr said to a group of assembled reporters, "We said early on he would testify. He shouldn't have, but we knew he would."[19]

On that point, Furr was accurate. On Thursday afternoon Hernandez announced that the next witness for the defense would be George Trofimoff. Nattily dressed in a gray suit, white shirt and maroon tie, he was the epitome of self-confidence as he took the stand. He gazed around the courtroom, smiling with a self-assured air as Hernandez began his questioning.

Hernandez first asked Trofimoff to tell the jury about his background, and he embarked on a long and detailed life story. His description of his early life was essentially the same as it is depicted in earlier chapters, and on the witness stand he proved himself to be a good actor. He became very sentimental describing his feelings as he recalled the many times he took the oath of allegiance.

"So, when I joined the Army on 19 July 1948, I raised my right arm and I was sworn in to, you know, the—the—the that we all have to give when we join the Armed Services . . . the next time I gave my oath of allegiance was when I became an American citizen. It was emotional, and it's very difficult to describe. But for the first time in my life I belonged someplace. The third time I gave this same oath when I got this commission . . . the Second Lieutenant's commission. And that ruled the rest of my life until now."[20]

Trofimoff continued with the long and detailed saga of his life, describing his experiences as he journeyed through Europe, his life in Paris, his immigration to America, and his service in the U. S. Army and as a civil service employee.

Hernandez asked him when he was assigned to Germany.

"January of 1961 I received a cable from Germany that my father had passed away . . . orders were cut for me to go on emergency leave to Germany . . . I went to the Civilian Personnel Office and asked them if they would have a job for me there because I wanted to take care of my stepmother . . . I got a job in Frankfurt."[21]

Hernandez asked him how many times he had been married.

"I have to admit I'm right now on my fifth and last marriage . . . I was married the first time when I was at Fort Bragg . . . a very nice young lady . . . we were married for less than a year . . . and then I went to Laos . . . So, my first wife left me because she couldn't join me in Laos.

"My second wife was in Hawaii . . . I was transferred to Korea, no dependents allowed . . . So, my second wife left me because she couldn't join me in Korea.

"My third wife is the mother of my three children . . . I don't know what she wanted, but after she stepped out on me a couple of times, I packed two bags and left.

"My fourth marriage . . . is one of those foolish things that many of us old men do . . . I married a girl that was 31 years . . . younger than I was.

"And then I met my, like I said, my current and last wife. She's sitting here in this room . . . I wish I could have met her 30 years earlier. Then, a lot of things would not have happened in my life that did."[22] This last statement seemed to be a slip on Trofimoff's part, as it might have been construed to be a confession. However, Furr either missed the implication of the statement or else decided not to take advantage of the comment.

Hernandez introduced several annual performance evaluation reports and commendations, and, as he viewed one glowing report, Trofimoff asked to see its date. He chuckled. "This when I allegedly started my espionage activities."[23]

The remainder of the day was spent with questions from Hernandez designed to have Trofimoff define the organizational charts of the 66th Military Intelligence Brigade and the operations, staffing and security of the JIC.

Trofimoff's testimony continued the next day, Friday, June 22, as he described JIC security measures, document-handling procedures, interrogation techniques, official courier procedures, and actions he took to establish control over classified documents and dispose of those becoming obsolete or unnecessary for the operation.

Hernandez asked Trofimoff to respond to the list of specific overt acts contained in the allegations. He vigorously denied each one. After the first was read, he said, "I would never even think of doing something like that . . . I could say a few drastic words which I'm going to refrain from, because I don't want to insult this court by using some vile language when I think of such accusations."[24]

Regarding his foster brother, he said, "If my brother, Igor, if he had ever mentioned to me—not recruited me or anything like that, but if he would have ever mentioned to me in any sort . . . in any way at all that he was in any way connected with the KGB, I would have told him, Igor, you have just lost your little brother . . . I most probably would have turned him in . . ."[25]

Trofimoff responded to the accusations of visiting different Austrian villages to meet with KGB officers. He readily admitted being in each village and had a ready explanation for each visit. He vehemently denied that he ever saw KGB officers during any of his trips.

During Hernandez' questioning, Trofimoff prefaced his answers with extensive comments and narrative before addressing each question. The judge issued a warning:

"Mr. Trofimoff, I'm going to ask you to answer the questions that are asked . . . you may elaborate on an answer, but if it has some relevance to the question that was asked . . . You need to stick to the point and answer the questions."[26]

Trofimoff's testimony continued with verbal sparring among Trofimoff, the two attorneys and the judge. The judge issued several warnings to Trofimoff, directing him to keep his comments relative to questions he was asked. Furr entered several objections to Trofimoff's statements, saying that Trofimoff attempted to "tell a story" prior to answering questions.

Hernandez introduced the matter of the videotapes of the meetings in the Melbourne hotel. From the beginning, Trofimoff insisted that the story he gave was a complete figment of the imagination—a fantasy.

Hernandez asked Trofimoff what he meant with his statement to Droujinsky regarding JIC documents "If I had 'em, you got 'em." "Why did you say that?"[27]

"I figured that someone had given them—so I might as well say I did it."[28]

Asked if his statement about having been awarded the Order of the Red Banner was true, Trofimoff replied, "No. In basic intelligence training I learned about Soviet uniforms and various awards, to include the Red Banner, so I decided to tell them I received it."[29]

Hernandez reminded Trofimoff that he said he needed money and asked if his financial situation had changed in the years after his first calls from Droujinsky.

"It had deteriorated. My wife and I had never owned a home together before, and we put our love into it (their new home). We were not familiar with the credit card system and we went 'hog wild.' We needed trees, a fireplace and many other things, and got deeper and deeper into debt."[30]

Trofimoff explained how he used his intelligence training to systematically concoct his "fantasy," saying, "I had to invent this story, even though I am not proud of it."[31]

Hernandez asked if he (Trofimoff) was present at Kalugin's testimony, and if he had ever met, seen, or had contact with him.

"I certainly was, and I have never seen him before."[32]

Regarding his statement in the videotapes that he had visited Yalta, he said, "Preposterous! That hotel was reserved for Russian elite. If I was scared to enter the German Democratic Republic, what about the USSR? I never heard of any agent being invited to a place like that—not even Philbin!"[33]

Furr commenced his cross-examination by asking Trofimoff why he didn't just "click" his telephone when the first call came from Igor.

"I'm a polite person. I don't click the person—the telephone just like that."[34]

Once, when the jury was absent, the judge said, "Mr. Trofimoff, you had something you wanted to say to me. I—I don't want to have any conversations with you in front of the jury because I have no idea what it is you're going to bring up."[35]

Trofimoff's frustration was evident in his reply: "I was asking for you to interfere with Mr. Furr in his dramatics because he's pointing his finger at me and waving (it) practically in my face, and I don't— I'm not used to that kind of treatment, sir."[36]

The judge replied that Furr had not left his podium and was not waving up in Trofimoff's face.

"That's true," Trofimoff replied, "but still it's extremely aggressive. I think he would be very unhappy if I would start answering my questions in the same manner."[37]

Many of the jurors exhibited their boredom with Trofimoff's long tirades, which often had little to do with the question being asked. During a break, the foreman sent a note to the judge:

"Your honor: Could we please have the witness answer only the questions asked without the narrative?"[38]

The judge complied with the jury's request, again cautioning Trofimoff to answer each question directly and eliminate any unnecessary comments or narrative.

By this time it was becoming clear that Trofimoff's plan, that is, to picture himself as a loyal and trustworthy citizen who was being treated unfairly by the prosecution, was beginning to backfire and the jury was becoming exasperated with his antics.

On Monday, June 25, the second half of Furr's cross-examination was devastating to Trofimoff. First, Furr retrieved several photographs of individuals that Trofimoff had identified as KGB officers during his meetings with Droujinsky—individuals he said he had worked with during his years of spying. In each instance, Kalugin or FBI agents, who had been called as witnesses, had identified the individuals as KGB officers during their testimony. As each picture was shown, Furr asked Trofimoff if it was just a coincidence that the men he picked out had been identified as KGB agents by other witnesses.

In each case, Trofimoff insisted that it was only a coincidence, but he became increasingly perturbed as Furr presented more pictures,

asking each time if it was only a coincidence that Trofimoff had identified each one. In a high-pitched voice loaded with anxiety, Trofimoff
said, "I told you before, I've never seen nor spoken with any of these
people before in my life."[39]

Furr continued. "Is it just a coincidence that Mr. Kalugin said you
were from noble Russian ancestry? And you said the same thing in
the undercover tapes?"[40]

Furr continued to introduce many comparisons of Trofimoff's
statements made in the videotapes to testimony of witnesses appearing at the trial. Trofimoff's face became increasingly flushed with
every comparison that was introduced.

Furr pointed out that Trofimoff told Droujinsky that he had photographed 50, 60, or 70 books and that Mitrokhin reported that
Antey's material exceeded 80 volumes. Kalugin reported that during
the 70s his (Trofimoff's) volume really picked up. "Is that all just a
coincidence?" Furr asked.[41]

In answer to Furr's questions, Trofimoff confirmed that he enjoyed
photography and liked to photograph his family. Furr asked him why
there were no pictures of his brother, Igor, in his house when he was
arrested.

Trofimoff's brow was wrinkled and he hesitated before responding. ". . . my whole photo album was almost empty . . . my kids were
against my marriage and the things they said about me when they
were asked by Germans made me so mad when I got back I threw out
every—every picture that I ever had of my children, my family and
everything else. I don't know why I don't have any pictures of my
brother."[42]

When you were arrested in Tampa, Furr asked, "Why did you tell
Special Agent Wagoner that you first received a call from someone
named Igor two months after Igor Susemihl passed away in
Germany?"[43]

"Mr. Droujinsky asked me how I was going to declare the money
that I was supposed to be getting. I told him, well, this is a good time
because my brother died and I can say that I got it from . . . Igor."[44]

When Furr asked Trofimoff why he lied to the FBI, telling them that
the money was coming from a previous loan, George replied,
"Because I wanted to avoid paying income tax."[45]

Furr rose and moved to stand behind Wagoner and another agent,
touching their shoulders. "You told . . . Special Agent Wagoner that
you had only spoken to Igor on the telephone on three occasions. Why

did you lie?"[46]

George responded that his entire story was a lie.

When Furr waved his arm toward the jury and asked Trofimoff if he had told the jury the truth, Trofimoff nodded affirmatively. "Yes, sir."[47]

"I have nothing further, your Honor." Furr resumed his seat.

After a few minor questions from Hernandez, the defense rested. Furr then announced that he was calling a rebuttal witness.

Brian Bebley (wearing a prisoner's orange jump suit) was called in to answer Furr's questions. He identified himself as a 24-year-old who had served 11 months of a 26-year sentence for possession of crack cocaine, grand theft of a firearm, and battery on a law-enforcement officer. He pointed to Trofimoff and said he had been his cellmate for three and a half months.

Furr asked Bebley what Trofimoff had told him.

"He told me . . . they accused him of selling secrets . . . military-based information . . . to an Archbishop to a church . . ."[48]

Furr hunched forward on the rostrum and asked Bebley whom Trofimoff had sold the information to.

Bebley answered, "An organization . . . like a three-letter word."[49]

Furr asked Bebley if he had heard of something called the FBI or CIA, but he did not recognize either. It was obvious that Furr deliberately avoided saying "KGB," allowing the jury to come to its own conclusion.

Furr asked Bebley what had happened in Florida.

"He told me that he was coming to Florida originally to meet a guy that he was supposed to get 40 or 50 thousand dollars for, for the information. At the time he didn't know it was an agent . . . But he told me that he told him everything."[50]

Trofimoff turned and faced the court with a look of genuine surprise on his face. He mouthed, "He's lying."[51]

After Bebley identified Trofimoff, Hernandez began his cross-examination. When Bebley testified that he was serving a 26-year sentence for a total of six felony convictions, Hernandez pointed out that Bebley's sentence could be reduced if Furr signed off on a motion for reduction of the sentence. Bebley answered "sure," when Hernandez asked if he would like a reduction in his sentence.

". . . if Mr. Trofimoff says, you know, this is what I'm being accused of, but I am innocent, you could . . . say, let me call Terry Furr . . . and say that George Trofimoff confessed to me . . . and if they're interested enough and call you as a witness, they just might file a motion for reduction of sentence, and it might result in—in you getting a substantial reduction, correct?"[52]

When Bebley agreed that he understood, Hernandez asked if he was sure that he could tell the difference between "Here's what I'm charged with, but I didn't do it," and "here's what I really did." Bebley said he was sure that Trofimoff really did the things he was accused of. While Bebley's testimony was not fully discredited, Hernandez raised enough questions to significantly reduce his credibility.

At this time the judge placed the trial in recess until the afternoon when closing arguments would be presented. She explained that the prosecution would go first, followed by the defense, with a final summary to be delivered by the prosecution. She cautioned the jury that statements made by the prosecution and defense in their closing arguments were not evidence.

When the court reconvened, before the jury was recalled, Hernandez repeated his motion for a judgment of acquittal, based on his charge of "outrageous government conduct." Again, the judge denied his motion.

As closing arguments began, Trofimoff appeared beleaguered with dark, sunken eyes and a thin face. The jolly optimism he had expressed throughout the trial was displaced by a worried, concerned expression.

Laura Ingersoll began the Government's closing argument.

George Trofimoff wasn't an accidental spy. He wasn't a casual spy, and he wasn't a sloppy spy. He was, in a very real sense, the perfect spy.

He had three things going for him: He had steady, constant access to what the KGB wanted, and he had it in an environment that he controlled. He had a safe private pipeline to the KGB to deliver the product and get paid. And he had what so many criminals don't have: self discipline, self control.[53]

The phrase, "a perfect spy" was immediately picked up by the media and appeared in almost every article written afterward. Ingersoll emphasized that Trofimoff knew which refugees were to be interviewed and when. From that knowledge he knew which reference documents would or would not be used on any given day. She continued:

This isn't a burglary case . . . Nobody has ever sug-

gested that the defendant was breaking into the JIC . . .
This is a crime that was committed in broad daylight
. . . The defendant . . . had unfettered access to the
Element's classified documents during the workday.
He sat in his locked office from time to time . . .
nobody checked his briefcase as he came and went.[54]

To emphasize the care Trofimoff took in covering his activities,
Ingersoll pointed out that he did not make copies of documents orig-
inating in the JIC but photographed only those documents that came
to him from higher headquarters. He removed their serial numbers
first, so they could not be traced to his JIC. He was also smart in handling his money, she noted:

. . . he spent every bit of the money he got from the
KGB, but he always took precautions.

. . . when a man representing himself to be a
Russian intelligence officer, he (Trofimoff) didn't hang
up . . . he laid out his entire KGB career to someone he
believed was a former KGB colleague. This is a really
a key point . . . The undercover agent never asked the
defendant if he had been a spy . . . It was a given that
the defendant had been a KGB agent . . . The defendant was reluctant . . . and he never rejected the
undercover's representation of who he was.

Repeating, she said, "The agent never asked the defendant if he
was a spy—that was a given. Trofimoff never rejected the premise
that there was a KGB problem and that he, as well as others, was in
danger."[55]

Noting that Trofimoff was reunited with his foster brother in 1968,
she pointed out that it all started in late 1969, and that there wasn't
much activity at the beginning. She pointed out that after Trofimoff
told Igor he needed money, the priest told him that he would loan it
to him, and later told him he didn't owe any money. "This, ladies and
gentlemen, is also just how it got started with Clayton Lonetree . . .
classic, classic KGB practice."[56]

In closing, Ingersoll said, "This man, ladies and gentlemen, fled
into this country's arms after World War II and spent 36 years with the
U. S. Army. He spent over half of that career as a loyal agent of the
KGB. He betrayed every hope and trust that his country placed in
him. Please keep in mind one thing the defendant said . . . He said,
'It's not that easy to bamboozle people in the United States.' "[57]

Hernandez began his summary comments by thanking the jury for their service, and then pointed out that, according to the rules, he would not be allowed to address them after he presented his closing argument. He emphasized the importance of Trofimoff's background, his hatred of the Communists, and his service to the U. S. Army. Discussing the charges against his client, Hernandez pointed out that the strongest part of the government's case, the videotapes, was based on two points: offers of money by the FBI undercover agent and Trofimoff's dire need for money.

Hernandez next attacked the testimony of Furr's rebuttal witness, the prisoner Brian Bebley. "He's not testifying . . . because he's an American patriot. He's testifying because . . . there's a thing called Rule 35. Rule 35 is a unique rule of the Federal Rules of Criminal Procedure that puts a lot of power in the hands of Mr. Furr . . ."[58]

Hernandez went on to explain that if Bebley testified as Furr wished, the government had the power to file a motion to get a substantial reduction in Bebley's sentence, even to reduce it to less than the ten-year minimum prescribed by law.

". . . George Trofimoff wanted to tell you in his own words what happened and why he said those things on the video . . . George Trofimoff is not and has never been a spy."[59]

He then displayed for the jury a list of several points that he claimed the government did not prove. "This man, George Trofimoff, is not guilty. I ask that you send him home to his wife."[60]

By then it was 5 p. m., but the judge decided to proceed with Furr's rebuttal.

Furr began as he assumed his favorite posture and addressed the jury:

> Ladies and gentlemen, the—the problem the defense has is a fundamental problem . . . their problem is the defendant. All right. Their problem is that he is a liar. He is a stone liar . . . The guy will not answer anything. He can't deal with the truth; he won't deal with the truth; he is a liar.[61]
>
> Kalugin might have been a bad guy in the past, but the fact is, what does he have to gain now? He can only buy a world of trouble by coming here and lying.
>
> The second part is the defendant's story: 'I talked with the undercover agent because I thought it would help me get some money from the Russian Orthodox

Church' . . .And I asked him about that . . . how is it
that a desire for some money from a church gets
moved along in a positive way by telling the representative of that church that you committed a massive
crime for 25 years, and that one of the princes of that
church, the equivalent of a Cardinal, a Metropolitan,
Archbishop—whatever he was—was in up to his eye-
lids with you?

When I heard that . . . I almost fell out of my chair.[62]

Furr continued, emphasizing significant contradictions in
Trofimoff's testimony, closing with the following:

To George Trofimoff, nobody matters—nobody—but
George Trofimoff. And if that isn't absolutely clear to
all of you, you haven't been paying attention. Your
decision is simple. You have—you have seen somebody do what he has done, you've seen the facts, and
you've had a chance to see him, as bad as that's had to
be. I want to thank you very, very much. Thank you.[64]

The judge then announced that the names of the alternate jurors
would be announced the next morning and declared the court to be in
recess.

Chapter
13

GUILTY!

In the final choice, a soldier's pack is not
so heavy a burden as a prisoner's chains..
—Dwight David Eisenhower,
Inaugural Address, January 20, 1953

In her extensive and detailed instructions to the jury, on Tuesday, June 26, Judge Bucklew explained the rules of law as they applied to the case before them.

"It will be your duty as jurors to decide whether the Government has proven beyond a reasonable doubt the specific facts necessary to find the defendant guilty of the crime charged in the indictment beyond a reasonable doubt."[1] She read a summary of the indictment and discussed the meaning of conspiracy, reasonable doubt, and the U. S. Statute of Limitations, pointing out that the United States had no statute of limitations for the crime of espionage. She explained that "John Doe" was allowed by the court to testify with a pseudonym and that the jury could accept his testimony accordingly.

"Any verdict that you reach back in the jury room . . . must be a unanimous verdict . . . should you decide at five o'clock you've not reached a verdict and you want to break apart for the day and come back tomorrow morning, you can do that . . . If you decide that you want to work later than five o'clock . . . you can do that . . . you can work as late as you want to work."[2]

She then named the three members of the jury who were excused and asked them to remain in their seats as the twelve other members left the courtroom. Her graciousness and respect for the jurors surfaced as she approached the three excused members to shake their hands and thank each one individually for their service.

It was 10:30 a. m. when the jury filed out, and at 12:05 p. m. they reported they had reached a verdict. In only 1-1/2 hours, the jurors had left the building for a coffee break, returned to have lunch with court-supplied sandwiches, and conducted their first and only vote. When the bailiff declared the court to be in session, Judge Bucklew entered and announced that, after calling the jury, she would ask if their decision was unanimous. If she was told that the answer was "yes," she would ask for the verdict sheet and then pass it to her assistant for publication.

When the members of the jury resumed their seats, Mark King, the foreman, verified that the vote was unanimous and passed the verdict sheet to the judge for review. The judge's assistant then read the verdict:

GUILTY!

With the announcement of the verdict, George, with a wry and resigned expression, turned to look at Jutta, her head buried in her hands, as if to say, "Well, I tried."

After the verdict, Judge Bucklew thanked the jury for their work and announced that sentencing would take place at 8:30 a. m. on September 27, 2001. Media representatives dashed out to file their reports, and after more than three long weeks, it was over. One of the most remarkable spy trials in American history drew to a close.

Jury foreman, Mark King, a heavy-set truck driver sporting a Van Dyke beard, said he felt as if he had been a part of history. "The mistake (Trofimoff) made was talking to this gentleman on the phone. He didn't hang up. Why not call the FBI? . . . He (Trofimoff) often seemed to be lying . . . His story did not jibe."[3]

Waiting for the verdict, Terry Furr was nauseated and Laura Ingersoll was "strung tight as a bow."

"I was nervous until I heard the words," Furr said the day after the verdict was reached. "It was an all-or-nothing case for both sides."[4] "This guy needed being caught . . . he needed being convicted."[5]

Hernandez, dejected, told the author that he still considered his client to be innocent, and he planned to appeal the decision. "We always tried to keep a very optimistic attitude. He was adamant that he was a victim. He chose to say some things that obviously came back to haunt him."[6]

The hearing to determine Trofimoff's sentence was conducted on September 27, 2001, in the U. S. District Court, Tampa, Florida, by U. S. District Judge Susan C. Bucklew, who had presided over Trofimoff's trial. He had been full of confidence and nattily dressed in business suits and ties during his trial, but now he appeared for the hearing with shackles on his ankles and clad in an orange prisoner's jump suit. Pale and thin with circles under his eyes, he appeared haggard and dejected, offering only a wan smile to his wife, Jutta.

Judge Bucklew's first order of business was to act on a motion filed by Trofimoff's attorney, Daniel Hernandez, requesting a new trial. She asked Hernandez to present his arguments and any evidence he had to support his motion. Hernandez' motion was centered on the testimony of Brian Bebley, an inmate of the jail in which Trofimoff was confined. Bebley had been introduced by the government unexpectedly at the end of the trial as a rebuttal witness, testifying that Trofimoff made a full confession to him prior to the trial. Hernandez said that the witness had been a complete surprise to him; he stated that, at the time of Bebley's appearance, he asked the judge for a recess so he could visit the jail and interview other inmates in order to verify or refute Bebley's testimony. Hernandez' request was denied by Judge Bucklew and the hearing continued.

Hernandez was able to identify another inmate in the jail occupied by Trofimoff and Bebley who would refute Bebley's testimony. This witness, Thomas Kincaid, was called by Hernandez to testify. When Hernandez asked for Kincaid's comments on Trofimoff, he replied that he had been in the jail with George for about eight months. "He was always reserved with his fellow inmates and always adamant about being innocent of the espionage charges."[7] When asked about prisoner Bebley, Kincaid said, "Bebley had a strong dislike for George."[8]

Hernandez argued that Bebley's testimony, coming at the end of the trial, was highly prejudicial to his client and had exerted a major influence on the jury. Because Kincaid's statements tainted Bebley's testimony, he maintained that a new trial was mandatory.

In Furr's-cross examination, Kincaid revealed that he was in jail for armed robbery. He believed that Bebley's testimony was offered solely to obtain a reduced sentence in return for his cooperation with the government. He further testified that Bebley had approached him, suggesting that he, too, testify against Trofimoff to get a lighter sentence. Kincaid maintained, however, that he refused to offer such testimony.

While it was clear that Bebley was not a strong witness for the prosecution, prosecutor Terry Furr made the point for the government in explaining that Bebley was only a corroborative witness whose testimony was not necessary to obtain a conviction. He maintained that the other primary evidence that had been introduced, including the two three-hour videotapes, the testimony of witnesses such as Kalugin, who identified Trofimoff, and the British BSIS agent who presented evidence from the Mitrokhin papers, would easily have resulted in a conviction without the testimony from Bebley.

Judge Bucklew agreed with the government and denied the motion for a new trial, asking for comments and arguments from each side prior to announcing Trofimoff's sentence.

Furr requested that before receiving motions for departures from the government's sentencing guidelines, the judge address the issue of Trofimoff's perjury, pointing out that the defendant had lied repeatedly in his testimony.

The judge agreed with Furr and addressed the defendant. "Mr. Trofimoff, you have the right to appear before me and deny your guilt—but when you are under oath, you have no right to lie. The jury did not believe your story, and neither do I. You committed perjury."[9]

Turning to the subject of Trofimoff's sentence, the judge explained that the United States' sentencing guidelines for crimes such as Trofimoff committed called for a minimum sentence of 324 months (27 years) to a maximum of 408 months (34 years). She pointed out that any sentence within the guidelines would probably be tantamount to life in prison for Trofimoff, but that she was obliged to ask for arguments from each side for any recommended upward or downward departure from the guidelines.

Hernandez requested downward departures from the guidelines for two reasons. One was Trofimoff's age. Rephrasing the judge's comment, he argued that without a downward departure, the minimum sentence would amount to a life sentence. The second reason was his physical condition, which would in all probability preclude his survival even with a minimum sentence. "Please pronounce a sentence which will enable this old gentleman to see the light of day,"[10] he pleaded.

Judge Bucklew was not swayed by Hernandez' arguments. "Age in itself is not normally admitted as a basis for downward departures. While I understand that Mr. Trofimoff has some medical problems, I do not consider his physical condition to be a valid reason for a downward departure. Accordingly, each of your arguments is denied."[11]

Prosecutor Furr offered five reasons for an upward departure from the guidelines.

First, a letter, dated September 24, 2001, from John P. Stenbit, Assistant Secretary of Defense, acting as a duly authorized designee

ASSISTANT SECRETARY OF DEFENSE
6000 DEFENSE PENTAGON
WASHINGTON, DC 20301-6000

2 4 SEP 2001

COMMAND, CONTROL,
COMMUNICATIONS, AND
INTELLIGENCE

The Honorable Susan C. Bucklew
United States District Judge
The Sam M. Gibbons United States Courthouse
801 North Florida Avenue
Tampa, FL 33602-4511

Dear Judge Bucklew:

I am writing, as a duly authorized designee of the President by virtue of my office, and on behalf of the United States Department of Defense, to convey our position that it is necessary for the protection of our national security that the defendant in United States v. George Trofimoff, No. 8:00-CR-197-T-24C (MDFL), be sentenced to a term of life imprisonment. This representation is submitted to you pursuant to Commentary 3 to Section 2M3.1 of the United States Sentencing Guidelines ("Guidelines"), in anticipation of the defendant's sentencing on September 27, 2001.

It our understanding that the application of the Sentencing Guidelines to this case would not necessarily result in a life sentence, notwithstanding the extent and gravity of the espionage activity of which a jury has found Trofimoff guilty. This Guidelines calculation is a function of the fact that the United States national defense information that Trofimoff sold to the Soviet Union over a period of two decades was classified at the level of Secret, rather than Top Secret, but Trofimoff himself has acknowledged that the only reason he did not turn over Top Secret information is that he did not have ready access to it. In our view, a sentence short of life imprisonment does not adequately address the scope and consequences of Trofimoff's actions, and would fail to serve as an appropriate deterrent for others who would contemplate violating a trust to protect our nation's security.

Accordingly, I respectfully request that you apply whatever upward departure is available under the Guidelines to ensure that a sentence of life imprisonment is imposed on George Trofimoff.

Sincerely,

John P. Stenbit

John P. Stenbit

Department of Defense letter to Judge Bucklew, requesting a term of life imprisonment for Trofimoff. (U.S. Justice Dept.)

of the President by virtue of my office, was addressed to Judge Bucklew. The letter said, in part, "In our view, a sentence short of life imprisonment does not adequately address the scope and consequences of Trofimoff's actions, and would fail to serve as an appropriate deterrent for others who would contemplate violating a trust to protect our nations security. Accordingly, I respectfully request that you apply whatever upward departure is available under the guidelines to insure that a life sentence is imposed on George Trofimoff."[12] (Prosecutor Furr later told the author privately that this was the first time he had ever seen that particular provision of the United States sentencing guidelines exercised.)

Second, conduct by the accused resulted in a significant disruption of government functions.

Third, public health and safety were endangered by Trofimoff's espionage activities.

Fourth, the time span of the defendant's espionage activities, stretching over some 25 years, is the longest in the history of the United States.

Fifth, Trofimoff's actions represent an extraordinary violation of the trust vested in him.

Judge Bucklew approved the first four reasons presented by the government but denied the extraordinary violation of trust, stating that it was, in reality, included in the first four. Turning to Terry Furr, she asked, "Are you requesting that I give the defendant a sentence of life imprisonment?"[13]

"Yes, I am. He has shown not one shred of remorse—not an iota. He became an American citizen 50 years ago and spent half of that time as a spy against his country."[14]

Before announcing her decision, the judge turned to the defendant and asked if he had anything to say. Trofimoff shuffled forward clumsily, hampered by his shackles. He surprised no one with his comments, in which he vehemently denied committing any of the offenses. He stated fiercely that he was not a traitor, but a true patriot and a good, loyal citizen of his adopted land, and that, until his dying day, he would never admit to committing any of the acts he had been accused of.

After Trofimoff's statement, Judge Bucklew announced that based on the government's recommendations, she would make an upward departure of one level in the sentencing guidelines, which would allow the imposition of a life sentence. In addition to the life sentence, she imposed a fine of $25,250, which was to be waived. She stated that the Federal Department of Prisons would determine where he would be incarcerated. Almost seven years after Trofimoff's first arrest by German authorities, it was all over.

A question frequently asked is why the government failed to offer Trofimoff a reduction in his penalty in return for his cooperation. At the end of the sentencing hearing, this question was posed to Prosecutor Furr, who answered, "Such offers are only made when a request for consideration is made by the defendant. In this case, Trofimoff never offered to admit his guilt or cooperate in any way, so the issue was never raised."[15]

An FBI source made similar comments to the author. "It's too bad that Trofimoff did not offer to come forward. He could have said, 'I did it, and if you want to know all I know, let's make a deal.' If he had done that, he would have saved himself a lot of agony and, more importantly, saved his wife from a lot of grief—exposure to the trial, the press, etc. She is a classy lady and certainly does not deserve what she has gone through."[16]

As soon as the sentence was imposed, Hernandez announced his plans to begin the appeal process, which would be initiated by a notice of appeal to be presented within ten days of sentencing.

Trofimoff was to be transferred (temporarily) to a Federal prison in Moorehaven, Florida. Later, he told Jutta that the federal prison was a vast improvement over Florida state and county jails, his homes for the last fifteen months.[17] He was then transferred to the maximum security section of a new Federal prison in Coleman, Florida, which was, according to Jutta, yet another improvement over the Moorehaven facility. Still maintaining his complete innocence, he began his long, lonely vigil, waiting for the wheels of the appeal process to turn.

After his conviction and sentencing to life imprisonment, Trofimoff became a legal expert as he studied all the legal material available to him in the prison library. In addition to the appeals entered by his attorneys, he prepared and submitted additional personal appeals in the hope (and belief) that he would be released some day. Despite his efforts, all of his appeals have been denied, and he remains in prison in perpetual denial—a bitter individual who maintains that he has been sorely mistreated by the United States legal process.

Jutta has finally acknowledged the harm that she suffered from her husband, and is determined to make a new life without Trofimoff. In all likelihood, he will spend the rest of his life in prison.

Chapter
14

THE ANATOMY
OF A SPY

If you have money, it doth not stay,
But this way and that it wastes amain,
What does it profit you, anyway?
Ill-gotton gain is nobody's gain.
—François Villon (1430–1484),
The Greater Testament. Seemly Lesson for the Good-for-Noughts.

Representatives of agencies involved in the Trofimoff investigation have been tight-lipped. Little, if any, official information pertaining to the investigation has been made public. However, information obtained at the trial, when combined with information obtained from other sources, provides a reasonably clear picture of the origin and particulars of that investigation, beginning with the defection of Vasili Mitrokhin to Great Britain in 1992.

When I first began compiling the story of the FBI investigation, Trofimoff's request for appeal was pending. With his case officially open, my request to the FBI to discuss the investigation with knowledgeable agents was denied. I pieced together my description of the investigation without any official input from participating agents.

Later, with Trofimoff's appeal denied, the FBI gave me permission to discuss the case with Special Agent Anthony (Tony) Wagoner, lead agent of the overall investigation. Agent Wagoner, involved with the investigation from the beginning and Trofimoff's arresting officer in Tampa, provided some details not originally available to me and confirmed others uncovered during my research.[1] The agents could not discuss other aspects of the investigation, such as the extent and types of surveillance exercised over Trofimoff, since they were not at liberty to discuss the agency's investigative techniques.

Mitrokhin's defection provided a treasure trove of secret extracts from KGB files that became available to the worldwide intelligence community. The KGB maintains individual files for every KGB agent, and any bit of information regarding each agent is diligently entered into his/her files. Agent Wagoner confirmed that the revelations from the Mitrokhin papers provided the trigger that started the investigation of Trofimoff's activities in Germany.[2] Two of the KGB files, described by the Government's witness "John Doe," were of particular interest to agents investigating Trofimoff. First, the Operational Cultivation (DOR) file is the KGB personal file for each agent that contains records pertaining to the agent's recruitment, etc. Second, the Working Production (RD) file contains records of all items ever produced by the agent. Over the years, Mitrokhin carefully copied and took to his home extracts of all agent records in the KGB files.[3]

A review of transcripts of the December 14, 1994 interrogations of Trofimoff and Susemihl by two German BKA agents leads to the conclusion that the investigation was initiated by the U. S. Army's Counter Intelligence (CI) operation. One anonymous source stated to me that, to the best of his knowledge, the investigation began sometime in 1994, shortly before the arrest of Trofimoff and his foster brother by German authorities. Further confirmation is provided by Agent Wagoner's statement that, when the Mitrokhin revelations became known, representatives of the FBI and U. S. Army CI agents briefed German investigators and later assisted the Germans in their investigation.[4]

Rocco Rosano, a retired U. S. Army CI Agent, once a member of the U. S. Army's 66th Military Intelligence Brigade (the organization responsible for the Nuremberg JIC), in an email to me, gave a slightly different version of how the investigation was started:

> CI has known about George Trofimoff for a very long time. It was an Army CI case long before it became an FBI case; the Army handed the case to the FBI under the "Silver Platter" rule. George retired and moved back to Florida, and at that time, the FBI took primary jurisdiction, although the Army still maintained a case officer assigned . . . there has been an Army CI Agent

assigned to the Trofimoff case for over a decade."[5]

When I asked Rosano to define the "Silver Platter" rule, he told me:

The 'Silver Platter' rule has two (commonly) accepted definitions. The first is when one agency has to
turn over a case to another agency under the DOJ
(Department of Justice) defined primary jurisdiction. The case being transferred to the new receiving
agency is accepted in totality with all the investigative material handed over on a 'Silver Platter.' The
Trofimoff case is an example where the FBI received
primary jurisdiction on a case that it did not develop. The second definition is when a case is handed
over with all the specifics included. The Hanssen
case is an example where U. S. Intelligence gave the
FBI the essential information to secure a conviction
on a 'Silver Platter.'[6]

The two German BKA agents who interrogated Trofimoff and
Susemihl separately appeared before the German Supreme Court
on December 15, 1994. Each requested that an arrest warrant be
issued for the two suspected spies. Agent Buchbender, who interrogated Trofimoff, said, "For the time being, the urgent suspicion is
based on information by a source of a U. S. Army office. The information is totally precise and covers the accused in all areas."[7]
Agent Zeitler, who interrogated Susemihl, said, "The strong suspicion rests on classified information presented by a reliable source of
a U. S. military office."[8] Each of these statements is compatible with
the information provided by agent Wagoner.

Neither German agent mentioned the FBI or a specific U. S.
Army unit or organization during their appearance before the
German Supreme Court. Later, when Special Agent Gary Pepper of
the U. S. Army's Intelligence and Security Command (Foreign
Counterintelligence Activity) appeared in the Trofimoff trial, he testified that in the summer of 1994 he was the senior agent in charge
of the Army's investigation.[9] Agent Pepper's testimony confirms
Rosano's conclusion that the U. S. Army's Counter Intelligence
operation initiated the Trofimoff investigation. In April 2003, Agent
Wagoner told me that the Army took the lead in Germany as it had
the most resources (manpower).[10] When the Trofimoffs moved to
the United States, responsibility for the case passed to the FBI under
the supervision of Special Agent Joe Navarro of the Tampa, Florida

FBI Office.[11]

One anonymous FBI source told me that, in addition to the German agents involved, the military (U. S. Army) and the FBI each had two permanent investigators assigned to the case. During the course of the investigation, this same source estimated that some 12 to 15 investigators/agents were assigned on a part or full-time basis. Agent Rosano told me that while the U. S. Army tended to keep a few dedicated agents assigned to the case over a long period, the FBI, with few experienced CI agents, rotated different agents through the case to give more of their agents "live" case time.[12]

In the videotaped interviews in Florida, Trofimoff stated that in 1987 his foster brother told him to stop his photography. Trofimoff says he assumed the Soviets were breaking away from him because of the "upheaval" in the Soviet bloc. However, there seems to be another, more significant (but unconfirmed), reason. Agent Rosano said:

> The FBI CI Program was penetrated by the Soviets during that period. The Soviets knew that Trofimoff was under FBI and Army CI investigation. They know everything there is to know about the FBI CI Program and the Army FCA (Foreign Counterintelligence Activity). It was an open window to the Soviets. That is why, during all those years, the Soviets never attempted to make contact with Trofimoff. Our (Army) CI folks (unaware that they were already compromised) were waiting to catch a live Soviet Case Officer attempting to make contact with George. But this wasn't going to happen. They (the Soviets) knew all about the case.[13]

There is also a strong suspicion that FBI Agent Robert Hanssen (later arrested as a traitor) became the source through which the Soviets learned of the American investigations of Trofimoff. Hanssen was charged with conducting espionage, starting in 1985, and CI Agent Rosano believes that Hanssen opened the door to the Soviets with Trofimoff. "Informed sources assert that Hanssen reactivated his contacts with Soviet special services in about 1985 (or thereabouts)."[14] Trofimoff states that in 1987 he received instructions from Igor to stop his activities; it is logical to assume that Igor's instructions resulted from the Soviet's knowledge of the

American investigations of his activities (information obtained from Hanssen when he "reactivated" his contacts). If this assumption is true, it is ironic that the FBI and Army investigations indirectly "saved" Trofimoff from being convicted and jailed in Germany. If the Russians had never known about the U. S. investigations of Trofimoff, it is unlikely that they would have told Igor to stop his espionage activities. Later, when the Germans got around to arresting Trofimoff and Igor, the espionage activity would still be going on, the German Statute of Limitations would not have expired, and the two alleged spies might well have spent the rest of their lives in a German prison. The Soviets, through Igor, tried to stop Trofimoff's espionage activities, but he states that he refused to stop until specifically instructed by Igor to destroy the camera and all other evidence.

Additional information obtained from unofficial but reliable sources reveals that, when the Trofimoffs moved to Florida, their telephone was tapped and all mail was intercepted, opened, read and/or photographed, and resealed by the FBI without any suspicion from Trofimoff or his wife. Other reports allege that aerial surveillance was employed and clandestine pictures were taken of Trofimoff as he bagged groceries at a local supermarket. Jutta told me that during a visit to Trofimoff's attorney in Tampa she saw boxes of taped telephone calls made to and from the Trofimoff residence, recordings which began when the Trofimoffs moved to Florida and continued until her husband's arrest. During the author's visit to Tampa in April 2003, Trofimoff said he saw the same material during discovery prior to the trial. Trofimoff said that all of his mail was intercepted and read after he moved to the United States.

While none of these reports of surveillance have been acknowledged or confirmed by FBI representatives, one would logically assume that such measures were in effect throughout the investigation. When I questioned Agent Wagner on this point, he declined to comment, saying he was not allowed to discuss details of FBI investigative methods.

With the Trofimoff's move to the United States, the Department of Justice became involved. Also, Assistant U. S. Attorney Terry Furr, from Tampa, and Laura Ingersoll, Senior Trial Attorney of the Internal Security Section of the Department of Justice in Washington, D. C. were assigned to the case.[15]

Everyone involved in planning the government's case realized that extraordinary steps would be required if this complex international case were to be successfully prosecuted. Threads from England, Germany, Austria, Russia, the United States, and even Scotland had to be brought together and woven into an airtight package that would assure the conviction of Trofimoff once he was arrested.

After extensive reviews and discussions with all involved in the case, the two prosecutors decided that the key to a successful prosecution was to get Trofimoff to tell his own story. They decided that a "sting" operation was the answer. Dimitry Droujinsky, a retired FBI agent who was a master of "False Flag" operations, was asked to join the team.

Droujinsky's results reveal there could not have been a better choice. Prosecutor Furr was so impressed that he kept transcripts of the agent's first three conversations with Trofimoff to read and savor later. The importance of the videotaped meetings with Trofimoff is underscored by the fact that responsible individuals said they could never have gone forward with the case without them.

Agent Wagoner emphasized that Trofimoff's arrest, trial and conviction sent a strong message to those contemplating crimes against the United States. "When individuals commit such crimes, regardless of when they are committed, they must realize that the FBI and other agencies will be unrelenting in their efforts to insure that the guilty parties will be punished for their crimes." He also praised the cooperation and support the FBI received from many other agencies involved, including German organizations. "We do not work alone. The final result could never have been achieved without the full cooperation of many U. S. and foreign participants."[16]

When the FBI arrested Trofimoff and charged him with espionage, I, my wife, and all who knew him viewed the news with disbelief. Trofimoff, originally a man without a country, was born in Berlin in 1927. His early years were perilous ones, and his entire life is the epitome of a classic hardscrabble, rags-to-riches story. Successful in all his endeavors, he was helped by all he came in contact with; good fortune followed throughout his life. An extremely likable and engaging person, he gained the respect and admiration of his coworkers, subordinates, and everyone he met along the way. Comments such as, "He was a good boss and a dedicated worker," were often repeated during his trial, as well as made privately to the author by those who knew him well. Some comments made by coworkers were prophetic: impulsive, romantic, egotistic, arrogant, and irresponsible were descriptions often volunteered.

In their Florida retirement home, the Trofimoffs were well-liked members of the community, regularly participating in the wide variety of activities available to all. However, with all his good characteristics, hints of a darker personality were present. Clues were there for all to see, but not as obvious before his arrest as they later emerged. He often displayed a strong ego (bordering on arrogance), and he was quick to flare up in anger when things did not go his way. Both my wife Doris and I observed his quick anger on several occasions when he exploded at Jutta for minor reasons, and members of the poker group Trofimoff and I organized became accustomed to his bursts of temper when his luck soured. On more than one occasion, friends of mine told of his violent temper on the tennis court where throwing his racket and often arguing vehemently on questionable points were apparently common-place. As a result of his attitude on the tennis courts, some members refused to play with him. "I play tennis for enjoyment," one resident told me, "and I don't want to argue point after point . . . I play for fun, not for blood."[17] Trofimoff wanted desperately to win at whatever game or sport he was playing, and his monster ego would not allow him to accept defeat graciously.

With Trofimoff's arrest, everyone unanimously asked one basic question: Why? Why would an individual, given so much by his adopted country, and so successful in his military and civilian careers, perform the acts of espionage with which he was charged? In addition to that basic question, as events preceding his arrest became known, many other questions arose, including the following:

How could he, on the one hand, proclaim his disdain and hatred for the Communists while proclaiming his patriotism and deep love for the United States, and at the same time, commit treason against his beloved country by giving military secrets to those he professed to hate? This dichotomy may never be fully understood.

Why, if he committed these crimes, did he expose himself by returning to America where there is no statue of limitations for the crime of espionage?

If he was truly innocent, why did he talk at length by telephone with an unknown person (who represented himself as a member of the Russian Embassy in Washington) for months and not report to the FBI or other authorities the letters and calls he received at his Florida home?

With an immense credit card debt and a large second mortgage on his home, why was he willing to risk his future for a promise of only some $23,000 from his Russian "friend," when that sum represented only a portion of his total indebtedness?

Why didn't he file for bankruptcy to solve his overwhelming financial obligations?

Answers to the basic dilemma and other allied questions are not easy to come by, but a look at his life history offers some clues.

Trofimoff's family plays a significant role in his character development. His grandfather, a wealthy member of the Russian nobility and General in the Imperial Russian Army, was killed fighting the Red (Bolshevik) Forces, and his grandmother starved to death under the Bolshevik regime. His father, who graduated from the distinguished Pagen Institute in St. Petersburg, served as a personal page in the family of Tsar Nicholas II and later distinguished himself in the Revolutionary War, fighting the Bolsheviks until he was forced to flee Russia. From the very beginning, the history of the Russian Revolution and role of the Trofimoff family was drilled into Trofimoff, and he became a fervent lover of "Mother Russia," despising the Bolshevik regime.

The young Trofimoff's life in wartime Berlin, a rigorous existence with many privations coupled with continuous exposure to his Russian noble heritage, served to expand and reinforce his love for his motherland and his hatred of the Communist regime. As Trofimoff matured, the poverty, deprivations, and hardships of his youth developed latent desires for more and more of the better things of life, desires that would be evident throughout his adult life. An additional influence was his nanny, Lydia, who constantly urged him to excel in school, helping him develop an attitude and belief that he would always be successful, no matter what difficulties he faced. Trofimoff's experiences with the youth organization "NORM" were also instrumental in increasing his love of "Mother Russia" and Russian nobility.

With Trofimoff's decision to evade the German draft and seek the security of the U. S. military, he met more hardships as he traveled alone on foot through farming communities, hiding from both German and Russian soldiers, and begging for work and food from impoverished locals. His successful evasion of the draft surely fostered the trait that enabled him to rationalize his actions and believe strongly that he could always, ethically and properly, avoid or deny any distasteful experience or situation. His every act, he convinced himself, was always justified.

He writes that as he traversed the countryside, he observed many atrocities committed by Communist forces, which further convinced him that the Bolsheviks and Communism represented an evil ideology. He encountered and was "adopted" by a U. S. Army unit, acting as an interpreter and helping wherever he was needed. During all phases of his journey from Berlin to Paris, he learned to be resourceful and take advantage of any person or situation that he encountered.

His two years in Paris and the good fortune experienced there reinforced his belief that whatever path he followed would work out to his advantage, and his ego grew with no bounds. His experiences with others from his same background, both his peers, the children of Russian aristocracy, and the older members of the Russian nobility he became associated with, further developed his love for "Mother Russia." This love of the country he considered to be his "Motherland" would be demonstrated throughout the rest of his life. It was a major factor that brought him under the spell of Soviet agents when, later, he was assigned to the Nuremberg JIC.

During those early years the young Trofimoff learned the secrets of survival, and as the years passed, he became the ultimate survivor, able to prosper under any and all adverse conditions. His early life was rigorous and demanding, helping him perfect his ability to survive any misfortune and nurture an ego that made him believe he could do no wrong. In his mind, he would always be successful in whatever situation or difficulty he found himself in, and his ego refused to let him admit that he was ever wrong.

His experiences in Europe exerted a strong influence on him, and in later years, he became so sure that what he was doing was right and acceptable that his personality bordered on that of a sociopath (an individual with asocial or antisocial behavior or character traits that refuses to believe that his activities and actions are wrong). Evidence of this trait and his ability to rationalize his actions was demonstrated in his videotaped discussions with the FBI agent he assumed to be a representative of the KGB. "In my opinion," he said during his meeting with the agent, "I was never a traitor because I never gave anything American to anybody." Even after his conviction and sentencing, he still maintains his absolute innocence and pure patriotism to the United States.

His extreme distaste for the Communist world was immediately evident when he first arrived in America. He spoke at the Quakers'

Meetings for Worship and to students in local universities of the bar-
barism of the Soviets and Communists and became agitated when he
experienced some differing opinions from the student groups he spoke
to. Both his actions and his words made it clear that he was grateful to
have been brought to America and was sincerely dedicated to fighting
Communism in all its forms.

After enlisting in the Army, receiving his citizenship and later a
commission, he became, to all appearances, a good soldier and a loyal
citizen who fully appreciated what his adopted country had done for
him. I, for one, am convinced that during his early years he was a fine,
dedicated soldier and loyal citizen who truly loved his adopted country and appreciated the assistance he received along the way. It was
only after his assignment to the Nuremberg JIC and his reunion with
his foster brother that the personality traits described above took control of his destiny, pulling him into the KGB web. Once embarked on
that journey, there was no turning back.

While handwriting analysis is not admissible in courts of law, an
experienced graphologist, Charles Richardson, a good friend of mine,
has this to say:

> Graphology, the study of how one reveals his/her per-
> sonality through their handwriting, is what many refer
> to as an inexact, or soft science. What is evolving is a
> science that is far more scientific than common sense
> reasoning initially led us to believe. I feel that graphol-
> ogy books will, in the future, be removed from the
> occult and supernatural section of bookstores, and be
> placed alongside psychology and psychiatry texts in
> stacks of leading medical school libraries.[18]

Clearly, any analysis of Trofimoff's handwriting could not be used
to prove or disprove his guilt in this case. However, Richardson's
analysis of that handwriting paints an interesting picture of Trofimoff:
Richardson never met Trofimoff and had only a cursory knowledge of
the charges levied against him, and after reviewing a full page of
George's handwriting, he reported these impressions:

> It is apparent that the writer is intelligent, organized,
> creative, clever, and controlling. George is energetic,
> compassionate, outwardly social, but inwardly pri-
> vate. The writing has a foreign origin to it. The person
> who wrote this was probably educated in a foreign
> country. Most likely Europe . . . perhaps the Middle

East, or a country with Middle Eastern ties, influenced the writer in his youth.

When you meet George you are impressed with his outward nicety. The gregarious, energetic, fun-loving nature of the writer is contagious and persuading. He is protective of his family and most private about his intentions. Probably an avid reader, he's one who enjoys subjects of an intellectual nature. George can be a most engaging personality. He has a knack of seeing the flip side of an issue. His thinking and logic may seem perverse, even strange to many.[19]

This description of Trofimoff, deduced by a person who had never met him, was extremely accurate and uncanny for anyone who knew Trofimoff, and particularly so for me, as I had known him on a day-to-

Colonel George Trofimoff in happier times. (Author's collection)

day, personal basis for several years. More important, in light of Trofimoff's indictment, Richardson's conclusions were an eerie but accurate prediction of Trofimoff's ultimate reaction and response to the espionage charges.

Richardson relates that Kathleen Urbina, a forensic graphologist with more than 25 years of experience studying the handwriting of convicted felons, identified 29 signs commonly found in felons' handwriting, i. e., signs or "markers" that have been verified by numerous other graphologists.[20] Richardson's analysis of the one page of Trofimoff's handwriting revealed a surprising 21 of Urbana's signs.

The sample first analyzed by Richardson was written shortly after Trofimoff's arrest in June 2000. A second sample, written several months later, was submitted to Richardson for analysis. In the second sample, the same 21 signs previously identified were still evident. Also, Richardson concluded that Trofimoff was a more disturbed, tense, and unhappy individual than before. Richardson pointed out how Barry Branston, an English graphologist, identifies in his book[21] 12 handwriting signs that point to tension. Richardson located 10 of those signs in the second sample. In addition, a handwriting analysis text cited by Richardson[22] lists a number of signs of unhappiness; Richardson reports that most of those signs are prevalent throughout the second sample. It is not surprising that Trofimoff would be tense after many months in prison waiting for his trial, but the fact that the second sample revealed tension and unhappiness that was not so noticeable in the first sample lends credibility to Richardson's analysis.

Some conclusions reached by Richardson in his analysis of the second sample follow:

> George is very tense, angry and hostile. Emotionally, he is about to go out of control. A host of handwriting signs appear in the second sample of George's writing that clearly point to an emotionally on-edge individual. Several signs have become noticeably accentuated, especially those that point to the writer being extremely tense. The intensity of bottled up feelings is so strong that the writer's emotions are boiling over, and he has reached the point of being hostile. When the graphologist looks past George's anger and hostility, he sees a person who is very unhappy . . . When one looks at the signs of criminality in this writing, coupled with obvious signs of stress and unhappiness, we see

> an individual who has the potential to cope with frus-
> tration in an anti-social way. Many signs in the writing
> point to an individual with incredible inner strength.
> He will not crack easily, but when he does, watch out![23]

Again, handwriting analysis is not currently admissible as evidence in United States courts, and it is clear that Richardson's conclusions will never used to prove (or disprove) Trofimoff's guilt. However, it is very interesting to see that, as Trofimoff's life story unfolds, the traits identified in Richardson's analysis become apparent, particularly after his arrest, during his pretrial confinement, and during the trial itself. The story of his life also helps one answer those questions raised at the beginning of this chapter, by identifying those personality traits that had an overwhelming influence on his actions:

• An almost fanatical love of "Mother Russia," ingrained during his early youth and intensified during his days as a foster child in Berlin, his travels to Paris, and his association with other members of the Russian nobility in that city.

• An immense, unsatisfied demand for the finer things of life.

• An unconquerable desire and capability to survive in any adverse situation.

• An unbounded ego that refuses to accept defeat in any form.

• An egocentric, narcissistic personality and an arrogance that justifies and rationalizes any action as acceptable.

• An incredible inner discipline and ability to live with, and keep hidden, an extensive dark side, while at the same time developing and maintaining a circle of friends who never suspected that aspect of his personality.

In the final analysis, the question remains—why did he commit these crimes and become the most senior member of the American military establishment to be accused of espeionage in modern times? Doctor Mike Gelles, US Naval Criminal Investigative Service, in his article, "Exploring the Mind of the Spy," gives some observations based on interviews with incarcerated spies:

> There was no single motive for espionage. The true
> motivation was always deeper than what commonly
> appeared on the surface—money, ideology, or revenge.
> For example, spies value money not just for what it can
> buy, but for what it symbolizes—success, power, and

influence. It is a balm for injured self-esteem. People commit espionage not just for money, but in a desperate attempt to fulfill complex emotional needs.

Money received for espionage was spent, not saved. Most spies were not paid enough for unexplained affluence to be a problem. The few who did receive lots of money spent it rather than save it, and unexplained affluence was a factor in their detection.

One thing that most spies have in common is inability to accept responsibility for their own actions. They always blame others for their problems, and minimize or ignore their own mistakes or faults.

The spies felt no guilt about their betrayal while they were conducting espionage, and sometimes not even after they were arrested, because they engaged in self-deceptive rationalizations. They rationalized that the information they passed was unimportant. It was just a business transaction, not betrayal of country. Or they felt that their incompetent supervisors were the ones who were really to blame for their problems.[24]

After researching and writing this story about Trofimoff's life, it is fascinating to learn that many of his personality traits that I recognized are mirrored in Dr. Gelles' article.

In my opinion, it all started when he encountered financial problems with his third wife, Alexa. His brother Igor was there at the opportune time to take advantage of his problems and weaknesses, and with the classic KGB recruiting technique, George was hooked. Once he began to realize that money was there for the taking, his love of the good life and his innate greed took control. As history has shown with so many other unfortunate souls, there was no way out. At that point his ego and sense of invulnerability worked together to develop Trofimoff's personality, and he began to believe that everything he did was justified. He "knew" he was a true, loyal son of "Mother Russia" and, at the same time he "knew" he was a dedicated patriot of his adopted country. In his mind everything he did was for George and his motherland, and nothing else mattered. Even today, alone in his prison cell for life, he is in a state of denial, steadfastly proclaiming his innocence.

Epilogue

BONDAGE

I live a life of emptiness
Surrounded by four walls
Imprisoned in a lonely cell
Freedom seldom calls.

I thirst, I drink, I satisfy
My hunger as it's needed
But in the feeding of my soul
In this, I am defeated.

Once I lived, laughed and loved
I knew a boundless joy
All the beauty I beheld
I managed to destroy.

I hurt the ones who loved me most
So unconditionally
My selfishness was my demise
I only thought of me.

I'm in solitary confinement
Never to be free
Sentenced to life without parole
And having to live with me.

Janice F. Walters

Bibliography

BOOKS

Amend, Karen Kristan & Ruiz. *Achieving Compatibility With Handwriting Analysis, Vol. I & II*. North Hollywood, CA: Newcastle Publishing Co., Inc., 1992.

Christopher Andrew (With Vasili Mitrokhin). *The Mitrokhin Archive and the Secret History of the KGB*. New York: Basic Books, A Member of the Perseus Books Group, 1999.

Edwin Black. *IBM and the Holocaust*. New York: Crown Publishers, Member of the Crown Publishing Group (Random House, Inc.), 2001.

Barry Branston. *Graphology Explained—A Workbook*. York Beach, Maine: Samuel Weiser, Inc., 1991.

Lucy S. Dawidowicz. *The War Against the Jews 1933-1945*. New York: Holt, Rinehart and Winston, 1975.

Oleg Kalugin (with Fen Montaigne). *The First Directorate, My 32 Years in Intelligence and Espionage Against the West*. New York: St. Martin's Press, 1994.

R. H. Bruce Lockhart. *British Agent*. New York and London: G. P. Putnam's Sons, 1933.

Kathleen Urbina. *Evidence From the Pen—Graphic Clues/Sinister Signs*. New York: GraphU Enterprises, 1998.

Alice Weiser and Jan Hargrave. *Judge the Jury. Experience the Power of Reading People*. Dubuque, Iowa: Kendall/Hunt Publishing Company, 2000.

PUBLIC DOCUMENTS

United Kingdom. *The Mitrokhin Inquiry Report. Intelligence and*

Security Committee. Presented to Parliament by the Prime Minister. Chairman, The Right Honorable Tom King, C H M P. June, 2000. (Available on the Internet).

U. S. Naval Command Investigative Service, Exploring the Mind of the Spy, Doctor Mike Gelles, October 3, 2004.

U. S. District Court, Middle District of Florida, Tampa Division: United States of America, v. George Trofimoff, Case No. 8:00-CR-197-T-24EAJ. *Government Transcript Exhibits –*
Volume 1. (Transcripts of telephone calls, 07/10/97-02/18/99.)
Ibid., Volume 2. (Transcript of first videotaped meeting, 02/24/99).
Ibid., Volume 3. (Transcript of second videotaped meeting, 02/24/99).
Ibid., Volume 4. (Transcripts of telephone calls, 08/13/99-06/02/00.)

U. S. District Court, Middle District of Florida, Tampa Division: United States of America, Plaintiff, vs George Trofimoff, a/k/a George von Trofimoff, a/k/a "Antey," a/k/a "Markiz," a/k/a "Konsul.," Defendant. Case No. 8:00-CR-197-T-24C. TRANSCRIPT OF TRIAL PROCEEDINGS BEFORE THE HONORABLE SUSAN C. BUCKLEW, JUDGE. 4 June 2001, Tampa, Florida, 9:03 a.m.
Ibid., 5 June 2001, Tampa, Florida, 9:30 a. m.
Ibid., 6 June 2001, Tampa, Florida, 9:28 a. m.
Ibid., 7 June 2001, Tampa, Florida, 9:30 a. m.
Ibid., 8 June 2001, Tampa, Florida, 9:30 a. m.
Ibid., 11 June 2001, Tampa, Florida, 9:30 a. m.
Ibid., 12 June 2001, Tampa, Florida, 9:28 a. m.
Ibid., 13 June 2001, Tampa, Florida, 9:50 a. m.
Ibid., 14 June 2001, Tampa, Florida, 9:29 a. m.
Ibid., 15 June 2001, Tampa, Florida, 9:43 a. m.
Ibid., 18 June 2001, Tampa, Florida, 9:30 a. m.
Ibid., 19 June 2001, Tampa, Florida, 9:33 a. m.
Ibid., 21 June 2001, Tampa, Florida, 9:30 a. m.
Ibid., 22 June 2001, Tampa, Florida, 9:32 a. m.
Ibid., 25 June 2001, Tampa, Florida, 9:28 a. m.
Ibid., 26 June 2001, Tampa, Florida, 9:49 a. m.

Federal Office of Criminal Investigation Nuremberg, Germany,

12/14/1994. ST 43-050563/94-3, GBA 3 BJs 1115/94-3, *Interrogation of an Accused*, George Trofimoff, 27 pages. (Entered in the Trofimoff trial as United States Government Exhibit 41B). (English language translation, Certified Copy).

Federal Office of Criminal Investigation, Munich Germany, 12/14/94. ST (Criminal Matter) 44 – 050 562/94, 3 BJs (Federal Justice Matter) 1116/94-3 (249). *Interrogation of the Accused*, Igor Iriney Susemihl, 23 pages. (Entered in the Trofimoff trial as United States Government Exhibit 43B). (English language translation, Certified Copy).

The Examining Judge of the Federal Supreme Court, 76125 Karlsruhe, Germany, December 15, 1994. 3 BJs 1116/94-3 (249), 2 BGs 290/94. *In the Preliminary Investigation against Igor Iriney Susemihl for Suspicion of intelligence agent activity*, 7 pages, conducted by Dr. Bode, Judge at the Federal Supreme Court as Examining Judge. (Entered in the Trofimoff trial as United States Government Exhibit 44B). (English language translation, Certified Copy).

The Examining Judge of the Federal Supreme Court, 76125 Karlsruhe, Germany, December 15, 1994. 3 BJs 1115/94-3 (249), 2 BGs 291/94. *In The Preliminary Investigation against George Trofimoff for Suspicion of intelligence agent activity*, 10 pages, conducted by Dr. Bode, Judge of the Federal Supreme Court as Examining Judge. (Entered in the Trofimoff trial as United States Government Exhibit 42B.) (English language translation, Certified Copy).

Germany, The Examining Judge of the Federal Supreme Court of Justice, 15 December 1994. 3 BJs 1115/94-3 (249), 3BJs 1116/94-3 (249), 2BGs 291/94, Court Order, *In the criminal investigation against 1. George TROFIMOFF and 2. Igor Iriney SUSEMIHL, because of Suspicion of secret service like spy activitie*s. (Unofficial English translation – 21 June 00/Ky)

DOCUMENTARY FILM

Columbia Broadcasting System, 60 Minutes II. *The Perfect Spy*. Fifteen Minute Documentary, March 27, 2002.

UNPUBLISHED MATERIALS

George Trofimoff, *Autobiography*, undated (consisting of more than fifty pages of handwritten and typed notes). Trofimoff's notes cover his family's history, his early life in Berlin, his time with a US Army unit, and his travel to Paris with that unit.

George Trofimoff, *Biography*, undated (consisting of more than one hundred pages of handwritten and typed notes). Trofimoff's notes cover his stay in Paris, his immigration to the United States, his early years in the U. S. Army, his service as a U. S. Civil Service employee, his assignment to the NATO Joint Interrogation Center, his arrest in Germany, his retirement and move to the United States, and his views on his arrest, trial, and conviction.

George Trofimoff, *Super Spy or Innocent Victim*, undated. A 33-page typewritten summary, written by Trofimoff while in prison, depicting, from his viewpoint, a chronological summary of the events which led to his arrest, trial, conviction, sentencing, and the subsequent appeals which were all denied. The summary concludes with the continued assertion of his innocence, and his strong belief that his conviction represents a serious miscarriage of justice, with violations of his constitutional rights of Due Process and a Fair Trial.

George Trofimoff, *Comments on Indictment*, undated. Trofimoff's comments on his indictment are in five enclosures (documents prepared by Trofimoff after his arrest in 2002):

    1. George Trofimoff, undated, *Legend to Organizational Chart*. A description of the elements of Trofimoff's organization, to include charts of organizational units and diagrams of the Nuremberg Joint Interrogation Center (JIC).
    2. *George Trofimoff*, undated, *Nuremberg JIC*. A detailed description of the organization and functions of the various elements of the JIC.
    3. George Trofimoff, undated. *Igor Susemihl*. A 1-pg. summary of Susemihl's life history.
    4. George Trofimoff, *Background*. A detailed 4-page history of Trofimoff, from his birth in Berlin on March 9, 1927, up to his arrest by German authorities in Nuremberg on December 14, 1994, and his retirement from Civil Service on March 3, 1995.

5. George Trofimoff, *Family Relationships and Political Beliefs.*

Andy J. Byers, *Trofimoff Trial Notes,* undated. Two stenographer's notebooks containing detailed notes taken during Trofimoff's trial, 6 June 2001–26 June 2001.

Andy J. Byers, taped interview with Jutta Trofimoff, undated (taped after the Trofimoff trial).

Appendix A

Decision of Judge Bode, German Supreme Court, 12 December 1994

Unofficial English Translation - 21 June 00/Ky

The Examing Judge
of the Federal Supreme Court of Justice

15 December 1994

<u>3 BJs 1115/94-3 (249)</u>
<u>3 BJs 1116/94-3 (249)</u>
2 BGs 291/94

<u>Court Order</u>

In the criminal investigation

against

1. George **TROFIMOFF**, born on 9 March 1927 in Berlin,
    living Daumerstr. 4 in 90409 Nürnberg,

2. Igor Iriney **SUSEMIHL**, born on 10 July 1919 in Tschernigow/
    Ukraine, living in Wien, Jauresgasse 2

because of

Suspicion of secret service like spy activities

The requests of the Federal Attorney General at the Federal Supreme Court of Justice for the issue of arrest warrant against the accused George Trofimoff and Igor Susemihl are

rejected.

<u>Reasons:</u>

There is no current strong suspicion against both accused that they conducted secret service like spy activities within the time of the statue of limitations according to para 99 StGB, Art. 7, Abs. 1 No. 4 4. StaÄG. For crimes according to para 99 StGB, a statue of limitations period of 5 years is effective (para 78 Abs. 3 No. 4 StGB). As the limitation of action was interrupted the first time on Dec. 12. 1994, by the decree of search directions, the criminal actions of the accused would have had to continue after Dec. 12, 1989. This is not substantiated. The office of the Federal Attorney based the

11

assumption of strong suspicion primarily on the source reports of the office of the German Intelligence Service of Dec. 5, 1994. The tactical time of the source reports, however, is end of the '70s/beginning of the '80s. Several personal indicators to the alias name "Antey" refer to the year 1978. Besides it is stated that the source is sure that the secret service like cooperation between "Antey" and "Ikar" lasted into the eighties. Closer and more concrete information regarding further crime periods cannot be assumed from the source reports. Also there is no credible evidence recognizable that proves that the accused accomplished secret service like activities in the sense of the allegations after Dec. 12, 1989 and therefore within the statute of limitations. The accuracy of the source reports has been confirmed in many details by the pre-investigations of the Federal Intelligence Service, but their tactical time is so far back that additional evidence is necessary to justify the strong suspicion also for the period thereafter, especially within the statute of limitations. This is missing. Regarding the accused Susemih, during the search a screw driver was found in a concealed place that with high possibility has been used for secret service like activities. It is evident that this container has not been used for a long time, so that criminal activities within the time of the statute of limitations cannot be established. Also the suspicious actions that appeared during the questioning of the witnesses Marion and Jutta Trofimoff [ex-wife and current wife, respectively] are not enough to warrant the strong suspicion. Both witnesses tried to conceal the personal contacts between Trofimoff and Susemihl. The reason for this can also be the previous behavior of the accused. Altogether there is no sound evidence that the secret service like connection between the accused and the KGB or its successors continued during the period covered by the statute of limitations. Strong suspicion in the sense of the requests for warrant of arrest is therefore not given. Therefore the requests have to be rejected.

Dr. Bode
Judge at the Federal Supreme Court of Justice

12

Appendix B

The United States Indictment for George Trofimoff

George Trofimoff Affidavit

UNITED STATES DISTRICT COURT
MIDDLE DISTRICT OF FLORIDA
TAMPA DIVISION

CASE NO. 8:00-CR-197-T-24C

UNITED STATES OF AMERICA

V.

GEORGE TROFIMOFF,

a/k/a George Von Trofimoff,

a/k/a "Antey," a/k/a "Markiz," a/k/a "Konsul"

INDICTMENT

The Grand Jury charges:

COUNT ONE

A. INTRODUCTION

At all times relevant to this indictment:

1. The defendant, GEORGE TROFIMOFF, a/k/a George Von Trofimoff, a/k/a "Antey," a/k/a "Markiz," a/k/a "Konsul," was born in Germany to Russian émigrés, and became a naturalized United States citizen in 1951. He enlisted in the United States Army in 1948 and received a commission in the United States Army Reserve in 1953. He was honorably discharged from active duty in the United States Army in 1956, and retired from the United States Army Reserve with the rank of Colonel in 1987. From 1959 through 1994, TROFIMOFF was employed by the United States Army as a civilian working in military intelligence, serving primarily in Germany.

2. Pursuant to Executive Order 12958 and its preceding Orders, information, the unauthorized disclosure of which could reasonably be expected to cause "damage to national security," must be classified as CONFIDENTIAL and properly safeguarded. Information, the unauthorized disclosure of which reasonably could be expected to cause "serious damage to the national security," must be classified as SECRET and properly safeguarded. Information, the unauthorized disclosure of which could reasonably be expected to cause "exceptionally grave damage to the national security," must be classified as TOP SECRET and properly safeguarded.

217

George Trofimoff Affidavit   Page 2

3. Throughout his career with the United States Army, TROFIMOFF held SECRET and TOP SECRET clearances, and received periodic briefings and acknowledged his responsibilities in handling classified information.

4. The United States, the Federal Republic of Germany, Great Britain, and others were member nations of the North Atlantic Treaty Organization (NATO), which provided for a common defense against the threat of military aggression.

5. Until in or around 1991, the principal military threat to the NATO countries was from the Union of Soviet Socialist Republics (Soviet Union) and its Warsaw Treaty organization (Warsaw Pact) allies, which included German Democratic Republic (East Germany), the Polish People's Republic, the People's Republic of Hungary, the Czechoslovak Socialist Republic, and the People's Republic of Bulgaria.

6. Since in or around 1991, NATO has guarded against potential threats from former republics of the Soviet Union, including the Russian Federation, and their allies.

7. As a member of NATO the United States had a military intelligence presence in Western Europe, including the 66th Military Intelligence Group (MIG).

8. A mission of the 66th MIG was to work together with the military intelligence services of other countries in collecting intelligence about Warsaw Pact countries. One source of this intelligence was interviews of refugees and defectors from Warsaw Pact countries. Some such interviews were conducted by military intelligence personnel assigned to Joint Interrogation Centers (JIC).

9. A JIC at Nuernberg in the Federal Republic of Germany was staffed by United States Army personnel as well as other United States, German, British, and French military personnel, From 1969 to 1994, the defendant GEORGE TROFIMOFF was the Chief of the United States Army Element at the Nuernberg JIC,

10. The United States Army Element at the Nuernberg JIC received classified information, including documents produced by members of the United States intelligence community such as the Defense Intelligence Agency.

11. As Chief of the United States Army Element at the Nuernberg JIC, TROFIMOFF had access to all classified information, including documents, received by and produced by the United States Army Element.

12. Among the classified documents related to the national defense of the United States which were maintained at the Nuernberg JIC were the following:

    (a) Intelligence Objectives, which listed current intelligence information required by the United States.

    (b) Intelligence Priorities for Strategic Planning, which identified and ranked the current intelligence needs of the United States military.

    (e) Soviet and Warsaw Pact Order of Battle documents which detailed the United States' current state of knowledge of Soviet and Warsaw Pact military organizations and capabilities.

    (d) Collection Support Briefs on specific topics such as the current chemical and biological warfare threat posed by the Soviet Union and its Warsaw Pact allies and others.

    (e) Intelligence Information Reports, which were reports of information responsive to identified intelligence collection requirements, obtained from various sources including interviews of refugee and defectors.

13. The Committee for State Security of the Soviet Union (*Komitet Gosudarstvennoy Bezopasnosti*, referred to as the KGB) was the principal intelligence and counterintelligence service of the Soviet Union

and was organized into Chief Directorates, Departments and Services. The KGB viewed the United States as the principal adversary, or main enemy, of the Soviet Union, and as the KGB's primary intelligence target.

14. Among the KGB's missions was counterintelligence, which was aimed at identifying and counteracting the threat posed to the security of the Soviet Union by hostile intelligence services, such as those of the United States. This mission required the KGB to obtain intelligence information about the state of adversaries' knowledge about the military preparedness of the Soviet Union and its Warsaw Pact allies.

15. A method by which the KGB obtained intelligence information about its adversaries was to recruit persons having authorized access to such intelligence information to provide it to the KGB, thereby giving the KGB the opportunity to identify, penetrate, and neutralize potential threats to the Soviet Union, and to conduct denial and deception.

16. The Russian Orthodox Church was an organized religious institution within the Soviet Union and had churches and officials, including clergy, both within the Soviet Union and abroad.

17. The KGB exploited the Russian Orthodox Church and its officials, including clergy, in furtherance of the missions of the KGB.

18. Igor Vladimirovich Susemihl, a/k/a Zuzemihl, also called "Iriney," was a priest of the Russian Orthodox church who served as the Archbishop of Vienna and Austria and Temporary Archbishop of Baden and Bavaria, and later served as Metropolitan of Vienna and Austria, and who resided in the vicinity of Munich, Federal Republic of Germany, until his death in 1999.

19. The defendant GEORGE TROFIMOFF was raised in Germany with Susemihl, who was also the son of Russian émigrés, and TROFIMOFF considered Susemihl to be his "brother." Beginning during the 1960s, TROFIMOFF and Susemihl met often and maintained a close personal relationship.

20. In or about 1969, after the defendant GEORGE TROFIMOFF became the Chief of the United States Army Element at the Nuernberg JIC, Susemihl recruited him into the service of the KGB.

21. Within the KGB, the First Chief Directorate (FCD) was primarily responsible for foreign intelligence.

22. Within the FCD, Directorate K was responsible for the KGB's counterintelligence mission abroad.

23. KGB officers who had counterintelligence responsibilities often operated abroad from diplomatic missions of the Soviet Union. These intelligence officers worked for Line KR of Directorate K.

24. The Order of the Red Banner is the oldest Soviet award and was presented to citizens and non-citizens for special bravery, self-sacrifice, and courage displayed in the defense of the socialist homeland, including special bravery and courage displayed in accomplishing special assignments, and special bravery and courage displayed in support of the state security of the Soviet Union.

25. Since 1992, the Russian Foreign Intelligence Service (*Sluzhba Vneshney Rezvedki Rossii*, referred to as the SVRR) has been the successor to the KGB as the foreign intelligence service of the Russian Federation.

B. The Agreement

26. Beginning on or about an unknown date which was at least 1969, and continuing through in or around the spring of 1995, both dates being approximate and inclusive, in the Federal Republic of Germany, the Republic of Austria, and elsewhere outside the jurisdiction of any State or district of the United States, the defendant,

GEORGE TROFIMOFF,
a/k/a George Von Trofimoff,
a/k/a "Antey," a/k/a "Markiz,"
a/k/a "Konsul,"

did knowingly and willfully combine, conspire, confederate, and agree with various other persons whose names are both known and unknown to the Grand Jury, to knowingly and willfully communicate, deliver, and transmit and to attempt to communicate, deliver, and transmit directly and indirectly to a foreign government, that is, the Union of Soviet Socialist Republics, and to representatives, officers, agents, and employees thereof, documents, photographs, photographic negatives, and information relating to the national defense of the United States, with intent and reason to believe that the same would be used to the injury of the United States and to the advantage of a foreign nation, in violation of Title 18, United States Code, Section 794(a).

C. The Manner and Means of the Conspiracy

27. It was part of the conspiracy that agents, representatives, officers, and employees of the KGB/SVRR would and did recruit individuals who had access to classified information relating to the national defense of the United States to obtain such information and transmit it to agents, representatives, officers, and employees of the KGB/SVRR. The persons recruited to conduct such espionage were called "agents-in-place."

28. It was further part of the conspiracy that agents, representatives, officers, and employees of the KGB/SVRR would and did pay money - including regular cash payments, bonuses, and special payments - to their agents-in-place, including the defendant GEORGE TROFIMOFF, in exchange for classified information relating to the national defense of the United States, including those documents described in Paragraph 12.

29. It was further part of the conspiracy that agents, representatives, officers, and employees of the KGB/SVRR would and did have meetings in the Federal Republic of Germany and the Republic of Austria with their agents-in-place for the purpose of obtaining classified information relating to the national defense of the United States, and in exchange would give these persons monetary payments and instructions for further espionage activities on behalf of the KGB/SVRR.

30. It was further part of the conspiracy that agents, representatives, officers, and employees of the KGB/SVRR would and did provide to their agents-in-place, and cause their agents-in-place to purchase, obtain, and use, equipment, including, but not limited to, photographic equipment and film, for the purpose of furthering their espionage activities on behalf of the KGB/SVRR.

31. It was further part of the conspiracy that agents, representatives, officers, and employees of the KGB/SVRR would and did cause its agents-in-place to secretly carry classified documents relating to the national defense of the United States, away from the locations where they were supposed to be kept, by utilizing briefcases and bags.

32. It was further part of the conspiracy that agents, representatives, officers, and employees of the KGB/SVRR would and did utilize agents and apparently innocent persons to spot, assess, and co-opt targets for recruitment as agents-in-place, and to introduce those persons to agents, representatives, officers, and employees of the KGB/SVRR.

33. It was further part of the conspiracy that officers and agents, representatives, officers, and employees of the KGB/SVRR and their agents-in-place, and their agents-in-place, would and did use innocuous explanations for their activities on behalf of the KGB/SVRR.

34. It was further part of the conspiracy that the KGB/SVRR would and did protect its agents-in-place through disinformation and other means.

35. It was further part of the conspiracy that the KGB/SVRR would and did assign to its agents code names which were periodically changed. The KGB/SVRR assigned to the defendant, GEORGE TROFIMOFF, the code names "Antey," "Markiz," and "Konsul," and assigned to Igor Susemihl the code name "Ikar."

36. Aleksandr Vasilyevich Blagov, a/k/a "Vlagov," was a KGB/SVRR officer who operated out of Soviet/Russian diplomatic missions in Europe and maintained contact with Igor Susemihl and others in furtherance of the missions of the KGB/SVRR.

37. It was further part of the conspiracy that agents, representatives, officers, and employees of the KGB/SVRR would and did continue to communicate with their agents-in-place after the agents-in-place had ceased providing intelligence information to the KGB/SVRR, in order to ensure continued loyalty and protection.

38. It was further part of the conspiracy that the defendant, GEORGE TROFIMOFF, and others would and did misrepresent, conceal, and hide, and cause to be misrepresented, concealed, and hidden, the acts done in furtherance of the conspiracy.

D. Overt Acts

39. In furtherance of and to effect the objects of the conspiracy, the defendant, GEORGE TROFIMOFF, did commit various overt acts, including but not limited to, the following: (Unless otherwise stated, these overt acts each occurred between at least 1969 and December 1994.)

(1) GEORGE TROFIMOFF secretly took classified United States documents relating to the national defense away from the Nuernberg JIC.

(2) GEORGE TROFIMOFF secretly photographed classified United States documents relating to the national defense.

(3) GEORGE TROFIMOFF secretly removed and replaced staples in classified United States documents relating to the national defense in order to photograph the documents' contents.

(4) GEORGE TROFIMOFF secretly returned classified United States documents relating to the national defense to the Nuernberg JIC.

(5) GEORGE TROFIMOFF purchased a Minox camera at the direction of the KGB, but "turned it back in" through Igor Susemihl because "it was too dangerous to have."

(6) GEORGE TROFIMOFF used a double-frame camera to photograph the contents of classified United States documents relating to the national defense.

(7) GEORGE TROFIMOFF made and used a device to place documents while he photographed them, "so the page would fit exactly."

(8) GEORGE TROFIMOFF possessed two goose neck lamps in 1994.

(9) GEORGE TROFIMOFF purchased film.

(10) GEORGE TROFIMOFF put rolls of exposed film back into their original boxes and glued the boxes shut.

(11) GEORGE TROFIMOFF stored boxes of exposed film at his home until he delivered them to Igor Susemihl or to KGB officers.

(12) GEORGE TROFIMOFF hand carried boxes of exposed film to Igor Susemihl.

George Trofimoff Affidavit   Page 6

(13) GEORGE TROFIMOFF hand carried boxes of exposed film to KGB intelligence officers.

(14) GEORGE TROFIMOFF maintained a regular relationship with and had frequent contacts with Igor Susemihl.

(15) GEORGE TROFIMOFF traveled to Amstetten, Austria, and met with a KGB officer.

(16) GEORGE TROFIMOFF traveled to Zell am See, Austria, and met with a KGB officer.

(17) GEORGE TROFIMOFF traveled to Bad Ischl, Austria, and met with a KGB officer.

(18) GEORGE TROFIMOFF traveled to Hallein, Austria, and met with a KGB officer.

(19) GEORGE TROFIMOFF traveled to in or around St. Johann, Austria, and met with a KGB officer.

(20) GEORGE TROFIMOFF met with KGB officer Anatoliy Tikhonovich Kireyev, a/k/a Kireev.

(21) GEORGE TROFIMOFF met with KGB officer Victor Aleksandrovich Chernyshev, a/k/a Tschernyshev.

(22) GEORGE TROFIMOFF met with KGB officer Yuriy Vasilyevich Lysov.

(23) GEORGE TROFIMOFF turned over to the KGB photographs of documents from the JIC which he believed would be of value to the KGB and could not be traced to him.

(24) GEORGE TROFIMOFF received periodic cash payments in Deutschmarks from Igor Susemihl, and from KGB officers.

(25) GEORGE TROFIMOFF received cash bonuses from the KGB.

(26) GEORGE TROFIMOFF received approximately 90,000 Deutschmarks from KGB.

(27) GEORGE TROFIMOFF used an oral recognition signal or statement, called a "parole", when he met with a KGB officer.

(28) GEORGE TROFIMOFF concealed from his wives his espionage activities and the true nature of the money he received from the KGB.

(29) GEORGE TROFIMOFF failed to report his relationship with Igor Susemihl, to the United States Army, as he was required to do.

(30) In or around December 1994, GEORGE TROFIMOFF and Igor Susemihl told authorities in Germany that money TROFIMOFF received from Igor Susemihl was personal loans.

(31) In or after December 1994, GEORGE TROFIMOFF discarded a tripod.

(32) GEORGE TROFIMOFF was awarded the Order of the Red Banner.

E. Venue

Venue is obtained by Title 18, United States Code, Section 3238.

All in violation of Title 18, United States Code, Section 794(c).

Forfeitures

1. The allegations contained in Count One of this Indictment are hereby realleged and incorporated by reference for the purpose of alleging forfeitures, pursuant to the provisions of Title 18, United States Code, Section 794(d).

2. From his engagement in any or all of the violations alleged in Count One, punishable by imprisonment for more than one year, the defendant shall forfeit to the United States, pursuant to Title 18, United States Code, Section 794(d)(1)(A) and (B), all of his interest in:

    a. Property constituting and derived from any proceeds the defendant obtained, directly or indirectly, as a result of such violations; and

    b. Property used and intended to be used in any manner or part to commit or to facilitate the commission of such violations.

3. If any of the property described above as being subject to forfeiture, as a result of any act or omission of the defendant:

    a. cannot be located upon the exercise of due diligence;

    b. has been transferred, sold to, or deposited with, a third party;

    c. has been placed beyond the jurisdiction of the Court;

    d. has been substantially diminished in value; or

    e. has been commingled with other property which cannot be subdivided without difficulty;

it is the intent of the United States, pursuant to Title 21, United States Code, Section 853(p), as incorporated in Title 18, United States Code, Section 794(d)(3), to seek forfeiture of any other property of said defendant up to the value of the above forfeitable property.

All in violation of Title 18, United States Code, Section 794.

    A TRUE BILL,

    _____
    FOREPERSON

DONNA A. BUCELLA
United States Attorney

_____
WALTER E. FURR, III
Assistant United States Attorney
Chief, Narcotics Section

_____
LAURA A. INGERSOLL
Senior Trial Attorney
Internal Security Section
United States Department of Justice

Endnotes

Chapter 1

[1]David Leppard, Jon Ungoed-Thomas, Paul Nuki, Gareth Walsh, and Clive Freeman. "Briton's Treachery Exposed by Keeper of KGB's Secrets: Defector Smuggled Out Copies of the 'Crown Jewels' of Soviet Espionage." *Sunday Times* (London), 12 September 1999.

[2]John McWethy, "An Intelligence Coup," ABC News, Washington, DC, Sept. 9, 1999.

[3]*Sunday Times*, loc. cit.

[4]ABC News, loc. cit.

[5]*Sunday Times*, loc. cit.

[6]Christopher Andrew (with Vasili Mitrokhin). *The Mitrokhin Archive and the Secret History of the KGB.* New York: Basic Books, Member of the Perseus Books Group, 1999. The details of Mitrokhin's meeting with the young female diplomat are found on pages 13-14.

[7]*Sunday Times*, loc. sit.

[8]Christopher Andrew (with Vasili Mitrokhin), loc. sit., pg. 14.

[9]ABC News, loc. sit.

[10]"John Doe," was the BSIS agent who testified during Trofimoff's trial. His true identity was never revealed during the trial, but it now seems that the individual could have been Professor Christopher Andrew, who coauthored *The Sword and the Shield* with Mitrokhin. His picture on the inside of the dust cover of that book bears no resemblance to the "John Doe" the author observed during the trial, but it is possible that "John Doe" was in fact Professor Andrew, heavily disguised.

[11]ABC News, loc .sit.

[12]Ibid.

[13]Ibid.

[14]Ibid

[15]Ibid.

[16]United Kingdom, *The Mitrokhin Inquiry Report.* Intelligence and Security Committee. Presented to Parliament by the Prime Minister. Chairman, The Right Honorable Tom King, C H M P. June 2000. (Available on the Internet).

[17]A summary of Mitrokhin items, introduced as Government Exhibit 116 during Trofimoff's trial, page 8 of 12.

Chapter 2

[1]George Trofimoff, Autobiography, undated, (consisting of more than 50 pages of handwritten and typed notes), p.1. Trofimoff's notes cover his family's history, his early life in Berlin, his time with a U. S. Army unit, and his travel to Paris with that unit.

[2]Ibid.

[3]Ibid.

[4]Ibid., p. 2.

[5]Wladimir's attendance at the Pagen Academy and his subsequent appointment to the Imperial Court has been verified by BLITZ St. Petersburg, a Russian-American company that provides genealogical searches, archival research and information services, using Russian State Historic Archives in St. Petersburg and Moscow. Documents obtained from the archives reveal that Wladimir graduated from the Pagen Corps Academy and was promoted to the rank of court-page, according to the Emperor's decision, on September 27, 1913. A handwritten document, dated October 17, 1913, signed by the Emperor, confirmed the appointment and gave Wladimir's marks in the academy.

[6]Trofimoff, loc. sit., p. 2.

[7]Ibid., p. 3.

[8]Ibid.

[9]R. H. Bruce Lockhart. British Agent. New York and London: G. P. Putnam's Sons, 1933, p. 227.

[10]Trofimoff, loc. sit., p. 1.

[11]Ibid., pp. 4, 5. The story of Trofimoff's acceptance by the Scharawoff family.

[12]Ibid., pp. 5, 6.

[13]Ibid., p. 6.

[14]Ibid.

[15]Ibid., p. 4a.

[16]Ibid., p. 7.

[17]Ibid., p. 4a.

[18]Ibid., pp. 9, 10.

[19]Ibid., p. 7.

[20]Ibid., Page 2a.

[21]Ibid., p. 8.

[22]Ibid.

[23]Ibid., pp. 8, 9.

[24]Ibid., p. 10.

[25]Ibid., p. 21.

[26]Lucy S. Dawidowicz,. The War Against the Jews 1933-1945. New York: Holt, Rinehart and Winston, 1975), pp. 101, 102.

Dawidowicz describes Kristallnacht: "That night (November 10, 1938) fires were ignited all over Germany, and the shattered plate glass that was to give the program its name littered the streets of German towns and cities. . . . Synagogues and Jewish institutions were burned to the ground . . . Nearly one hundred Jews were killed, and thousands more subjected to wanton violence and sadistic treatment."

[27]Edwin Black, IBM and the Holocaust (New York: Crown Publishers, Member of the Crown Publishing Group [Random House, Inc.], 2001), pp. 142-144.

[28]Trofimoff, loc. sit., pp. 11, 12.

[29]Ibid., p. 12.

[30]Ibid., pp. 12, 13.

[31]Ibid., p. 13.

[32]Ibid., p. 14.

[33]Ibid.

[34]Ibid., p. 15.

[35]Ibid., pp. 15, 16.

[36]Ibid., p. 17.

[37]Ibid., p. 19.

[38]Ibid., p. 20.

[39]Ibid.

[40]Ibid.

[41]Ibid., pp. 21, 22.

[42]Ibid., p. 22.

[43]Ibid., p. 21.

[44]Trofimoff's aunt and cousin were both among the thousands of Dresden citizens perishing in the firestorm resulting from a massive air raid on February 22/23, 1945. The date of this raid was verified by personal flight records of U. S. Air Force Colonel (Ret) Vito Fierro, who piloted a B-24 bomber in the raid.

Chapter 3

[1]George Trofimoff, Autobiography, undated (consisting of more than 50 pages of handwritten and typed notes), p. 23. Trofimoff's

notes cover his family's history, his early life in Berlin, his time with a
U. S. Army unit, and his travel to Paris with that unit. Trofimoff's
description of his journey from Pilsen to Paris begins on page 23 of his
notes. This chapter (3) is based entirely on his notes as the author was
unable to locate anyone who could verify their accuracy. When
Trofimoff speaks, the quotation comes directly from his written jour-
nal.

[2]Ibid

[3]Ibid., p. 24.

[4]Ibid., p. 24a.

[5]Ibid., pp. 24a, 24b.

[6]Ibid., p. 24b.

[7]Ibid., p. 26.

[8]Ibid., p. 27.

[9]Ibid.

[10]Ibid., p. 28.

[11]Ibid.

[12]Ibid., pp. 28, 29.

[13]The author was unsuccessful in his attempts to locate the records
of this unit.

[14]Trofimoff, loc. cit., p. 30.

[15]Ibid., p. 31.

[16]Ibid., pp. 31, 32.

[17]Ibid., p. 32

[18]Trofimoff, loc. cit., p. 35.

[19]Ibid., p. 35.

[20]Ibid., p. 36.

[21]Ibid.

[22]Ibid.

[23]Ibid., p. 37.

[24]Ibid., p. 38.

[25]Ibid.

[26]Ibid., p. 37.

[27]Ibid., p. 38.

[28]Ibid.

[29]Ibid., p. 39.

[30]Ibid.

[31]Ibid.

[32]Ibid.

[33]Ibid., p. 40.

[34]Ibid.
[35]Ibid.
[36]Ibid.
[37]Ibid., p. 41.
[38]Ibid.
[39]Ibid.
[40]Ibid., p. 42.
[41]Ibid., p. 43.
[42]Ibid.
[43]Ibid., pp. 43, 44.
[44]Ibid., p. 44.
[45]Ibid.
[46]Ibid., p. 45.
[47]Ibid., p. 41.
[48]Ibid., pp. 45, 46.
[49]Ibid., p. 46.
[50]Ibid. p. 47.
[51]Ibid.

Chapter 4

[1]George Trofimoff, Biography, undated (consisting of more than 100 pages of handwritten and typed notes), p. 47. Trofimoff's notes cover his stay in Paris, his emigration to the United States, his early years in the U. S. Army, his service as a U. S. Civil Service Employee, his assignment to the NATO Joint Interrogation Center, his arrest in Germany, his retirement and move to the United States, and his views on his arrest, trial, and conviction. His description of his experiences in the United States begins on p. 47 of these notes.
[2]Ibid., p. 47.
[3]Ibid., pp. 47, 48.
[4]Ibid., p. 48.
[5]Ibid.
[6]The confusion in Trofimoff's arrival time resulted from the cable he sent the Butterworths prior to his departure from Amsterdam. His notes say that his cable gave his arrival time at La Guardia Field as "4.25 Dec," without specifying the date. Jean Robinson, in her comments on the book, wrote that they (the Butterworth family) "presumed it meant Christmas Day."
[7]Trofimoff, loc. sit., p. 48.

[8]Jean Robinson, one of Uncle Paul's daughters, provided comments on an early draft of this book. Her notes, dated May 2, 2001, describe the Butterworth's family home, Sunset Farm, as "a community of many widely separated houses on the edge of West Hartford. It had ancient oaks, maples, hemlocks, pines, a neighborhood spring-fed swimming pool and a tennis court."

[9]The Butterworth sisters still live in New England. I have corresponded with each, and they have confirmed Trofimoff's notes depicting the time he spent with their family in Connecticut.

[10]Trofimoff, loc. sit., pp. 48, 49.

[11]Ibid., p. 49.

[12]Ibid.

[13]Ibid., p. 50.

[14]Ibid., pp. 50, 51.

[15]Ibid., p. 51.

[16]Ibid., p. 52.

[17]Ibid., pp. 52, 53.

[18]Ibid., p. 54.

[19]Ibid.

[20]Ibid., p. 55.

[21]Ibid., p. 56.

[22]Ibid., pp. 56, 58.

[23]An article in the Hartford Courant dated July 20, 1948, titled "Enlistment Is Explained By Russian," gives some details of Trofimoff's travails as a young lad traveling through Europe. It includes a picture depicting him with two other youths taking the oath of allegiance, administered by a Major Frederick G. Wilkin, Officer-in-Charge of the Hartford Recruiting Station.

Chapter 5

[1]George Trofimoff, Biography, undated (consisting of more than 100 pages of handwritten and typed notes), p. 1. Trofimoff's notes cover his stay in Paris, his emigration to the United States, his early years in the U. S. Army, his service as a U. S. Civil Service employee, his assignment to the NATO Joint Interrogation Center, his arrest in Germany, his retirement and move to the United States, and his views on his arrest, trial, and conviction. The descriptions of his experiences in this chapter are based solely on his notes, except for those events that are confirmed by other sources (supported by footnotes).

[2]Ibid., pp. 1, 2.

[3]Ibid., p. 2.

[4]Ibid.

[5]Ibid., p. 3.

[6]Ibid.

[7]Ibid., pp. 3, 4.

[8]Ibid., p. 4.

[9]Ibid.

[10]Ibid.

[11]"RA -- All the Way" ("Regular Army -- All the Way") was a catch phrase used by many "Regular Army Soldiers," who had enlisted as opposed to those who were drafted.

[12]Noncommissioned Officers.

[13]Quoted by permission of Colonel, U. S. Army Reserve (Ret) Nicholas M. Getmanov.

[14]Trofimoff, loc. sit., p. 5.

[15]Ibid., p. 6.

[16]Ibid.

[17]Ibid., p. 7.

[18]Ibid.

[19]Ibid., p. 8.

[20]Ibid.

[21]Ibid.

[22]When he began his training, Trofimoff received an honorable discharge from his U. S. army rank of Sergeant First Class, and was called to duty as a Second Lieutenant in the Army's active reserve. He was instructed to wear civilian clothes rather than an officer's uniform. He would retain that status until a few months after reporting to his new assignment when he was again placed in the inactive reserve and assigned to the U. S. State Department (The International Cooperative Administration or ICA) as a U. S. Army Civil Service Employee.

[23]Ibid., pp. 8, 9.

[24]Ibid., p. 10.

[25]Ibid., p. 12.

[26]Ibid., p. 16.

[27]Ibid.

[28]Ibid., pp. 22, 23.

[29]The team was impressed by the friendly welcomes they received from all Laotians as soon as they realized they were Americans, not Frenchmen. The French had by this time become unpopular through-

out Indochina and were not welcome anywhere.

[30]Ibid., p. 43.

[31]Ibid., p. 33.

[32]Ibid., p. 34.

[33]Ibid., p. 52.

[34]Ibid., p. 54.

[35]Ibid.

[36]Ibid.

[37]Ibid., p. 55.

[38]Ibid., p. 56.

[39]Ibid., pp. 57, 58.

[40]Ibid., p. 2a.

[41]Ibid., p. 3a.

[42]Ibid., pp. 3a, 4a.

[43]A Metropolitan is the equivalent of a Cardinal in the Roman Catholic Church.

[44]Trofimoff, loc. sit., p. 12a.

[45]Ibid.

[46]Ibid., p. 6a.

[47]Ibid., p. 8a.

[48]Ibid., pp. 8a, 9a

Chapter 6

[1]George Trofimoff, *GT Biography,* undated (consisting of more than 100 pages of handwritten and typed notes), p. 47. Trofimoff's notes cover his stay in Paris, his emigration to the United States, his early years in the U. S. Army, his service as a U. S. Civil Service Employee, his assignment to the NATO Joint Interrogation Center, his arrest in Germany, his retirement and move to the United States, and his views on his arrest, trial, and conviction.

[2]George Trofimoff, *Comments on Indictment,* Encl. 2, the Nuremberg JIC, undated, Trofimoff's comments on his indictment are contained in five enclosures (documents prepared by Trofimoff after his arrest in 2002). Descriptions and functions of JIC elements are drawn from this document.

[3]The German BND (Bunde Nachrichten Dienst) is the approximate equivalent of the U. S. CIA.

[4]Trofimoff, loc. cit., p 6.

[5]United States District Court, Middle District of Florida, Tampa

Division: United States of America, Plaintiff, v. George Trofimoff, a/k/a George von Trofimoff, a/k/a "Antey," a/k/a "Markiz," a/k/a "Konsul.," Defendant. Case No. 8:00-CR-197-T-24C. *TRANSCRIPT OF TRIAL PROCEEDINGS BEFORE THE HONORABLE SUSAN C. BUCKLEW, JUDGE.* 5 June 2001, Tampa, Florida, 9:30 a.m. Page 219.

[6]Ibid., 6 June 2001, Tampa, Florida, 9:28 a. m., pages 68, 69.

[7]Ibid, 21 June 2001, Tampa, Florida, 9:30 a. m., page 40.

[8]Trofimoff, GT Biography, p. 9a.

[9]Ibid., pp. 9a, 10a.

[10]Ibid., pp.10a, 11a.

[11]Ibid., p.12a.

[12]Ibid., pp. 13a, 14a.

[13]Federal Office of Criminal Investigation, Munich, Germany, 12/14/94. *Interrogation of the Accused,* Igor Iriney Susemihl, 23 pages.(Entered in the Trofimoff trial as U. S. Government Exhibit 43B). (English language translation, Certified Copy).

[14]U. S. District Court, Middle District of Florida, Tampa Division: United States of America v. George Trofimoff, Case No. 8:00-CR-197-T-24EAJ. *Government Transcript Exhibits* - Volume 3. (Transcript of second videotaped meeting, 02/24/99 PM.). Pp. 61, 63.

[15]Ibid, pp. 63, 66.

[16]Ibid, pp. 66, 67.

[17]Trofimoff, loc. sit., pp. 14a, 6a.

[18]Ibid., p. 16a.

[19]Ibid., p. 16c.

[20]Ibid.

[21]Ibid., p. 16a.

[22]During the time Trofimoff was the author's neighbor in Florida, he remained very bitter. On more than one occasion, he said, defiantly, "I have no children. They will have nothing to do with me, and as far as I'm concerned, they don't exist. My only family is Jutta and her daughter, Sandy."

[23]U. S. District Court, Tampa, loc. cit., 21 June 2001, page 29.

[24]Quotations attributed to Drozda were obtained during a personal interview with the author shortly after the completion of the Trofimoff trial.

[25]Ibid.

[26]Ibid.

[27]U. S. District Court, Tampa, loc. cit., 21 June 2001, page 63.

[28]Comments made by an anonymous JIC interrogator to the author

shortly after completion of the Trofimoff trial.

[29]Ibid.

[30]All of Mrs. Drozda's quotations are from a telephone discussion the author had with her shortly after the conclusion of the Trofimoff trial.

[31]Ibid.

[32]Ibid.

[33]Ibid.

[34]Ibid.

[35]Ibid.

[36]Ibid.

[37]Trofimoff, GT Biography, loc. cit., pp. 18a, 19a.

[38]Ibid., p. 17b.

[39]Ibid., p. 19a.

[40]Trofimoff, loc. cit., p. 20a.

[41]Ibid.

[42]Ibid., p. 24a.

[43]Ibid., p. 26a.

[44]Ibid., p. 26a, 27a.

[45]Ibid., p. 28a.

[46]Andy J. Byers, Personal interview, undated, (audiotape), with Jutta (after the Trofimoff trial).

[47]Ibid.

[48]Ibid.

[49]Trofimoff, loc. sit., p. 28a.

[50]Ibid., pp. 28a, 29a.

[51]Byers, loc. cit.,

[52]Ibid.

[53]Ibid

[54]Trofimoff, loc. sit., p. 29a.

[55]Ibid., pp. 29a, 30a.

[56]Byers, loc. cit.

[57]Ibid.

[58]Trofimoff, loc. sit., p. 30a

[59]Ibid., pp. 30a, 31a.

[60]Ibid., p. 33b.

[61]Ibid., p. 33a.

[62]Ibid., p. 34a.

[63]Ibid., p. 35a.

[64]Byers, loc. cit.

[65]Ibid., pp. 35a, 36a.

Chapter 7

[1]The BKA is the German Federal Office of Criminal Investigation, equivalent to the FBI.

[2]NATO is the acronym for the North Atlantic Treaty Organization.

[3]George Trofimoff, Biography, undated (consisting of more than one hundred pages of handwritten and typed notes, p. 38a. Trofimoff's notes cover his stay in Paris, his immigration to the United States, his early years in the U. S. Army, his service as a U. S. Civil Service employee, his assignment to the NATO Joint Interrogation Center, his arrest in Germany, his retirement and move to the United States, and his views on his arrest, trial and conviction. All quotations attributed to Trofimoff come from these notes, unless otherwise indicated by footnotes.

[4]Personal interview, undated (audiotape), with Jutta by the author (after the Trofimoff trial).

[5]Ibid.

[6]Ibid.

[7]Ibid.

[8]Ibid.

[9]Trofimoff, loc. sit., p. 38a.

[10]The BSIS (British Secret Intelligence Service) corresponds to the U. S. CIA. It is also known as MI6, the organization made famous by the fictional spy, James Bond.

[11]Trofimoff, loc. sit., pp. 39a, 40a.

[12]Federal Office of Criminal Investigation, Nuremberg, Germany, 12/14/1994. ST 43-050563/94-3, GBA 3 BJs 1115/94-3, *Interrogation of an Accused,* George Trofimoff, 27 pages. (Entered in the Trofimoff trial as United States Government Exhibit 41B). (English language translation, Certified Copy). pp. 1-5.

[13]Ibid., p. 5.

[14]Ibid., p. 6.

[15]Ibid., p. 7.

[16]Ibid., p. 9.

[17]Ibid., p. 9.

[18]Ibid., p. 11.

[19]Ibid., p. 11.

[20]Ibid., pp.12, 13.

[21]Ibid., p. 15.
[22]Ibid., p. 15.
[23]Ibid., p. 16.
[24]Ibid., p. 21.
[25]Ibid.
[26]Ibid.
[27]Ibid., p. 22.
[28]Ibid.
[29]Ibid., p. 24.
[30]Ibid.
[31]Ibid.
[32]Ibid., p. 25.
[33]Ibid., p. 26.
[34]Trofimoff, loc. sit., p. 40a.
[35]Ibid., pp. 40a, 41a, 42a.
[36]Federal Office of Criminal Investigation, Munich, Germany, 12/14/94. ST (Criminal Matter) 44 - 050 562/94, 3 BJs (Federal Justice Matter) 1116/94-3 (249). *Interrogation of the Accused,* Igor Iriney Susemihl, 23 pages. (Entered in the Trofimoff trial as United States Government Exhibit 43B). (English translation, Certified Copy). pp. 2, 3.
[37]Ibid., p. 4.
[38]Ibid., pp. 4, 5.
[39]Ibid., p. 5.
[40]Ibid., pp. 5, 8.
[41]Ibid., p. 8.
[42]Ibid.
[43]Ibid., p. 9.
[44]Ibid.
[45]Ibid.
[46]Ibid., pp. 9, 10.
[47]Ibid., p. 11.
[48]Ibid.
[49]Ibid., p. 12.
[50]Ibid., p. 13.
[51]Ibid.
[52]Ibid.
[53]Ibid., p. 14.
[54]Ibid., p. 15.
[55]Ibid., pages 15, 16.

[56]Ibid., p. 16.
[57]Ibid., pages 16, 17.
[58]Ibid., p. 18.
[59]Ibid.
[60]Ibid., p. 20.
[61]Ibid.
[62]Ibid., p. 1.
[63]Ibid., p. 2.
[64]Ibid.
[65]Ibid., p. 3.
[66]Ibid.
[67]Ibid., p. 5.
[68]Ibid.
[69]Ibid., p. 6.

[70]The Examining Judge of the Federal Supreme Court, 76125 Karlsruhe, Germany, December 15, 1994. BJs 1116/94-3 (249), 2 BGs 290/94, *In the Preliminary Investigation against Igor Iriney SUSEMIHL for Suspicion of intelligence agent activity,* 7 pages, conducted by Dr. Bode, Judge at the Federal Supreme Court as Examining Judge, (Entered in the Trofimoff trial as United States Government Exhibit 44B). (English language translation, Certified Copy).

[71]Ibid., p. 2.
[72]Ibid., pp. 2, 3.
[73]Ibid., p. 3.
[74]Ibid., pp. 3, 4.
[75]Ibid., p. 4.
[76]Ibid., p. 5.

[77]The Examining Judge of the Federal Supreme Court, 76125 Karlsruhe, Germany, December 15, 1994. 3 BJs 1115/94-3 (249), 2 BGs 291/94. *In the Preliminary Investigation against George TROFIMOFF for Suspicion of intelligence agent activity,* 10 pages, conducted by Dr. Bode, Judge of the Federal Supreme Court as Examining Judge. (Entered in the Trofimoff trial as United States Government Exhibit 42B). (English language translation, Certified Copy). Points emphasized by Buchbender appear on pages 6-7.

[78]Ibid, p. 7.
[79]Ibid.
[80]Preliminary Investigation against Igor Iriney SUSEMIHL, loc. cit., p. 6.
[81]Ibid.

[82]Germany, The Examining Judge of the Federal Supreme Court of Justice, 15 December 1994. 3 BJs 1115/94-3 (249), 3BJs 1116/94-3 (249), 2BGs 291/94, Court Order, *In the criminal investigation against 1. George TROFIMOFF and 2. Igor Iriney SUSEMIHL, because of Suspicion of secret service like spy activities*, (Unofficial English translation – 21 June 00/Ky)

[83]Ibid., pp. 11, 12.

[84]Personal interview, undated (audiotape), with Jutta by the author (after the Trofimoff trial).

[85]Ibid.

Chapter 8

[1]George Trofimoff, *Super Spy or Innocent Victim*, undated, p. 4. A 33-page typewritten summary, written by Trofimoff while in prison, depicting, from his viewpoint, a chronological summary of the events, which led to his arrest, trial, conviction, sentencing, and the subsequent appeals, which were all denied. The summary concludes with the continued assertion of his innocence and his strong belief that his conviction represents a serious miscarriage of justice with violations of his constitutional rights of Due Process and a Fair Trial.

[2]Standard Form 50-B, Notification of Personnel Action, 12/23/94. Effective date, 12/31/94. Signed by Annette Weiss, for Elmer F. Williams, Director, Civilian Personnel Operations. Copy provided by Robert J. Fiore, Esq.

[3]U. S. District Court, Middle District of Florida, Tampa Division: United States of America v. George Trofimoff, Case No. 8:00-CR-197-T-24EAJ. *Government Transcript Exhibits* - Volume 2. (Transcript of first videotaped meeting, 02/24/99 AM.), pp. 30, 31.

[4]Personal interview, undated (audiotape), with Jutta by the author (after the Trofimoff trial).

[5]Ibid.

[6]Robert J. Fiore, e-mail, (ohaireandfiore@hotmail.com), Monday 26 March 2001, to Andy J. Byers (ajircc@juno.com), subject: George Trofimoff.

[7]George Trofimoff, Biography, undated, pp. 43a and 44a, (consisting of more than one hundred pages of handwritten and typed notes), Trofimoff's notes cover his stay in Paris, his immigration to the United States, his early years in the U. S. Army, his service as a

U. S Civil Service employee, his assignment to the NATO Joint Interrogation Center, his arrest in Germany, his retirement and move to the United States, and his views on his arrest, trial and conviction.

[8]Ibid., p. 44a.

[9]Jutta Trofimoff, loc. sit.

[10]George Trofimoff, loc. sit., p. 45a.

[11]Ibid., pp. 45a, 46a.

[12]Ibid., p. 46a.

[13]Ibid., pp. 46a - 47a.

[14]Jutta Trofimoff, loc. sit.

[15]George Trofimoff, loc. sit., p. 47a.

[16]Jutta Trofimoff, loc. sit.

[17]Ibid.

[18]Trofimoff made these unrecorded statements to the author; they are not in his handwritten notes.

Chapter 9

[1]George Trofimoff, *Biography*, undated (consisting of more than one hundred pages of handwritten and typed notes), pp. 48a, 49a. Trofimoff's notes cover his stay in Paris, his immigration to the United States, his early years in the U. S. Army, his service as a U. S. Civil Service employee, his assignment to the NATO Joint Interrogation Center, his arrest in Germany, his retirement and move to the United States, and his views on his arrest, trial, and conviction.

[2]In Russian archives "Trofimov" is the spelling used for Trofimoff's ancestors. When the spelling was changed is unknown. Trofimoff states that, in Germany, those with noble ancestry have "von" inserted in front of the last name. While assigned to the Nuremberg JIC, some of his coworkers, knowing of his pride in his noble Russian lineage, presented him with a plaque inscribed "Colonel George von Trofimoff." He retained that plaque and installed it on his mailbox in front of his Melbourne home.

[3]U. S. District Court, Middle District of Florida, Tampa Division: United States of America, Plaintiff, v. George Trofimoff, a/k/a George von Trofimoff, a/k/a "Antey," a/k/a "Markiz," a/k/a "Konsul." Defendant. Case No. 8:00-CR-197-T-24C. *TRANSCRIPT OF TRIAL PROCEEDINGS BEFORE THE HONORABLE SUSAN C. BUCKLEW, JUDGE.* 8 June 2001, Tampa Florida, 9:30 a. m., pp. 197- 201.

[4]Trofimoff, loc. sit., pp. 48a, 49a, 50a.

[5]Ibid., pp. 10, 11.

[6]Ibid.

[7]Ibid., p .21.

[8]Ibid., p. 24.

[9]Trofimoff Biography, loc. sit., pp. 50a , 51a.

[10]Ibid., pp. 51a, 52a.

[11]Ibid., p. 53a.

[12]U. S. District Court, Middle District of Florida, Tampa Division. United States of America v. George Trofimoff, Case No. 8:00-CR-197-T-24EAJ. *Government Transcript Exhibits* - Volume 1, telcall 020498, p. 5.

[13]Ibid., p. 8.

[14]Ibid., pp. 14 - 17.

[15]Ibid.

[16]Ibid., pp. 28, 29.

[17]Ibid., p. 38.

[18]Ibid., pp. 42, 43.

[19]Ibid., p. 46.

[20]Ibid.

[21]Ibid., p. 47 and p. 50.

[22]Ibid., p. 50.

[23]Trofimoff Biography, loc. sit., p. 56a.

[24]U. S. District Court, loc. sit., Volume 1, telcall 08/26/98, p. 3.

[25]Ibid., pp. 8, 10.

[26]Ibid., p. 10.

[27]Ibid., pp. 10, 11.

[28]Ibid., p. 12.

[29]Ibid., p. 20.

[30]Ibid., pp. 21, 22.

[31]Ibid., p. 36.

[32]Ibid., pp. 36, 37.

[33]Ibid., pp. 38, 39, 40.

[34]Ibid., pp. 43, 44, 45.

[35]Ibid., p. 48.

[36]Ibid., pp. 49, 50.

[37]Ibid., p. 58.

[38]Ibid., pp. 63, 64.

[39]Ibid., pp. 66, 67.

[40]Ibid., pp. 74, 75.

[41]Ibid., pp. 75, 76.

[42]Ibid., pp. 77 and 83.

[43]Trofimoff Biography, loc. sit., pp. 58a, 59a, 61a, 63a.

[44]Ibid., p. 64a.

[45]U. S. District Court, loc. sit., Volume 1, telcall 021899, p. 2.

[46]Ibid., p. 4.

[47]Ibid., pp. 4, 5

[48]Ibid., p. 5.

[49]Paula Christian, "Verdict Ends Pursuit of 'Perfect Spy,' " *The Tampa Tribune*, Final Edition, June 28, 2001, p. 1.

[50]U. S. District Court, loc. sit., Volume 2, first videotaped meeting 02/24/99, p. 4.

[51]Ibid., 2/24/99 AM, p. 15.

[52]Ibid., p. 16.

[53]Ibid., pp. 31, 32.

[54]Ibid., pp. 45, 46.

[55]Ibid., pp. 66, 67.

[56]Ibid., p. 72.

[57]Ibid., p. 77.

[58]Ibid., p. 79.

[59]Ibid., p. 86.

[60]Ibid., pp. 86, 87.

[61]Ibid., pp. 92, 96.

[62]Ibid., p. 101.

[63]Ibid., p. 105.

[64]Ibid., pp.104, 105.

[65]Ibid., pp. 125, 126.

[66]Ibid., pp. 129, 132.

[67]Ibid., pp. 173, 178.

[68]U. S. District Court, loc. sit., Volume 3, second videotaped meeting, 02/24/99, pp. 22, 23.

[69]Ibid., p. 23.

[70]Ibid., pp. 23, 24, 25.

[71]Ibid., p. 32.

[72]Ibid., pp. 62, 63.

[73]Ibid., pp. 63, 65.

[74]Ibid., pp. 66, 67.

[75]Ibid., p. 68.

[76]Ibid., p. 80.

[77]Ibid., pp. 81, 82.

[78]Ibid., p. 83.

[79]Ibid., p. 98.

[80]Ibid., pp. 138, 139.

[81]Ibid., p. 141.

[82]Ibid., p. 142.

[83]Ibid., p. 156.

[84]Ibid., p. 201.

[85]Ibid.

[86]Ibid., pp. 207, 209.

[87]Ibid., pp. 228, 229.

[88]Ibid., pp. 229, 230.

[89]Ibid., pp. 248, 250.

[90]Ibid., pp. 256, 257.

[91]Ibid., pp. 258, 259, 262.

[92]Ibid., p. 264.

[93]Ibid., p. 266.

[94]Ibid., p. 273.

[95]Trofimoff *Biography*, loc. sit., p. 103a.

[96]U. S. District Court, loc. sit., pp. 276 - 277.

[97]Ibid., pp. 284, 286, 287.

[98]Ibid., p. 288.

[99]Ibid., pp. 290, 291.

[100]Ibid., pp. 291, 292, 294, 295.

[101]Ibid., p. 302.

[102]Ibid., pp. 311, 312.

[103]Ibid., p. 339.

[104]Ibid., p. 341.

[105]Trofimoff *Biography*, loc. sit., p. 128a.

[106]U. S. District Court, loc. sit., Volume 4, Transcripts of telephone calls, telcall 081399, pp. 3, 5, 6.

[107]Ibid., pp. 14, 15.

[108]U. S. District Court, loc. sit, telcall 090999, p. 3.

[109]Ibid., p.10.

[110]Ibid., pp. 19, 20.

[111]U. S. District Court, loc. sit., telcall 110499, p.17.

[112]Ibid., pp. 19, 23.

[113]Ibid., pp. 28, 29.

[114]Ibid., p. 31.

[115]Ibid., p. 36.

[116]Ibid., pp. 36, 40.

[117]Ibid., p. 40.

[118]Ibid., pp. 40, 41.
[119]Ibid., p. 50.
[120]Ibid., p. 53.
[121]Ibid.
[122]Ibid., pp. 55, 56.
[123]Ibid., pp. 56, 58.
[124]Ibid., pp. 59, 60.
[125]Ibid., p. 83.
[126]U. S. District Court, loc. sit., telcall 120899, p. 4.
[127]Ibid., p. 9.
[128]Ibid., pp.18, 20.
[129]U. S. District Court, loc. sit., telcall 012100, p. 2.
[130]Ibid., pp. 3, 5, 7.
[131]Trofimoff *Biography,* loc. sit., p. 136a.
[132]U. S. District Court, loc. sit., p. 2.
[133]Trofimoff *Biography,* loc. sit., p. 137a.
[134]U. S. District Court, loc. sit., telcall 051000, pp. 2, 4.
[135]Ibid., pp. 5, 7, 8.
[136]Trofimoff *Biography,* loc. sit., p. 137a, 138a.
[137]U. S. District Court, loc. sit., telcall 06/02/00, p. 14

Chapter 10

[1]These comments are from by an FBI agent who was involved in the case who requested anonymity.

[2]George Trofimoff, *Biography,* (consisting of more than one hundred pages of handwritten and typed notes), undated, p.138a. Trofimoff's notes cover his stay in Paris, his immigration to the United States, his early years in the U. S. Army, his service as a U. S. Civil Service employee, his assignment to the NATO Joint Interrogation Center, his arrest in Germany, his retirement and move to the United States, and his views on his arrest, trial and conviction.

[3]Personal interview, (audiotape), by the author with Jutta, undated.

[4]George Trofimoff, *Biography,* loc. cit., pp. 138a, 139a.

[5]U. S. District Court, Middle District of Florida, Tampa Division: United States of America, Plaintiff, vs George Trofimoff, a/k/a George von Trofimoff, a/k/a "Antey," a/k/a "Markiz," a/k/a "Konsul," Defendant. Case No. 8:00-CR-197-T-24C. *TRANSCRIPT OF TRIAL PROCEEDINGS BEFORE THE HONORABLE SUSAN C. BUCKLEW, JUDGE.* 15 June 2001, Tampa Florida, 9:43 a. m., pp. 23-26.

[6]Ibid., p. 26.
[7]George Trofimoff, Biography, loc. cit., pp.139a, 140a.
[8]Ibid., p. 140a.
[9]Personal interview, loc. sit.
[10]Ibid.
[11]Comments from an FBI agent, loc. sit.
[12]Ibid.
[13]Unrecorded discussion with attorney Daniel Hernandez, June 20, 2000.
[14]George Trofimoff, *Biography,* loc. cit., pp.141a, 142a, 148a.
[15]Personal interview, loc. sit.
[16]Ibid.

Chapter 11

[1]Paula Christian, "Spy Trial to Give Rare Look at KGB," *The Tampa Tribune,* Tampa, Florida, June 4, 2001.

[2]U. S. District Court, Middle District of Florida, Tampa Division: United States of America, Plaintiff, vs George Trofimoff, a/k/a George von Trofimoff, a/k/a "Antey," a/k/a "Markiz," a/k/a "Konsul." Defendant. Case No. 8:00-CR-197-T-24C. *TRANSCRIPT OF TRIAL PROCEEDINGS BEFORE THE HONORABLE SUSAN C. BUCKLEW, JUDGE.* 4 June 2001, Tampa Florida, 9:03 a.m., pp. 211-212.

[3]U. S. District Court, loc. sit., 5 June 2001, p. 14.

[4]A measure of Trofimoff's ability to get along with others was comments this marshal was heard to make. "George is well-liked by all the guards. He is a real gentleman and highly respected by all of us."

[5]Trial Proceedings, loc. sit., p.18.
[6]Ibid., p. 41.
[7]Ibid., pp. 51, 52.
[8]Ibid., pp. 53, 54.
[9]Ibid., pp. 55, 56.
[10]Ibid., p. 58.
[11]Ibid., p. 65.
[12]Ibid., p. 68.
[13]Ibid., pp. 69, 70.

[14]As the government's case unfolded over the next three weeks, Hernandez' prophecy proved to be well founded as the government prosecutors pulled all the stops in making their case. Clearly, with the

embarrassments recently faced by the FBI, neither that agency nor the government wanted to take any chances with this case!

[15]Trial Proceedings, loc. sit., pp. 70, 71..

[16]Paula Christian, "Lies Uncloak Cold War Spy," *The Tampa Tribune*, Tampa, Florida, June 27, 2001.

[17]Paula Christian, "Spy Trial to Give Rare Look at KGB," *The Tampa Tribune*, Tampa, Florida, June 4, 2001.

[18]U. S. District Court, Tampa, loc. sit., p. 219.

[19]U. S. District Court, Tampa, loc. sit., 6 June 2001, p. 12.

[20]Ibid., p. 17.

[21]Ibid., p. 21.

[22]Ibid., pp. 23, 24.

[23]Ibid., p. 27.

[24]Ibid., p. 28.

[25]Ibid., p. 34.

[26]Ibid., pp. 68, 69.

[27]Ibid., p. 77.

[28]Ibid., p. 75.

[29]Ibid., p. 111.

[30]Ibid., pp. 172 - 173,

[31]Ibid., p. 196.

[32]Ibid., pp, 202, 206.

[33]Ibid., pp. 221, 222, 227, 228.

[34]The Examining Judge of the Federal Supreme Court, 76125 Karlsruhe, Germany, December 15, 1994. 3 BJs 1116/94-3 (249), 2 BGs 290/94. *In the Preliminary Investigation against Igor Iriney SUSEMIHL for Suspicion of intelligence agent activity*, 7 pages, conducted by Dr. Bode, Judge at the Federal Supreme Court as Examining Judge. (Entered in the Trofimoff trial as U. S. Government Exhibit 44B.) (English language translation, Certified Copy).

[35]The Examining Judge of the Federal Supreme Court, 76125 Karlsruhe, Germany, December 15, 1994. 3 BJs 1116/94-3 (249), 2 BGs 290/94. *In The Preliminary Investigation against George Trofimoff for Suspicion of intelligence agent activity*, 10 pages, conducted by Dr. Bode, Judge of the Federal Supreme Court as Examining Judge. (Entered in the Trofimoff trial as US Government Exhibit 42B.) (English language translation, Certified Copy).

[36]U. S. District Court, Tampa, loc. sit., 7 June 2001, p. 53.

[37]Ibid., pp. 60, 61.

[38]U. S. District Court, Tampa, loc. sit., 8 June 2001, p.18.

[39]Ibid., p. 19.
[40]Ibid., p. 50.
[41]Ibid., p. 59.
[42]Ibid., p. 60.
[43]Ibid., p. 64.
[44]Ibid., p. 101.
[45]Ibid., p. 184.
[46]Ibid., pp. 185, 186.
[47]Ibid., p. 189.
[48]Ibid., p. 215.
[49]Ibid.
[50]Ibid., p. 217.
[51]U.S. District Court, Tampa, loc. sit., 11 June 2001, p.16.
[52]Ibid., pp. 17, 18.
[53]Ibid., p. 18.
[54]Ibid., p. 60.
[55]Ibid.
[56]Ibid., p. 290.
[57]U. S. District Court, Tampa, loc. sit., 12 June 2001, pp. 4, 5.
[58]U. S. District Court, Tampa, loc. sit., 15 June 2001, pp. 60, 61.
[59]Ibid., p. 86.
[60]Ibid., p. 90.
[61]Ibid., p. 91.
[62]Ibid., p. 93.
[63]Ibid., p. 131.
[64]Ibid.
[65]Ibid., p. 133.
[66]Ibid., pp, 170, 171.
[67]U. S. District Court, Tampa, loc. sit., 18 June 2001, p.12.
[68]Ibid., p. 31.
[69]Ibid., p. 32.
[70]Oleg Kalugin (with Fen Montaigne). *The First Directorate, My 32 Years in Intelligence and Espionage Against the West.* New York: St. Martin's Press, 1994.
[71]Andy J. Byers, Trofimoff Trial Notes, undated. Two stenographer's notebooks containing detailed notes taken during Trofimoff's trial, 6 June 2001-26 June 2001. Book 2, p. 4.
[72]Ibid.
[73]Ibid.
[74]Ibid., p. 5.

[75]Ibid.
[76]Ibid.
[77]Ibid.
[78]Ibid., p. 6.
[79]Ibid., pp. 7, 8.
[80]Ibid., p. 9.
[81]Ibid., p. 10.
[82]Ibid., pp.10, 11.
[83]Ibid., p. 11.
[84]Ibid., p. 12.
[85]Ibid.
[86]Ibid., p. 13.
[87]Ibid.
[88]Author's personal unrecorded conversation with Kalugin, September, 2002.
[89]Byers, loc. sit., pp. 4, 15.
[90]Ibid., p. 15.
[91]Ibid.
[92]U. S. District Court, Tampa, loc. sit., 19 June 2001, p.141.
[93]Ibid., p. 154.
[94]Ibid., pp. 154, 155.
[95]Ibid., p. 157.

Chapter 12

[1]U. S. District Court, Middle District of Florida, Tampa Division: United States of America, Plaintiff, vs George Trofimoff, a/k/a George von Trofimoff, a/k/a "Antey," a/k/a "Markiz," a/k/a "Konsul.," Defendant. Case No. 8:00-CR-197-T-24C. TRANSCRIPT OF TRIAL PROCEEDINGS BEFORE THE HONORABLE SUSAN C. BUCKLEW, JUDGE, 21 June 2001, Tampa, Florida, 9:30 a.m., p.13.
[2]Ibid.
[3]Ibid. p. 16.
[4]Ibid. p. 17.
[5]Ibid. p. 19.
[6]Ibid. pp. 18, 20.
[7]Ibid. p. 20.
[8]Ibid. p. 29.
[9]Ibid. p. 40.
[10]Ibid. p. 46.

[11]Ibid.

[12]Ibid. p. 102.

[13]Ibid. pp. 103, 104.

[14]Ibid. pp. 104, 105.

[15]Ibid. p. 105.

[16]Ibid. p. 109.

[17]Byers, Private unrecorded discussion with Frenkel during a break in the trial.

[18]Byers, Unrecorded discussion with Furr during a break in the trial.

[19]Furr, Unrecorded comments made by Furr to a group of reporters.

[20]U. S. District Court, Tampa, loc. sit., pp. 148, 149.

[21]Ibid., p. 155, 156.

[22]Ibid., pp. 173, 177.

[23]Ibid., p. 194.

[24]U. S. District Court, Tampa, loc. sit., 22 June 2001, p.35.

[25]Ibid., p. 43.

[26]Ibid., pp. 53, 54.

[27]Andy J. Byers, Trofimoff Trial Notes, undated. Two stenographer's notebooks containing detailed notes taken during Trofimoff's trial, 6 June 2001-26 June 2001. Book 2, p. 51.

[28]Ibid.

[29]Ibid.

[30]Ibid., p. 52.

[31]Ibid., p. 54.

[32]Ibid., p. 55.

[33]Ibid.

[34]U. S. District Court, Tampa, loc.sit., 22 June 2001,. pp. 142, 143.

[35]Ibid., p. 160.

[36]Ibid., p. 161.

[37]Ibid.

[38]Byers, trial notes, loc. sit., p. 57.

[39]U. S. District Court, Tampa, loc. sit., 25 June 2001, p.11.

[40]Ibid., p. 22.

[41]Ibid., p. 28.

[42]Ibid., p. 39.

[43]Ibid., p. 43.

[44]Ibid., pp. 43, 44.

[45]Ibid., p. 44.

[46]Ibid., p. 47.

[47]Ibid., pp. 47, 48.

[48]Ibid., p. 69.

[49]Ibid.

[50]Ibid., p. 71.

[51]Byers, trial notes, loc. sit., p. 64.

[52]Ibid., pp. 77, 78.

[53]U. S. District Court, Tampa, loc. sit., 25 June 2001, p. 113.

[54]Ibid.

[55]Ibid., pp. 122, 125.

[56]Ibid., p. 127.

[57]Ibid., p. 168.

[58]Ibid., p. 219.

[59]Ibid., p. 222.

[60]Ibid., p. 223.

[61]Ibid., p. 227.

[62]Ibid., pp. 226, 227.

[63]Furr, unrecorded comments, loc. sit.

[64]U. S. District Court, Tampa, loc. sit., pp. 239, 240.

Chapter 13

[1]U. S. District Court, Middle District of Florida, Tampa Division: United States of America, Plaintiff, vs George Trofimoff, a/k/a George von Trofimoff, a/k/a "Antey," a/k/a "Markiz," a/k/a "Konsul," Defendant. Case No. 8:00-CR-197-T-24C. *TRANSCRIPT OF TRIAL PROCEEDINGS BEFORE THE HONORABLE SUSAN C. BUCKLEW, JUDGE,* 26 June 2001, Tampa Florida, 9:49 a.m., p. 4.

[2]Ibid., pp. 20, 21.

[3]Paula Christian, "Lies Uncloak Cold War Spy," *The Tampa Tribune,* Tampa, Florida, June 27, 2001.

[4]Paula Christian, "Verdict Ends Pursuit of 'Perfect Spy,' " *The Tampa Tribune,* Tampa, Florida, June 28, 2001.

[5]Christian, "Lies Uncloak Cold War Spy," loc.sit.

[6]Andy J. Byers, Private discussion with Hernandez after the trial.

[7]Andy J. Byers, *Trofimoff Trial Notes,* undated. Two stenographer's notebooks containing detailed notes taken during Trofimoff's trial, 6 June 2001—26 June 2001. Book 2, p. 95.

[8]Ibid.

[9]Ibid., p. 94

[10]Ibid., p. 93.

[11]Ibid.

[12]John B. Stenbit, Assistant Secretary of Defense, 6000 Defense Pentagon, Washington, D. C. 20301-6000. Letter, dated September 24, 2001, to the Honorable Susan C Bucklew, U. S. District Judge, The Sam M. Gibbons U. S. Courthouse, Tampa Florida.

[13]Byers, loc. sit., p. 94.

[14]Ibid.

[15]Ibid., p. 92.

[16]Andy J. Byers, telephone discussion with FBI Special Agent Navarro after the trial.

[17]Soon after Trofimoff was moved to the Moorehaven prison, his wife, Jutta, visited him. She reported that his comments were that his new quarters were "Paradise." She was able to speak with him face-to-face through glass as opposed to contact through TV monitors which had been the case in Florida jails. She reported that the prison was brand new, spotlessly clean, and served good food. Where George was confined, there were only six inmates sharing two showers, and they had access to more than 20 channels on a TV set.

Chapter 14

[1]Andy J. Byers, Telephone conversation with FBI Special Agent Anthony Wagner, 20 April, 2003.

[2]Ibid.

[3]U. S. District Court, Middle District of Florida, Tampa Division: United States of America, Plaintiff, vs George Trofimoff, a/k/a George von Trofimoff, a/k/a "Antey," a/k/a "Markiz," a/k/a "Konsul," Defendant. Case No. 8:00-CR-197-T-24C. *TRANSCRIPT OF TRIAL PROCEEDINGS BEFORE THE HONORABLE SUSAN C. BUCKLEW, JUDGE.* 4 June 2001, Tampa Florida, 9:03 a.m, pp. 34, 36.

[4]Byers, loc. sit.

[5]Rocco Rosano, email message: Re: Was Trofimoff Polygraphed? 21 June 2001.

[6]Rocco Rosano, email message: Re: George Trofimoff, 31 July 2001.

[7]The Examining Judge of the Federal Supreme Court, 76125 Karlsruhe, Germany, December 15, 1994. 3BJs 1116/94 - 3 (249), 2BGs 290/94. *In the Preliminary Investigation against George Trofimoff for Suspicion of intelligence agent activity,* 10 pages, conducted by Dr. Bode, Judge of the Federal Supreme Court as Examining Judge. Entered in

the Trofimoff trial as U. S. exhibit 42B. (English language translation, Certified Copy), p. 7.

[8]Germany, The Examining Judge of the Federal Supreme Court, 76125 Karlsruhe, Germany, Dec. 15, 1994. 3BJs 1116/94-3 (249), 2BGs 290/94. *In the Preliminary Investigation against Igor Iriney Susemihl for Suspician of intelligence agent activity,* 7 pages, conducted by Dr. Bode, Judge at the Federal Supreme Court as Examining Judge. (Entered in the Trofimoff trial as U. S. Government Exhibit 44B.) (English language translation, Certified Copy). p. 6.

[9]U. S. District Court, Tampa, loc. sit., 5 June 2001, p. 76.

[10]Byers, (Wagner), loc. sit.

[11]Andy J. Byers, Telephone discussion with FBI Special Agent Navarro after the trial was over.

[12]Rocco Rosano, email message: Re: Trofimoff Book, 20 April 2002.

[13]Ibid.

[14]Ibid.

[15]Paula Christian, "Verdict Ends Pursuit of 'Perfect Spy,' " *The Tampa Tribune,* Tampa, Florida, June 28, 2001.

[16]Byers (Wagner), loc. sit

[17]A confidential, anonymous comment made by a member of IRCC.

[18]Charles Richardson, *Graphology Analysis of George Trofimoff,* undated, p. 1.

[19]Ibid.

[20]Kathleen Urbina. *Evidence From the Pen—Graphic Clues/Sinister Signs,* New York: GraphU Enterprises, 1998.

[21]Barry Branston, *Graphology Explained—A Workbook,* Samuel Weiser, Inc., York Beach, Maine, 1991.

[22]Amend, Karen Kristan & Ruiz, *Achieving Compatibility With Handwriting Analysis Vol. I & II,* North Hollywood, CA, Newcastle Publishing Company. Inc., 1992.

[23]Richardson, loc. sit., p. 3

[24]Gelles, Dr. Mike, Exploring the Mind of the Spy, US Naval Command Investigative Service, October 3, 2004, p. 4.

Index